COUGHING IN INK

The Demise of Academic Ideals

Philip F. Lawler

UNIVERSITY
PRESS OF
AMERICA

Copyright © 1983 by

University Press of America, Inc.

P.O. Box 19101, Washington, D.C. 20036

Library of Congress Cataloging in Publication Data

Lawler, Philip F.
  Coughing in ink.

  Bibliography: p.
  1. Universities and colleges--United States.
2. Academic freedom--United States. I. Title.
LA227.3.L38   1983   378.73   83-1081
ISBN 0-8191-3051-6
ISBN 0-8191-3052-4 (pbk.)

To My Parents

The Scholars

By William Butler Yeats

Bald heads forgetful of their sins,
Old learned, respectable bald heads
Edit and annotate the lines
That young men, tossing on their beds,
Rhymed out in love's despair
To flatter beauty's ignorant ear.

All shuffle there; all cough in ink;
All wear the carpet with their shoes;
All think what other people think;
All know the man their neighbor knows.
Lord, what would they say
Did their Catullus walk that way?

ACKNOWLEDGEMENTS

The ideas contained in this book were formed and refined in conversations and arguments with a variety of friends over a period of many years. I can particularly recall enlightening talks with Dean Ernest Gordon and Alberto Coll at Princeton. Since the bulk of the first draft was produced while I was employed with the Concerned Alumni of Princeton, I am endebted to that organization and to my colleagues there, Harding Jones and Will Swigart. Invaluable encouragement came from David Asman and from the world's least typical mother-in-law, Elizabeth Day Edwards. Dan O'Meara read early drafts, criticized, and exhorted me to continue. At their most helpful moments, none of these friends realized that they were contributing directly toward this publication; I hope they are not too appalled by the use I have made of their ideas.

That first draft was refined, edited, and finally set into type while I worked at the Heritage Foundation. I am grateful to Heritage not only for the help I have received in preparing this work, but also — far more importantly — for the opportunity to work with an organization which, far better than our contemporary American universities, serves the goals of true education in its best sense.

Jean Scheel and I supported each other at the Foundation, working long overtime hours to finish our respective books. And at the eleventh hour Steve Manacek and Corey Crume ferretted out references that I had lost.

My wife, Leila Marie Lawler, is the ideal editor. She does not cut, paste, and rewrite; she sees and explains the argument that I have not quite fully brought to light. If I tried to explain the ways in which she had guided, encouraged, and supported me, this would become a very long book.

CONTENTS

INTRODUCTION

For as long as I can remember, I have loved learning, and hated school.

That double-edged observation, so routinely expressed by boys in grammar school, becomes heresy when uttered by a college student. So when I first voiced my feelings bluntly, as a Harvard junior, I encountered a predictably stunned reaction. I had been talking with a counselor at the college's career planning office, discussing my prospects for graduate study. The counselor was visibly unnerved by my confession. If I hated school, how could I contemplate graduate work and an academic career? Because I loved to learn. But if I loved to learn, why did I hate school? Ah, there was the rub; I had never noticed a terribly strong connection between school and learning.

Through grammar school and high school, through four years of college and two years of graduate study, I wondered whether I was unique. American educators employ a powerful and aggressive rhetoric. The mythology surrounding colleges and universities depicts a vibrant, exciting life of the mind. Was it possible that most students enjoyed that exciting quest for truth, while I somehow remained unmoved? Could my classmates and instructors perceive a clear relationship between school and learning which somehow eluded me? Gradually but inexorably, I reached a negative conclusion, and from that conclusion, with appropriate pains of labor, this book is born.

The academic mythology permeates every phase of our educational system. In grammar school, teachers tell their bored students that secondary school will open a new horizon. It does not. But in secondary school those same bored students are assured that college brings a welter of intellectual pursuits and an unlimited opportunity for exploration. The college catalogues promise an unending series of new discoveries, revealing insights, probing questions; college courses will be freewheeling seminars, or no-holds-barred academic disputations. The portrait is attractive; the life of the mind has tremendous appeal. But once again students will be disappointed. Reality diverges from mythology. Our universities enjoy no such intellectual ferment. American higher education is more often pedestrian, unimaginative, and routinized.

The sentiments expressed in this book are not often heard. The countervailing rhetoric is strong, and the risks of heresy are palpable. But I firmly believe that most students and professors share my fundamental complaint. American colleges are not what they claim to be. Our system of higher education is not exciting, nor does it encourage the life of the mind. The Emperor is wearing no clothes.

Notice, please, what I am *not* arguing. I do not deny that many professors and students find academic life exciting. Some scholars are so sincere, so energetic, that they manage either to ignore or to transcend the limitations of university life. Others take genuine pleasure in arcane scholastic research. Still others, by dint of a perverse act of will, lower their sights until they see nothing of interest beyond the realm of their own academic disciplines. Finally, some scholars fall under the hypnotic effect of the ubiquitous rhetoric; having heard so often that their university is rife with excitement, they come actually to believe it.

Nonetheless, contemporary collegiate life is not exciting. Surely there are hundreds of potential scholars who abandon their plans for an academic career because they find the university's atmosphere stultifying. Some of the most ambitious and idealistic students lose their taste for scholarship, or their patience with the academic rigmarole. And as these idealists drop out of school, they abandon the field to their less imaginative classmates: the same plodders who, in their turn, drive their own best students away from scholarship. The net effect has been observed by many prominent critics of education: a disproportionate number of the most devoted students leave school and choose other careers. Sincerity, insightfulness, and a taste for adventure can actually be handicaps for a potential scholar. Of course there are exceptions, but ordinarily the university does not accommodate swashbuckling types.

If the academic life does not bring adventure, what then is its allure? Does knowledge bring happiness? I put that very question to a group of friends several years ago. There were perhaps ten of us. All were beginning our final year at Harvard College, all scholarship students in good academic standing. The group was reasonably representative of the undergraduate population: a potpourri of diverse backgrounds, personalities, and academic interests. Yet despite this diversity, the group responded to my question with one voice: Knowledge does not make one happy. On the contrary, every one of my classmates argued that evening that knowledge brings unhappiness. The more they learned, the less happily they confronted life. Perhaps I overemphasize that incident. We were veterans of academe's most turbulent era, much given to bursts of existential despair. Perhaps today's undergraduates approach their studies with a more sanguine trust that studying will bring them happiness. But I wonder. I wonder how many students view knowledge as a consolation, rather than as a psychological burden.

In fact, I wonder how many students abandon their studies precisely because they doubt their ability to remain cheerful in the face of the scholarly travail. There is a view, prevalent in academe, that life is fraught with sorrow, and that knowledge brings with it a grimmer, starker understanding of our pitiable human condition. That such a view could prevail is an indictment of the atmosphere fostered by our schools, and I will pursue that indictment at some length later in this book. For now my point is simply that if students view collegiate study as a means to life-time happiness, they are courting disappointment.

Where, then, is the attraction? Surely not in the value of a college degree on the marketplace. (Here, and throughout the book, I am speaking of the liberal arts, not of pre-professional or vocational training.) The labor force is crowded with college graduates, many of them searching desperately for suitable work. If a bachelor's degree was once a ticket to financial security, it no longer serves that function. In fact, some economists will argue that today's high-school senior might be more successful, financially speaking, if he joins the labor force immediately rather than entering college. The cost of a college education has become staggering, and although college graduates earn higher salaries, the difference might not be enough to recoup the investment in tuition, fees, and time.

Once again, then: Where is the attraction? Total up the cost of tuition, room and board, books, travel, and miscellaneous college fees. Add the price the student pays for not joining the labor force — the income he could have earned had he chosen a full-time job rather than a year in college. Multiply by the four years most students take to complete their degree requirements. The total cost is sobering; at the most expensive private schools it exceeds $85,000. Discounting inflation, most students will never make a more expensive investment in their lives. Why do students choose college? Why do they choose one school over another? Where do they find the information on which they base their decisions?

Viewed from the economic perspective, American higher education constitutes an enormous industry, surpassing even the automobile industry in size. But think of the difference in how the two industries disseminate information about themselves. No doubt automobile advertisements can be misleading, but manufacturers also release reams of factual information, and consumer groups compare the available products. With a minimum of individual effort any shopper can compare cars and choose the one best suited to his own needs. What is still more important, every automobile buyer knows with reasonable accuracy what he wants from his car. Not so in academe. College brochures bear a remarkable similarity; even the photographs (idyllic campus scenes, couples strolling on the mall, shirtsleeved professors conferring with students) are virtually interchangeable. Every college touts its outstanding faculty, its modern facilities, its lively social ambiance. Despite its theoretical commitment to the spread of knowledge, the education "industry" provides precious little information about itself.

So how do students choose? What makes one school different from another? Why attend Harvard rather than the University of Michigan? Duke rather than Texas Tech? Berkeley rather than Haverford? A school's reputation is at best a partial index of its strength, and sometimes a grossly misleading one. College catalogues provide only the vaguest notions of the school's unique mission. A few fortunate students receive specific information about a number of schools (outstanding athletes, ironically, have very solid grounds for comparison of scholarship offers), but most students choose their college without really understanding its strengths and weaknesses.

But the students are not to blame. It is the colleges that provide the indistinguishable brochures and the platitudinous descriptions. Only a handful of schools articulate a comprehensive approach to undergraduate education. The overwhelming majority of our colleges and universities do not encourage students to think about what sort of education they want. Small wonder, then, that so many students are disenchanted with college, confused by their studies, and uncertain about their futures. Where there is no common understanding about the aims of education, there can be no sense of unifying purpose; the schools cannot enjoy the excitement of pursuing a shared mission.

Now we come to the crux of the problem. Why do our universities have so little interest in analyzing their own goals? This book is an extended meditation on that question. It is my earnest belief, gained from years of observation and participation, that American higher education has lost its way. My thoughts are drawn from reading and reflecting on educational theory, and from my own academic career. The conclusions I advance here did not come easily; they are the product of years of confusion, frustration, and the sort of intellectual odyssey so typical of my generation. The three universities with which I am most intimately familiar all possess reputations of the very first rank, but I believe their troubles are indicative of the entire system of higher education. As an undergraduate at Harvard, a graduate student at the University of Chicago, and an education writer at Princeton, I observed the common faults that plague the entire system. Not many schools escape these problems; most schools encounter the same problems in more virulent form. Finally, as an undergraduate during the tumultuous '60s, I had the opportunity to see how the college community reacted to extreme pressure — always an instructive index of an institution's character.

Already I can hear my critics' lament: "All this talk about

theory is fine, but where are your practical suggestions? What reforms can the university undertake?" This book will not satisfy such critics. Contemporary educational literature abounds with proposals for the reform and reinvigoration of the liberal arts. Many of those proposals are wrongheaded, some of them sound; from time to time in this book I shall comment on them. But I shall not add any dramatic new suggestions.

If I were preparing for a mountain-climbing expedition, rest assured that I would check all the equipment. If I found any mechanical defects, I would surely have the equipment repaired. But even before I did that, I would want to be certain that every member of the expedition agreed as to what mountain we should climb. More basic still, I would demand some proof that the mountain in fact exists. In American higher education today, there is no common understanding about which mountain should be tackled. Some people even argue that there is no mountain. I do not propose, therefore, to analyze the equipment.

A university, as I understand it (and everyone who speaks or writes on the subject *claims* to agree), should be a community of scholars seeking after wisdom. Such an institution could be large or small, structured or informal, old or new. The form does not matter.

What does matter is that members of the university community must share a common set of ideals. Whether it is Plato's Academy, or the University of Bologna in the Middle Ages, or Oxford at the turn of the century, the great university emphasizes a common cause and a common commitment to the pursuit of truth. A healthy univeristy is a thoroughly idealistic institution; idealism is the fuel on which academic life runs. Conversely, universities without ideals are thoroughly decrepit institutions. This book argues that American universities are just such decrepit institutions. So the question of reform is too far advanced; no real reform is possible until the university recovers its ideals. First let us locate the mountain; then we can inspect our climbing equipment.

And why should *I* write a book about higher education? I am, after all, not a professor, nor an administrator, nor even (any longer) a recent graduate. No, I am writing this book as an academic dropout, a representative of that widespread opinion that collegiate life is not exciting. I have grievances to file. I have endured eighteen years of formal schooling, and four more years of life on the fringe of academe. Through it all, I have been disappointed consistently. I am writing for the people who hate school.

But not for those who hate learning. If I did not place an extremely high value on knowledge, and an even higher value on truth, I could leave the universities to their own confusion. My frustration stems precisely from my belief that our schools do not encourage the growth and preservation of knowledge, or promote the search for truth. I am writing, then, for the idealists who cannot live within the strictures of contemporary schools.

In writing this book I have not solved — not even attempted to solve — the crisis in American higher education. (There are many other, better books that describe what a collegiate education should be; I list several of them in my bibliography.) I know, from bitter experience, that confusion is the first and worst of the obstacles confronting a disaffected student. He knows his school is failing him, but he doesn't know how, or why. All too often an unhappy student recognizes the problem too late: after his schooling is finished, or nearly finished, and he is powerless to recoup his lost time and energy. For such a student, I hope this book can be a useful guide. Once he understands the problem, then he can set about the larger task of framing his own solution.

One final point. Some prudent readers will wonder how I can undertake to change the ideals that rule American colleges without first changing the ideals that rule American society as a whole. After all, colleges do not operate in an ideological vacuum. Their options are limited by the attitudes students acquire in secondary schools. And secondary schools are limited in turn by the attitudes acquired in grammar schools. And grammar schools by kindergartens. Even kindergartens are restricted by the values parents instill in their children. By the time students arrive in college (so the argument runs), their ideals and attitudes are already largely determined.

True enough. Yet the people who teach in grammar schools

and secondary schools — and the opinion-makers who influence parents — are themselves college graduates. And if grammar school instructors mold students' educational expectations, those instructors received their own ideas from the universities they attend. So one could turn the argument around completely, and point it in the opposite direction. Thus, one could argue that it is impossible to reform the nation's grammar schools — impossible to reform society as a whole — without first reforming the universities.

Which comes first, the chicken or the egg? Do the universities form societal attitudes, or do societal attitudes govern the universities? I shall not presume to answer that question; I do not know. The process of changing society's attitudes is terribly complex. One can throw up one's hands at the complexity, and lapse into quietism. One can despair, and conclude that society's opinions will never change. Or one can begin somewhere.

To me, higher education seems a reasonable place to start.

CHAPTER ONE

Academe in Revolt

> Had the American university *before* 1964
> done its work properly . . . the reaction to the
> crisis of most educated Americans, whether
> anarchists or conservatives in their politics,
> would have been uniform: a reassertion of the
> university's true function and a message to
> those concerned that it is not only outrageous
> but ridiculous to transform it into a theater of
> existential drama.
>
> *Adam Ulam*[1]

The idea of this book germinated on Thursday morning, April 10, 1969. I was in a rut. Literally. The grounds of Harvard Yard, softened by the spring rains, had been gouged by a fleet of buses — buses carrying hundreds of policemen to the infamous University Hall Bust. A few hours after that cataclysmic event I found myself wandering through the bus tracks, wondering how it had all come to pass. How had Harvard, the archetypal Ivory Tower, suddenly become a battleground?

Perhaps I was being presumptious, believing that I could answer the question by myself in my lowly freshman mind. Certainly I was being melodramatic, comparing the scars in the sod with the scars in the University's collective psyche. But presumption and melodrama were very fashionable in those days. The habit of sober reflection had disappeared, the first casualty of the Bust. For several weeks thereafter, life at Harvard was dominated by slogans, by intimidation, and by the theater of the absurd.

Harvard's student uprising was not the first — nor the worst — of the series that made campus unrest a national issue. Revolutionary protests had already become a staple of the Berkeley campus diet; Mark Rudd had gained national headlines the previous year when Columbia students turned that university into a battleground. But the national media professed amazement when the uproar inundated Harvard. "It couldn't happen here" had been the standard incantation, and now suddenly it had happened. The element of surprise served some journalistic purposes; sensational stories sell. ("Rebels Maul Harvard Deans," one Boston newspaper headline screamed).[2] In fact, the Harvard Bust was thoroughly predictable.

Spring riots are a Harvard tradition. After a long winter, pent-up undergraduate exuberance overspills, inevitably creating a minor civil uproar. Traditionally the spring riot had taken a relatively harmless form: a panty raid at Radcliffe, say, or a massive food fight in the Freshman Union. University officials would chuckle quietly while their municipal counterparts fumed. (When the riot reached its zenith, a few participants would find themselves running from angry Cambridge policemen into the friendly and understanding arms of the university's own security officers.) But in the middle '60s the spring riots took on a mildly political flavor. First there was a semiserious protest against the university's decision to print diplomas in English rather than in Latin; then a slighly more earnest demonstration to "Save the Sycamores" that stood in the projected path of a new throughway. In 1968 the political element had been both dominant and nasty: radical students, led by members of the Students for a Democratic Society (SDS), heckled and threatened former Defense Secretary Robert S. McNamara, refusing to let his limousine pass.[3] The stage was set for the events of 1969.

The class of freshmen living in Harvard Yard during the academic year 1968-69 was arguably the most radical class, politically, in recent Harvard history. As so many analysts have noted, we were raised on a diet of optimism about American society and its ability to solve all social problems; then the shocking events of the late '60s destroyed that optimism. We came to college armed with a sense of angry purpose, a corps of traduced idealists dedicated to the recovery of that roseate social vision. Of course no such statistic is or was available, but I feel sure that at least 75 percent of Harvard's freshmen that year (myself included) fully expected to become President of the United States.

Perhaps the Admissions Officer had been naive, selecting such a volatile group of potential activists. But the Housing Office evidently sensed the danger, and took steps to insulate the administration from any upheavals. The highest concentration of radical freshmen occurred in dormitories on the fringes of the Yard, while the two entryways facing University Hall (the college's administrative center) housed an unrepresentative aggregation of quiet, apolitical types. (Least anyone doubt that the Housing Office played such Machiavellian games with room assignments, let me add that in my own entryway of about 60 freshmen, *exactly* one third were Protestant, one third Catholic, and one third Jewish; the division among private, public, and parochial school graduates was also precisely even. Coincidence?) By virtue of my uncontroversial secondary school career, I was placed on the first floor of Thayer Hall, in an entry just fifty feet from the deans' offices in University Hall. So I had a convenient first-hand view of April's events.

Political tension had been brewing throughout the year, with SDS leading the radical forces. By early April, the campus controversy was reaching a critical level. SDS accused the university of complicity in the Vietnam war and oppression of the working people of Cambridge, and condemned the campus ROTC program. Leaders of the organization were discussing the possibility that they might sieze an administration building forcibly, to dramatize their protest. At a stormy meeting on Tuesday, April 8, the SDS membership voted down a proposal to seize University Hall. The more militant leaders then scheduled a new vote on the same resolution, to be held at noon on Wednesday, *inside* University Hall.[4]

After the Tuesday night meeting, SDS members marched through the Yard, stopping in front of University Hall to chant "ROTC must go" at the deserted windows. Subsequent reports of the Harvard Bust have somehow ignored the one salient fact about that demonstration: it failed. The overwhelming majority of freshmen in the Yard, whatever their political convictions, were utterly unsympathetic toward SDS at that time. When the marchers reached the Yard, around midnight, groups of freshmen straggled out of their domitory rooms to investigate the clamor, listen briefly, and return muttering to their studies or their beds. A substantial number stayed in the Yard, jeering and taunting the demonstrators. The march had been an effort to gain support for the SDS demands. The response was pathetic.

However, while the march failed, the implicit threat worked like a charm. By calling attention to the rumors about a building takeover, the SDS leaders turned campus attention toward themselves. Remember, this was happening ten years ago. Building takeovers were not yet a campus routine. The SDS proposal was a leap into an unknown territory. No one knew what would happen if the building were occupied; no one knew how the administration would react. Many students argued that a forcible occupation would prove impossible: that administration officials would guard their offices with force if necessary. Others, notably a few football players, expressed their ample willingness to evict any demonstrators. For several hours after the demonstration, on into the early hours of morning, excited little knots of undergraduates and professors discussed the possibilities and ramifications. The pace of events forbade the formation of consensus, but amid the general uncertainty two themes seemed clear. The majority of freshmen thought it was all a bluff. And the overwhelming majority condemned the idea.

Wednesday classes reflected the uncertain mood of the campus community. My geology instructor had chosen to forego his usual lecture in favor of a freewheeling discussion of the prospects for disruption. Midway through the hour a dishevelled undergraduate burst through the door to announce that SDS was preparing its assault. Since rumors were abounding, the professor suggested that we assume the report was inaccurate; an SDS member in the class endorsed that plan. But when we left the building at the end of the hour, a mob was surrounding the Hall, and an SDS leader, armed with a bullhorn, was congratulating his comrades for having "liberated" the building. The deans were out, SDS in. I hurried to lunch, gulped something down, and returned.

The crowd around University Hall grew steadily all that afternoon, as student filtered in from around the campus to witness the spectacle. To attend classes that afternoon was unthinkable; the events in the Yard were historic. Newspaper and television reporters mixed with the crowd, along with political activists from all over the Boston area. By now the SDS leaders were passing the bullhorn around, one to another, taking turns haranguing the spectators. The rhetoric was so strong, the slogans so dominant, that the speakers were interchangeable. The crowd buzzed with conversation, none of it inspired by the speeches. Observers traded witticisms, most of them at the demonstrators' expense. Someone in a nearby dormitory turned up his stereo, and the Beatles song "Revolution" blared across the Yard. ("You say you want a revolution./Well, you know, we all want to change the world.") The crowd laughed, applauding. A carnival atmosphere was beginning to take hold. Frustrated SDS leaders finally changed their tactics, abandoning the bullhorn to march around the Yard, chanting slogans and urging sympathetic onlookers to join their ranks.

Suddenly the mood became serious. Tensions erupted onto the surface. Some students joined the SDS march, despite their distaste for the organization's tactics. Their classmates heckled them as they marched by, full of uncertain moral afflatus. The groups began to polarize. When the marching stopped, the new radical recruits were greeted with hoots and shoves on their way back to their rooms. They returned the insults disgustedly. A few scuffles erupted. A muscular student grabbed the SDS flag, and his friends hustled it away.

So SDS had accomplished its first objective. The student community had split along political lines, and political rivalries had overcome personal friendships. Classmates and neighbors looked at each other with newfound distaste, suddenly judging each other as politically backward, or immoral, or subversive, or some combination of those qualities. With its strident, escalating rhetoric, SDS had forced students to choose between two extreme postures. No middle ground, no genteel disagreement, was possible. Nor could anyone remain neutral. The survival of the university, and the continuation of the war, were at stake (or

seemed to be). Students must choose to support either the
revolutionaries inside University Hall or the U.S. involvement
in Vietnam. That was the choice SDS offered, and suddenly
students were accepting that dichotomy. Naturally, most undergraduates were perplexed.

Evening arrived, and the atmosphere grew more relaxed.
Inside University Hall the demonstrators began to worry about
food. Franklin Ford, the dean of the college faculty, had closed
the gates around the Yard, and only freshmen (that is, residents)
were being admitted. So if the demonstrators left for dinner,
they could not return. Soon they began pouring into domitories,
borrowing freshmen identification cards. Then the crowd began
to settle down for the evening. University policemen and deans
were sprinkled through the crowd, observing quietly. Curious
undergraduates began wandering through the occupied building
to see the scene inside. Rock music welled up from inside the
dormitories, then from inside the Hall itself. The carnival atmosphere returned.

Once again the rumor mill began to churn. Early in the evening
I heard that policemen were massing in the fire station across the
street from the Yard. I strolled over to check the rumor. No signs
of unusual activity. But the speculation would not die. No one —
not even the deans around the steps of University Hall — knew
what the University's response would be. But everyone expected
a quick confrontation. The administration could not allow such a
direct assault on its authority, and the political mood off campus
dictated a prompt return to order. President Pusey was reported-
ly meeting with other authorities; alumni opinion was demanding
a strong response. The tension grew, despite all the frivolity.
Those of us close to the scene were living in almost feverish
expectancy.

Shortly after midnight, I noticed that a few deans were leaving
their posts in the Yard. Did they know something? Had they
been summoned for a secret summit? I speculated with my
friends. Soon no prominent university official was in sight. Perhaps the deans just needed their sleep. Or perhaps a bust was
imminent. But a bust would prove difficult in the darkness. I
turned all the evidence over and over, offering new analyses to

my friends and listening to their own theories. Finally, at three in the morning, I went to bed.

The alarm exploded inside my head. I punched at my clock; then, fully awake, realized that the unbearable clamor was coming from the fire alarm. It was throbbing inside my brain, threatening my self-control. I jumped to my feet and began to pull on some clothes. My roommate was already doing the same, his eyes still heavily lidded.

"Is is a bust?"

"No, it's a fire."

I was sure it wasn't a fire. But I had to leave the building quickly, to escape the reverberating alarm. The alarm stopped ringing, and I relaxed. Then it began again. I sprinted out the dormitory door onto the front steps, out of its range.

Of course there was no fire. The demonstrators had set off all the alarms when they heard the police were coming: at 4:15. They wanted an audience for their martyrdom. No police vehicles were visible anywhere near the Yard, but the demonstrators were convinced. Fearing tear gas, they tore up proffered bed sheets, and filed into our communal bathroom to soak the rags in water, thereby fashioning crude gas masks. A steady stream passed by me for several minutes. All were excited, apprehensive, frightened.

At 4:45 a handful of students burst running across the Yard, coming from the gate nearest the fire station. The sentries, with their final warning. The police were on their way. A frenzy of activity, and the demonstrators clambered back into the Hall, closing the doors. Fear wrapped the Yard; local policemen were notoriously unfriendly toward Harvard students, and we anticipated violence. A handful of students, outraged by the administration's decision to call in the police, sat on the steps of the Hall in a silent show of sympathy for the demonstrators.

Then, amid the uproar of chanted slogans, a police cruiser appeared just beside me, turned up the footpath, and drove into the center of the Yard. And another. Even with ample warning, the shock was palpable. The police had opened an unused gate; now they were driving across the lawn beside the Hall. Another two or three cruisers arrived, each one bearing police and univer-

sity officials. Then came a minibus full of helmeted police. And
then a full-sized bus, carrying perhaps 60 riot-geared State
troopers. And another. And another. Then a few small buses,
and a long succession of police wagons from every city and town
in the vicinity. The vehicles formed a phalanx facing the shouting
demonstrators, and discharged their passengers. At first the
police formed a ring around their vehicles, keeping student
onlookers at a distance. Then the ranks of State troopers formed:
about 200 baby-blue uniforms, helmets, and oversized clubs, in
precise formation, facing the rear steps of the Hall.

The scene was surrealistic. The light blue wave of police, all
identical behind their face masks, confronted the screaming,
disorganized students chanting on the steps and inside the building. Heads poked out of windows all around the Yard. Clusters
of students on the dormitory steps shouted that the police must
leave. A frantic woman nearby kept shouting, sobbing, "They're
not people," until a weeping companion led her away. The police
sergeants shouted instructions to their troopers. Their superiors
issued final warnings to the demonstrators, all lost in the uproar.
Cacophonous, pervasive din filled the air. And when the troopers
began to march toward the Hall, the noise and the light and the
chaos all built toward a crescendo. The eerie dawn light con-
firmed the air of unreality.

As the troopers neared the Hall, squadrons of local cops
lengthened their cordons to prevent any other would-be demonstrators from approaching the building. The police line stretched
in front of the steps to the nearby dormitories, encircling the
area for the upcoming battle. Then one unit peeled off from the
main line and headed around the Hall toward the west steps,
where a few silent demonstrators sat. I followed at a distance to
watch. I expected rough treatment, but the encounter left me
horrified. The local police waded into the handful of unresisting
demonstrators, swinging from the heels. One dazed student was
thrown headlong down the stairs, blood trickling from the side
of his mouth.[4] In a matter of seconds, the cops were implanted
on the steps. Shaken, I headed back toward my original vantage
point on the steps of Thayer Hall.

Suddenly, without warning, the police line converged on us.

They were rushing spectators. Having just returned from my foray, I was in the front lines. Before I could react — before I could burrow through the wall of people outside the door of the building — one cop planted his stick in my back and pushed. He and his cohort worked a violent, effective pattern: a shove to knock the victim off balance, then a full windup and swing for the head. Unfortunately, I was directly in front of one of these club-happy constables. Fortunately, his aim was poor. The first blow landed on my ear; another coupled with a second shove, staggered me. But the momentum of the crowd swept me forward, up the stairs, and into the sanctuary of Thayer Hall. I recovered my balance just as I passed through the doors. Now I felt safe; surely the police would not enter the dormitory itself. I turned around. And saw a club descending toward my head. I must have moved slightly before it landed, bouncing painfully off my temple. That was enough. As the cops poured into the hallway, pounding on the walls with their clubs, I stumbled into my room and slammed the door.

Dazed, I sat alone for several minutes, vaguely conscious of the alarums and excursions outside my window. When at last I ventured back to the doorway, the Bust was a *fait accompli.* The police had bundled the demonstrators out of the University Hall and into the waiting wagons. Now the blue lines were constricting, as the police retreated toward their buses. There were sporadic isolated incidents, as individual officers charged into the crowd in pursuit of some unusually insulting observer. But the Bust itself was done.

When the police arrived, the mood of the onlookers had changed dramatically. By invoking legal force rather than moral suasion, the administration lost a great deal of support from the student body. And as undergraduates watched their classmates pummeled, the administration had called in the police; now the administration would bear the responsibility for police excesses. And the excesses were many. Ironically, the State troopers who entered University Hall were, by most reports, a good deal less violent than the untrained local policemen who wielded their clubs outside. So dozens of innocent bystanders were assailed, while radical ringleaders enjoyed comparatively mild escorts to the local jail. (Only much later did I learn that several top SDS officers had slipped out of the Hall just before the Bust, so that they could continue directing radical activities without the inconvenience of arrest.) To those of us who had not been involved in the earlier confrontations, the whole affair seemed sinister: the hushed conferences of the deans; the shocking appearance of police battalions in sheltered Harvard Yard; the raid at dawn. Events had been whirling past, leaving no time for reflection. Now we were too sleepy to be logical, but not too sleepy to be resentful. As the police prepared to leave, clusters of students stood on dormitory steps shouting obscenities, while the cops laughed and jeered in turn. The campus was thoroughly polarized.

From that point forward, a tiny group of radical students controlled Harvard's agenda. SDS provided a focus for the general resentment, and before the confusion surrounding the Bust had abated SDS spokesmen were firmly in command of student opinion. Whenever they issued a statement — and they issued many — some students would immediately agree, others violently disagree; but everyone would take notice. Political controversies were all-important; ordinary scholarship seemed trivial by comparison. SDS had won the battle.

On Wednesday morning, before the building takover, the typical Harvard undergraduate had opposed SDS and Richard Nixon with roughly equal fervor. By Thursday afternoon, after the Bust, campus opinion had taken a quantum leap to the left of the political spectrum. Now hundreds of students sided with the SDS demands, and accused Harvard of complicity in the Vietnam war. And so, by a weird soritical construction, Harvard students accepted another SDS argument: that the university must be closed. Perhaps a majority of students abhorred the use of police violence. Perhaps a majority favored the discontinuation of the ROTC program. Perhaps a majority opposed criminal punishment for the demonstrators who had been arrested in University Hall. But the strike was not called on those grounds. Harvard undergraduates began a student strike because of the war in Vietnam.

On Wednesday morning SDS had been a small campus organization. Now its leaders controlled the most powerful forums at Harvard, almost by default. Flushed with success, radicals reached for new levels of activism, new revolutionary vistas, in a grotesquely one-sided debate that was to continue throughout my college career. To anyone outside the swirl of events, the rhetoric must have seemed impossibly inflated, and the violence of the radical arguments must have been stunning. Immediately after the University Hall Bust, a graduate student named Alan Gilbert called on all students to attack President Pusey's residence with rocks and bricks.[5] A series of preposterous rumors circulated, alleging that the Dean of the college, a quiet, affable man named Fred Glimp, had chortled sadistically as he watched the police club defenseless demonstrators. Another rumor brought the hideous but plausible report that black undergraduates planned to set fire to the bookstacks of Widener Library. When Dean Franklin Ford suffered a heart attack, many students actually cheered the news. The campus was virtually at war, with radical students aligned against administrators, against teachers . . . against the university itself.

In his introduction to *The Secret Agent*, Joseph Conrad explained that he had intentionally constructed a metaphor of utter frightful anarchy. He could imagine nothing so redolent of chaos as the event he depicted in that novel: the assault on Greenwich Observatory. As he explained it, he intended the scene to horrify the reader. The nihilists were not merely attacking an institution; they were lashing out against order, against logic . . . against reason itself. Conrad chose Greenwich Observatory as his symbol of disinterested study: the epitome of an institution devoted to order and reason for their own sake. To attack such an institution, Conrad felt, was the greatest possible rejection of our culture, and the most hideous threat anarchists could muster.[6] Could not the same be said of the radicals who led the assault on Harvard? Ultimately they were not simply protesting against the war in Vietnam. They were demanding the cessation of studies, scoffing at the life of the mind, struggling to abolish the pursuit of knowledge. They called themselves students, and yet they rebelled against the reflective academic style. They called themselves political activists, and yet they would not confront the established powers in the political realm. No; they assailed the university — the province of reason and reflection.

But for all its violent and horrifying implications, this war was a war of theater: of words rather than actions. After all, the "enemy" was a university, not an army. And for that matter, the "rebels" were students, most of them thoroughly dependent on their parents' largesse. (The median family income of SDS members was notably higher than the Harvard average — and the Harvard average was, of course, very very high.[7]) Radical students wanted so badly to be revolutionaries! Inside the "liberated" University Hall, demonstrators debated with utmost seriousness such questions as whether or not the occupants should smoke marijuana, or play rock music. Would the new revolutionary society permit such activities? Or should the students be too serious, too full of revolutionary zeal to enjoy such base amusements?

To his everlasting credit, Harvard President Nathan Pusey gave the student rebels the attention they deserved. "Walter Mittys of the Left," he called them, as he wondered aloud whether anyone could possibly take the SDS demands seriously.[8] But blunt men like Pusey were in short supply, and few scholars defended the President against the onslaught that followed his statements. Pusey became a pariah; campus sages mournfully noted that he was "out of touch" with the students. He was forced to alter his personal habits, entering and leaving his office by the underground steam tunnels to avoid confrontations with hostile students. His resignation was assured long before he formally announced it. And the new president would be a diplomat, who could accommodate himself to students more readily. Pusey was a symbol of the old regime. He would have to go.

After the Bust — for three years after the Bust — the rhetoric continued apace, equally absurd in its mock-revolutionary vein. Writing in the *Harvard Crimson,* the undergraduate newspaper, executive editor Nick Gagarin announced, "Any radical movement at Harvard should base itself on our own needs — the needs of the oppressed student class."[9] (*Oppressed* student class?) "Guerilla theatre" troupes sprang up, invading dining halls and common rooms to bring their revolutionary message home to the complacent residents. When classes were held, radical students interrupted with provocative questions for the professors, demanding to hear a defense of the university's multifold transgressions. Leaflets, slogans, shirts with the red-fisted strike symbol silk-screened on the back — all became a regular part of campus life. The logic was preposterous, and yet the message found fertile ground: the university was an oppressor, the students oppressed; American society was fundamentally sick, racist, fascist; the people who ran Harvard were the same malevolent magnates who supervised the prosecution of the Vietnam war; the revolution was already underway.

Enough. Yes, the political spectrum was impossibly skewed. Perhaps one further incident will serve to summarize the insanity that prevailed during those years. The incident occurred two years after the Bust, when a band of radical students marched from Boston to Cambridge, smashing windows and looting ("trashing" had some obscure revolutionary justification) as they marched. Arriving in Harvard Square, the marauders began aiming for the windows of Holyoke Center, the most prominent building in the area. But the lower floors of Holyoke Center house the university's infirmary, and one brave nurse appeared at the door to scold the vandals. "Hey, stop that," she shouted angrily: "There are sick people in here." "Hey, man," retorted one scraggly demonstrator, "The whole society's sick." And while his companions applauded this display of wit, he launched another rock.

Violence, political tensions, and student strikes played havoc with my undergraduate career. During my freshman, sophomore, and junior years, the spring semester withered in the face of a strike; only in my senior year did final examinations proceed on schedule. Academic rigor was unfashionable; the few professors who unflinchingly demanded it were derided with the ubiquitous label "fascist." Karl Deutsch was called a "fascist," although Deutsch had seen a boyhood friend shot down at his side as the two of them distributed anti-government literature in Hitler's Germany. Samuel Beer, the kingpin "fascist" of the faculty, was once the president of the Americans for Democratic Action. Many professors tried to meet the students halfway, and attempted to meld contemporary politics with their ordinary subject matter. A few capitulated entirely. Once I registered for a course in social philosophy, unaware that the instructor was an avid SDS supporter, and the enrollment nearly matched the SDS list. Each lecture, I learned, was to be an impromptu forum for radical rhetoric. The focus of the course never wavered from the alleged racism, imperialism, and sexism of American society and the problems of the impending revolution. Since Marxist theory as popularly understood maintained that the students would unite with the working class, SDS members eagerly proclaimed the worker-student alliance, oblivious to the hatred shown them by blue-collar workers. (My term-time job involved working in Harvard's janitorial crew; when SDS learned that I actually *was* a worker-student, I enjoyed a brief unwanted popularity.) Even the rituals of Commencement and Class Day were disrupted by a variety of radical demonstrations and counter-events. For three years, in that circus atmosphere, academic discipline was virtually unknown.

The clear majority of students never supported these disruptive assaults on the university itself. On the contrary, most were anxious to redeem the academic life — to show that we could be morally sensitive without joining the revolt. But we were too quiet, too frightened and intimidated by the radical rhetoric. We preferred quieter, reflective discussions to the hurly-burly of the political sphere.

As a result, the years of wildness did bring some tangible intellectual benefits. Colleges are highly traditional institutions, and often the crusty routine of lectures and papers deadens the thrill of new learning. Changes come at a snail's pace; as the old saw put it, if the Edsel had been a college course, it would still be offered today. But the theatrical fury of the campus revolt brought every pat assumption into question. Originality gained a new supreme status. And we wanted, desperately, to justify the academic routine in the eyes of political activists. So students and even professors aired radical new ideas, while their colleagues listened with unwonted interest. In an atmosphere permeated with revolutionary zeal, an atmosphere in which people debated seriously over the remodeling of society, it seemed only reasonable to remodel the university — to question, say, the grading system and the academic calendar.

So the grading system and the academic calendar were discussed. But more then that. Students asked fundamental questions about the purposes of the university. Why should all classes last one semester, and end with the same sort of exam? Why should all students spend the same four-year period earning their degrees? Why shouldn't students receive academic credit for their employment, or their political experience? Idealism and a keen whimsical sense prompted still more basic questions. Why should there be classes at all? Why not transform the school into a communal artistic or political enterprise? What, in the last analysis, was the purpose of higher education?

Now admittedly most of these questions were hopelessly naive. A short, sober discussion of the university's role would have cleared the air. But by asking those questions — by calling for such a discussion — we were presenting the academic world with a powerful opportunity. Now is the time. The university could reinforce its claims against the radical onslaught; scholars could justify their work with a fresh new argument. With their certainties thrown into tumult, students were ready to hear any new idea, any new informing purpose that might shape their attitude toward academe. A fresh wind was blowing through the academic marketplace.

Then that wind grew stale, because the idealistic questions never provoked a satisfactory answer. The whimsical insights never elicited a pragmatic reply. The freewheeling discussions of undergraduate life, bereft of any practical conclusions, began to bog down. Students could find no new connection between their fiercely idealistic beliefs and their humdrum classroom subsistence. So the campus grew cynical. After the first radical political outbursts, student activists had turned their attentions back toward the school itself; now they lapsed again into an exclusively political approach. Within a few short years, apathy regained its pre-eminent position in campus affairs.

Now, a decade later, the American campus is quiet again. So quiet that today's college students must find the notion of a student revolution difficult to comprehend. Even those of us

who lived through the wildest of the campus disturbances recall
the events with a sense of unreality. And yet, unreal as it may
seem now, we students did expect to see a revolution. We honestly expected that the conflicts so obvious on campus would swell
up and engulf the whole society. Some of us were happy with
that prospect, other frightened by it; but the overwhelming
majority expected a series of radical changes in American society.

Somehow, the revolution never came. Society weathered the
storm. The ferocity of radical protests dwindled, long before the
Vietnam war ended. The media lost their fascination with campus upheavals. We had expected some sort of showdown between
the forces of change and the existing institutions; we had thought
the social revolution would reach a climax, and for better or
worse the ideological conflicts would be resolved. No such thing
happened. The era of campus revolt simply faded.

So nothing was resolved. The radicals did not overthrow
society; neither did society repudiate the radicals. No one won.
No one lost. The whole awful battle was fought in vain.

Or so it would seem. But the calm atmosphere on campus
today is deceptive.

The Danish philosopher Kierkegaard once wrote that a revolutionary age would attack all of society's institutions frontally,
overthrowing them with sheer intimidating power. But such a
direct attack would allow the forces of tradition to arm themselves for the defense. A cunning age would leave the institutions
in place, never threatening them directly. Instead, the cunning
age would undermine the society's institutions, subvert them,
leave them bereft of their power and their dignity. The institutions would still stand, but they would be parodies of their
former selves.[10]

Mine is a cunning generation.

During the late '60s, student radicals threatened the very existence of the university as an institution. In their desperate efforts
to avoid a direct, decisive confrontation, college administrators
hastened to accommodate the radicals on every possible issue. As
long as the university itself survived, the administrators would be
happy. So today the universities have survived as institutions, but
the old sense of purpose and discipline is gone; the universities

have sacrificed their ideals. Today, student rebellions usually peter out quickly. Why? Because the administration capitulates so quickly that the radicals have no time to organize.

I know, these statements seem extreme. After all, the campus is quiet today. Or so it is said.

But it is not quiet. Today students routinely organize the sort of political protests that earned horrific headlines a decade ago. In 1969 students at Harvard occupied University Hall, and virtually every newspaper in the country carried headlines describing the event. Three years later, students at the same college occupied the same building, and virtually no one outside Harvard Square heard about it. Today's student protests are no less strident, no less immoderate. But the protests have become commonplace, and so they no longer seem threatening. In 1969, Harvard's campus revolt seemed frightening in part because it disrupted the established order of things. No one knew what to expect, and the uncertainty compounded the shock. But now the campus protests *are* the established order of things, and everyone knows what will happen. Nothing will happen.

To illustrate my point, I submit the case of one single student: a recent Princeton graduate named Adhimu Changa. (Born Lawrence Hamm, Changa took his new name at the suggestion of his mentor, the poet Amiri Baraka, also known as LeRoi Jones.) I choose Changa because I think his case dramatizes how today's university responds to a radical activist.

During his sophomore year, Changa and two accomplices disrupted a campus lecture by Boston politician Louise Day Hicks. The trio chanted slogans and criticisms constantly, so that the audience could not hear Hicks' remarks. How did Princeton respond? The university issued a half-hearted warning. (One graduate student, acting on his own against the advice of the university's officials, successfully prosecuted Changa and his friends under the terms of a New Jersey statute forbidding the disruption of public assemblies).[11] During his junior year, Changa in a public speech referred to the Trustees of Princeton as "bloodsucking capitalist leeches." A dean of the university, asked for his comments on the speech, replied blandly that Changa had made a very thoughtful presentation.[12] During his senior year,

Changa led a group of protesting students who forcibly occupied
Nassau Hall, the campus administration building. Several administrative officials pledged their support; again no meaningful disciplinary action resulted. But that was not enough. Unsatisfied
with the coverage his group was receiving in the campus newspaper, Changa issued a bold threat: "We've got your names;
we've got your numbers. We're going to deal with you pencil-
scratchers."[13] Soon thereafter, he led a group of protestors into
the newspaper's editorial offices, for another short occupation.
Again, no disciplinary result. In fact, at Commencement the same
campus newspaper conferred its highest accolade on: Adhimu
Changa.

Now these are only isolated incidents, taken from the undergraduate career of one isolated activist. Changa made many
other contributions to the radical cause, and there are many like
him on other campuses. But think about it. Through it all, the
university refrained from substantive disciplinary action. In fact,
when his preoccupation with disruptive demonstrations made it
impossible for him to finish his senior thesis on time, the university understandingly granted him an extension. Princeton officials
professed nothing but respect for Changa; when he closed out his
undergraduate career by disrupting the alumni parade, the Dean
of Students stepped out of line of march to shake his hand.
Today Adhimu Changa is a graduate student. At Princeton.

Yet this same young man had interrupted lectures, insulted
Trustees and deans, threatened students, occupied buildings,
and openly proclaimed his dedication to the goal of violent communist revolution. What more could he have done? What would
it take to provoke a school like Princeton? *What would it take?*

Yes, the universities have survived as institutions. But they are
weak, cynical institutions, unwilling or unable to come to their
own defense.

Today the wages of cynicism are falling due, both in our
schools and in our society. My classmates and contemporaries
are assuming powerful positions, beginning to spread their
influence to another new generation. These are the same men and
women who, ten years ago, wholeheartedly endorsed revolt; now
they are taking prominent positions in the government they had

pledged to overthrow. In 1969 James Fallows was the President of the *Harvard Crimson,* whose editorials referred to the federal administration as an "outlaw government"[14]; in 1979 Fallows was the chief speechwriter for President Carter. These same people, who once despaired of finding a moral justification for academic life, are now earning tenure at leading universities. Alan Gilbert (remember the firebrand who wanted to stone Harvard's President)? is now teaching political science.[15] The very activists who threw society into turmoil are now collecting society's benefits.

Am I bitter? Yes. I resent watching the old revolutionaries bask in the privileges they once condemned, while those of us who avoided disruptive activities — and therefore never attracted attention — work laboriously for the same recognition. The violent students of those days have prospered, while the law-abiding have struggled.

But if I am bitter, I am much more frightened. Frightened because a cynical generation is taking the reins of our society. Very few member of my generation have ever publicly admitted what I now freely admit: that, as a generation, we were profoundly tragically *wrong.* Our attacks on American society were ill-conceived, ill-fated. Even those of us who did not participate in the disruptions share in the blame. As Edmund Burke said, "All that is needed for evil to triumph is that good men do nothing." My generation hurt society immeasurably. Still, without apology — without even renouncing its destructive intent — that generation is now taking its turn at leadership. How much integrity will our institutions retain, when they are led by revolutionaries *manqués*? How much moral force will our society preserve, when its leaders are the same people who once unblushingly advocated its destruction? A society led by cynics is inevitably decadent.

Why did such an unusually idealistic generation become such a cynical one? Because its idealism was frustrated; it could not find a comfortable set of ideals. In academe, for instance, when students questioned the role of the university they received no adequate answer. The universities had lost their bearings; they could not justify their mission in straightforward, compelling, moral terms. Of course there were those who defended the academic tradition, and even those who pointed out its idealistic underpinnings. But most educators — administrators and professors alike — could not provide an argument explaining scholarship in idealists' language. So the questions dangled unanswered until students, assuming that no answer existed, forsook their righteous ambitions. That is the answer I had sought in that rut ten years ago: The Harvard Bust, and the countless similar episodes, occurred because in an age of idealism the universities could not satisfy the demands of the undergraduate conscience.

That same inability still afflicts American universities. The spate of radical activity never did cease; it simply lost its theatrical impact. Students still routinely occupy campus buildings, picket university ceremonies, and flout college discipline. Today such transgressions are viewed with jaded equanimity by all involved. (Many of the deans who should be administering discipline were once campus radicals themselves.) The issues vary, but the underlying objections remain the same. Students accuse the university of complicity with unsavory corporate powers, or investment in repressive foreign regimes, or acquiescence in improper social conditions. Almost invariably, it is the *moral* stature of the university that is questioned. And almost invariably, the university does not answer the radical charges directly. True, radicals often lose the individual battles; administrators often steadfastly uphold their policies. Nevertheless, the universities never deter such criticism; they never take the offensive to recover moral currency. If one issue evaporates, another will emerge to replace it by the following semester. Student activists never lack a cause.

Through it all, the schools refuse to counterattack — refuse to proclaim righteously the positive moral value of the university. Many professors uphold the ethics of scholarship; many more question the social and political assumptions on which the radical arguments are based. But very few pause to debate the wider question of institutional morality. The old rhetoric still prevails, arguing the ascetic virtues of those who seek the truth. But the practice belies that rhetoric. Students and professors view the university not as a crusading community, but as an ethically neutral institution. Once the rhetoric has run its course, administrators go back to talking of a value-free scholarship. They speak not from a lofty moral perch, but from the same pragmatic political stance that characterizes any other large organization. Our universities cannot — or will not — defend themselves on moral grounds.

CHAPTER TWO

The Leisure Class

> And to ask the American professorite to restructure itself is as sensible as if one had asked Marie Antoinette to establish a republican government in France. Whether or not it coincided with her long-term interests was immaterial; the poor woman couldn't even conceive of the possibility.
>
> *Irving Kristol*[1]

Even before his term in the Eisenhower cabinet began, Charles Wilson earned his own private niche in American history by uttering the notorious phrase, "What's good for the country is good for General Motors, and vice versa."[2] Today no image-conscious corporate executive would make the same gaffe; none would dare suggest that the company's interests and the national interest are identical. Yet every year congressmen hear an argument that would mirror Wilson's statement exactly, but for three distinguishing features. First, the speaker is not a businessman, but a college or university executive. Second, he speaks not of General Motors, but of Harvard or Michigan State. Third, his remarks do not infuriate political writers as Wilson's statement did. No one minds at all.

Why not? If Wilson's statement was considered blasphemous, why are the educators' arguments accepted so complacently? True, the country depends on General Motors (among others) to build automobiles. In either case, the country requires the service provided, but not necessarily on the supplier's terms. Just as every business has its own special corporate concerns, so too every college faculty has vested interests. And just as businessmen occasionally neglect the public interest while pursuing personal gain, so too professors occasionally neglect their students' educational needs while they pursue their own academic careers.

Educators generally claim a special immunity from supervision, whether by government, by alumni, by students, or by anyone else. Only college professors, they argue, are qualified to judge the country's educational needs. That argument, so readily accepted by so many analysts, is simply illogical. Professors receive their positions because they are judged proficient in one academic discipline, not in any overall understanding of the educational process. Even if the professor has earned his credentials in the field of education, he does not necessarily understand the broad educational needs of the society. Each academic department trains students to pursue a career in that particular area. Even education departments merely train future educators. No academician possesses the breadth to encompass all fields and be social arbiter to boot. Within their own department, the scholars should reign supreme. But what is good for the department, or for the university — as seen through the eyes of academic specialists — is not necessarily good for the country.

Nonetheless, educators defend their fiefdom admirably. The American professoriate has a unique opportunity to lobby for its own interests. For the four years that a student spends in college, academicians have a near monopoly on his attentions. They teach him that the academic approach surpasses all other forms of conduct — that any attacks on academic processes arise out of ignorance and Know-Nothingism. Since the college faculty shares a common set of interests, no one on campus contests this view. The student accepts the professors' view, and retains it in his later life. In all probability, he never devotes much attention to collegiate education, once he himself has passed through the experience. So his views retain the impress of his college mentors. Since most of the nation's most influential citizens are college graduates who have undergone this four-year lobbying process, the academicians' viewpoint survives intact.

No wonder, then, that when pollsters ask college students to rate the integrity of various professions, the students give high ranking to their scholarly overseers. Professors rank near the top of the list, judged by students to be models of professional probity. Lawyers and businessmen — notably absent from the collegiate scene where the ideological campaign is waged — rank near the bottom of the poll.[3] Somehow, when such poll results are released, the media fail to notice that the survey audience is biased toward academicians. Certainly a group of young corporate acolytes would rate business ethics more favorably; when a group of students rates its instructors the result is predictable. Academe, understandably enough, has a very high opinion of its own virtues.

But sometimes the self-congratulatory afflatus gets out of hand. In April 1973, after years of ballyhoo, Princeton University released a report by its Commission on the Future of the College. It had been an ambitious study, authorized to inspect every aspect of undergraduate life in minute detail. Listen to its conclusion about the moral status of the university: "It is difficult to imagine a more bountiful ethical system that is implicit in the norms that sustain the process of inquiry."[4]

"It is difficult to imagine" a better ethical system? These are scholars, now, who are writing this report. They presumably know of the world's great religions, of the laws of Solon and Confucius. Yet they have difficulty imagining an ethical system more bountiful than . . . their own. The arrogance of the statement is breathtaking. Imagine a lawyer making the same statement. ("It is difficult to imagine a more bountiful ethical system than is implicit in the norms that sustain the juridical process.") Or a doctor. (". . . that sustain the process of surgery.") Editorial writers across the country would wring their hands and rend their garments, and rightly so. How could one profession presume that its ethical status so thoroughly transcended all others as to make comparison inconceivable? No one blinked at the Princeton report.

Nor is Princeton alone. W. Allen Wallis, the chancellor of the University of Rochester, committed a comparable enormity in a 1962 essay, writing, "The process of seeking knowledge is, in a great university, a way of life, with ethical ideals as lofty and aesthetic values as inspiring as exist in any aspect of our culture."[5] At least Wallis qualified the claim somewhat; he includes only the "great" universities in his Olympian category. It seems that the most prestigious universities must be the repositories of the True Religion, while the lesser colleges act the part of those myriad cults that siphon off its moral currency.

How could we test these extraordinary claims? One convenient method would be to examine the behavior of the people who embrace this ethical system. Does their moral conduct indicate a superior guidance? Does it accord with the behavior that system would predict? Of course no ethical system, no matter how bountiful, can make men perfect. The more serious question is whether it raises the moral tone of its followers. Christians lapse into sin, but the Christian religion teaches them to recognize their sins and battle against further temptations. The most pious Christians betray their faith now and then, but the Church can point to countless indications of an overall moral uplift: not only the saints, but the entire community of believers.

In the case of the academic profession, the moral uplift is not at all clear. It is bad enough that many professors abuse their positions; it is worse that their colleagues rarely criticize or reprimand them. Perhaps the academic ideal is a lofty one, but it is one that is widely disregarded. Is this an ideal professors truly cherish, or only one to which they allude in their self-indulgent arguments?

The normal conduct of academic business stands in sharp contrast to the ideals apologists cite. Faculty political maneuvers are legendary for their pettiness. Academic conventions are notorious for their cutthroat competition and backstabbing. Young aspirants to teaching positions are treated like so many cattle, shunted from one interview to another at an exhaustive pace in a process that leaves the losers embittered. If the appointment is secured, the problems are just beginning. College faculties devise elaborate pecking orders and byzantine political alliances to thwart attempts at curriculum reform. One highly respected sociologist, who also belongs to a national advertisers' association, reports that he finds more cooperation among the scions of Madison Avenue than among his sociology colleagues. If the idealized professoriate is a guild of scholars selflessly united in the cause of truth, the reality flouts that ideal.

Obviously, not every professor comes to the profession out of a sincere love for learning. The teaching profession is attractive for its own rewards; most professors have a fairly easy life. The hours are good: five or six classroom hours per week, at the most, plus a few more hours for consultations and meetings. The professor's independence is unmatched; scholars choose and pursue topics of their own choosing, and their superiors rarely ask for an account of their time. Ordinarily professors have wide latitude in designing the content of their own courses, so that they may avoid the areas that bore or trouble them. Thus the typical professor spends perhaps ten hours a week performing required duties, many of which he designates for himself; his remaining working hours are entirely at his own disposal. Not a bad schedule, by any normal criteria.

Radical political thinkers flock to academe in terrific numbers, and for evident reasons. Inside the Ivory Tower, the professor can rail against the capitalist system without facing the consequences of his thoughts. He can shout all day about the iniquities of privilege, and then wander home to his comfortable evening with the books. He can rail against the rich and against elite institutions, while wealthy parents paying tuition support him in his job at an elite institution. He can become an expert about oppression without ever undergoing oppression himself. With a minimum of danger, he can preach revolution — even become a revolutionary hero — without risking his own creature comforts. Safe behind his podium and his desk, safe behind the smokescreens of tenure and academic freedom, he can urge other people to make the necessary sacrifices for political upheaval; he himself undertakes no nuch onerous task. Maybe he engages in a demonstration or two, or even spends a night in jail after some well publicized act of civil disobedience. But has any Marxist professor renounced his salary, or risked his life for the cause he espouses?

For scholars with more ordinary voices, the academic life offers similar protection from the ordinary costs of those vices. The schools are crowded with young women — or men, if that is the preference. Alcohol flows freely on campus, and a tenured professor has no need to abstain. (In three years at my Harvard upperclass House, I never saw the House Master sober). For the younger set, the proximity of a large student community effectively guarantees the supply of marijuana and harder drugs. In short, the academic life provides an easy way to prolong the carefree student years, avoiding new responsibilities.

Professors complain incessantly that they are paid less generously than their friends in other professional occupations. True enough, professors earn less than doctors or lawyers. But both doctors and lawyers — especially as they embark upon their careers — surrender almost all control over their own time. Doctors may be called to the hospital at any time of the day or night; lawyers work long hours on cases chosen by their superiors in the firm. What other profession offers the same generous fringe benefits that the university affords: a three-month vacation for beginning employees, the cultural and social attractions of a campus community, university-paid insurance — and occasionally housing, sabbatical leaves?

And then we are back to tenure. Once a professor has cleared the initial obstacles, he becomes virtually immune from his critics. In theory, a tenured professor, like a tenured judge, could be dismissed for neglect of duty or for moral turpitude. In practice, only the grossest violations of professional conscience result in any such censure: professors routinely overlook their colleagues' peccadilloes. Consequently, after the first frenzied rush to secure tenure, countless scholars lapse into a humdrum career, merely going through the motions of teaching and scholarship. In the less prestigious colleges, many professors neglect their scholarship entirely. Many publishers' representatives, touring the countryside to peddle their house's latest textbooks, find that they are more conversant in the discipline than the teachers who buy the books.

Even at the most famous universities some professors fall into a very noticeable rut. Harvard's Donald Fleming is a highly respected historian, an eminent researcher, whose course in American intellectual history I took during my sophomore year. Once, having missed a lecture, I borrowed notes from a friend who had taken the course the previous year. Comparing our notes for some other classes, I found a striking similarity, and pursued the clue. Sure enough, I learned that Fleming gives the same identical lectures, verbatim, every year. Even his jokes are the same for every succeeding class. Why could Fleming not have published these well worn lectures in book form, saving us the trouble of attending his classes? Because then Harvard would not have paid him; he was required by university regulations to teach this course. But he was not required — and his colleagues did not urge him — to spend any time in preparing new lectures. So he did not.

But I was fortunate. Fleming's lectures, old as they were, were nevertheless interesting and informative. The real victims are the students whose teachers did not have any real insights to offer even when they first began teaching; as these lesser scholars fall into their own academic ruts, their lectures lose any semblance of originality or utility.

No supervisor peers over the instructor's shoulder as he addresses his captive audience. No inquiring public peruses his tax returns, or demands a justification for his expenditures from the public till. His hours are short, vacations long, colleagues understanding, critics impotent. The professoriate is the unrecognized leisure class of our society.

Almost invariably, whenever critics raise an ugly issue, the professors call up their one consistent defense. Any advice from outside academe, they insist, is unacceptable. It would infringe upon academic freedom. Scholars must be allowed to pursue their researches wherever they lead, free from outside interference. That argument would be convincing if academic research were in fact untrammeled, and scholars welcomed debate on any subject with equal fervor. But the academic horizon is actually quite narrowly limited by the professors themselves, and some arguments are quickly stifled by the very people who demand academic freedom. Some subjects are declared taboo, and those who pursue them are subject to vicious pressures from their own academic colleagues.

The limitations on academic freedom do not come in the form of rules and regulations. Rather, unpopular professors are harassed and intimidated by pickets, protests, and disruptions. Dozens of top-flight academicians, plagued by such problems for years, have simply stopped appearing on college campuses. Yet the faculties stand idly by, refusing to punish the miscreants and enforce the rule governing freedom of speech on campus. Harvard's James Q. Wilson, several years ago, lamented the result: "The list of subjects that cannot be discussed in a free and open forum has grown steadily, and now includes the war in Vietnam, public policy toward urban ghettos, the relationship between intelligence and heredity, and the role of American corporations in certain overseas regimes."[6] That list is intact now, and growing.

At about the same time that Wilson made that statement, a Harvard colleague, Richard Herrnstein, was invited to address a class at Princeton. Herrnstein was a psychologist whose views on the connection between race and intelligence had provoked ferocious criticism. Princeton's radical students, hearing of the invitation, vowed to disrupt Herrnstein's appearance and call him to account for his ideological waywardness. As it happened, the guest lecture would have had nothing to do with the controversial topic; Herrnstein was slated to discuss the training of laboratory pigeons. No matter; the radicals promised a confrontation. Eventually, when Princeton officials refused to provide him with the protection he needed, Herrnstein cancelled his scheduled appearance.[7]

If one subject is absolutely off limits for discussion on campus, it is the subject of academic freedom itself. Students and faculty members may criticize any institution in society — any institution, that is, except the university itself. The university will accommodate a mild protest, but one may not question its fundamental orientation. The student who suggests new courses, or who protests limitations on enrollment, is within the pale; at least he implies that the college should allow new constituencies to enjoy its services. But when a student questions the integrity of the university itself, the reaction is swift and suppressive. At Princeton, for instance, after the Herrnstein fiasco, a conservative undergraduate group protested that by allowing the intimidation of Professor Herrnstein the university had sacrificed its claim to academic freedom. Princeton officials responded in a pother, branding the complaints as "inaccurate" and "irresponsible."[8] Critics may accuse the university of racism, of oppression, of insensitivity, or of immorality; they may not accuse it of hypocrisy. One cannot argue that the university is not open to all competing ideas. That criticism strikes too close to the truth, and academicians react with vicious *ad hominem* attacks. The teaching profession will encourage criticism on every other front, but it will not subject its one most cherished assumption to the same scrutiny. Nothing is sacred in academe, except academe itself.

When the university's own ox is gored, academic freedom counts for nothing. Even tenure counts for nothing. In 1953, a tenured professor named Frank Richardson bewailed the loss of academic standards at the University of Nevada.[9] He was summarily dismissed. (Richardson sued and won his case, no thanks to academe or its votaries.) And Richardson's case is only the most flagrant example. How many other scholars have been harassed, hounded out of their schools, denied appointments or degrees, merely because they rebelled against the prevailing academic orthodoxy? How many students have dropped out of the academic orbit because they know the academic Establishment will not tolerate their views? How many honest scholars have recanted their trenchant criticisms in the face of administrative disapproval? The number, if it could be calculated, would be high indeed.

No matter where it begins, any discussion of the scholar's job keeps coming back to one focal point: tenure. That old academic shibboleth, however, is an anachronism in today's universities. Once the persecution of scholars was a real and constant threat, but today the Inquisition has long since passed. Can anyone honestly imagine that our government would ever persecute a philosopher — if it could find one? Professors cite the alleged ravages of the McCarthy era. Yet even during that episode very few professors actually lost their jobs. And — what is much more to the point — very few universities forthrightly condemned McCarthy and supported their maligned professors. Today, on the infrequent occasion when political considerations come into play, the university stands idly by. Tenure is obsolete.

If only the universities took academic freedom seriously, the argument for tenure would sound duly impressive. When scholars put their careers on the line, risking public disdain at every turn, they should have some special protection from passing political upheavals. But tenure is the sort of instrument useful only to an idealistic institution — one that wholeheartedly protects the freedom it claims to serve. Given the cavalier attitude of the contemporary American universities, one must doubt the rhetoric invoking the rule of tenure.

A cynical analysis of tenure yields a very different understanding of the entire idea. Look upon the university as an ordinary business, with the same manpower needs as every other industry. Hiring and firing inevitably pose problems in this industry, as in every other. The industry needs a steady flow of young laborers, yet it cannot afford to pay for the permanent services of all the young talent it attracts. So the industry must find a commodious way to fire people — or, if you prefer, to terminate their employment. The tenure system solves the problem on all counts. The new professors stay for two, or three, or five years, and then face the watershed decision: they will either receive tenure, and stay on until retirement, or they will, in effect, lose their jobs. As long as everyone understands the process in advance, all the potential ugliness is removed from the process for firing employees. Scholars realize that they may not find employment at the same university forever; their superiors know that they will not suffer too long if a new recruit is incompetent or unpersonable. The whole matter proceeds smoothly. And of course once a professor receives tenure, the university simply declares the problem solved; a tenured professor is considered fit for duty, no matter how obviously the facts contradict that judgement. After tenure is bestowed, the gentlemen's club that constitutes the professoriate pretends that its hiring-and-firing needs have been fulfilled. And indeed they have, if the object of the process is to smooth over potential difficulties. The tenure process preserves academe free from the nasty scenes that afflict all other industries.

People writing in this iconoclastic vein usually point out that Socrates himself would never receive tenure at an American university today. Quite so. But the usual argument misses the reason. It is true, as the argument traditionally runs, that Socrates would be cited for his failure to publish. But the more compelling reason against appointing Socrates to a professorial chair is that he would constantly vilify the American university. The academy today claims to derive its moral force from Socrates' example, when in fact Socrates spent his career fighting against the very same forces that nourish contemporary colleges. Eventually, those very forces put Socrates to death.

During his public career Socrates clashed constantly with the competing schools known as the Sophists and the Rhetoricians. The common assumption of those two schools was the assumption that knowledge should be used as a means to an end. The Sophists and Rhetoricians taught students to reason and speak persuasively, to marshall arguments cogently, so that they could have their way in political and financial disputes. Knowledge, to them, was an instrument of power. Against this assumption Socrates posed the theory that one should study not to acquire knowledge, but to seek wisdom. And wisdom, to Socrates and his followers, was not a means to an end but an end in itself. In the Socratic model one studies out of love for wisdom (the word "philosophy" means exactly that: love for wisdom), nothing else.

To Athenian society, Socrates' ideas sounded seditious, dangerous. If young men devoted themselves to the love of wisdom, they might begin to question the power and righteousness of the city-state. Their faith and patriotism might waver. The Sophists and Rhetoricians had never questioned these basic values; they merely helped students to run society more efficiently, without worrying about the society's justice or morality. Of course the competing teachers fulminated against Socrates and his methods of inquiry, accusing him of exercising an "immoral influence" on his youthful students. Socrates, as we all know, was eventually tried, found guilty, and executed by the Athenian authorities on just those charges.

Now can there be any doubt that today's universities play the role of the Sophists and Rhetoricians, while falling back on Socrates for their own indulgence? The universities' advertisement is plastered on subway walls throughout the country: "To get a good job, get a good education." College catalogues and brochures cite the chances of increasing one's salary, or entering into a more exciting career. Even the most esoteric research projects go where the government funds lead. American universities criticze society incessantly (Socrates, by the way, did so rarely), but they do not resort to the higher morality of the Truth, except as a rhetorical gesture.

If I have pursued this subject at some length (and of course such cursory analysis does no justice to the competing Athenian philosophers), I have done so to make a fundamental point. American universities have no right to claim Socrates' mantle. If they were less hypocritical, they would set about justifying his execution. And yet at the same time, the university certainly did first grow out of Socrates' ideal. Therefore the contemporary American universities have betrayed their origins, and lost their ideals.

What claim do the universities have on our loyalties, then, if we adhere to the original Socratic ideal? In his fascinating book *Zen and the Art of Motocycle Maintenance* Robert Pirsig, a some-time university professor, confronts just that problem. Imagine a church building, Pirsig instructs us. Suppose the congregation disappears, and the church is sold. Now suppose the new owners convert the building into a bar. Will that bar be a holy place? [10]

The academic community engages in palpable hypocrisy when it trots out the old defense of academic freedom. Perhaps at one time the universities were citadels of truth, and custodians of the Socratic legacy. Today they are not. Perhaps at one time the universities resisted all political entanglements, and ensured vigorous debate on all topics; today they do not. The exemptions and privileges that accrued to the university in times past do not automatically devolve upon the very different institutions that exist today.

Clark Kerr has impeccable credentials as a proponent of latter-day universities; he was president of the University of California before assuming his present position at the head of the Carnegie Commission. His book *The Uses of the University* is a veritable paean to modern education; even the title, emphasizing the "Uses" of the university rather than Newman's "Idea," is a tacit bow to the new academic approach. Yet even Kerr sees the uncertainty of the genealogy that links modern universities with the Athenian Academy. "The modern academician likes to trace his intellectual forbears to the groves of Academe," Kerr writes; "but the modern university with its professional schools and scientific institutes might look equally to the Sophists and Pythagoreans."[11] As Kerr goes on to point out, comparison with the other Greek schools is not insulting in itself; Sophists and Pythagoreans served a vital role in Hellenic culture. But when professors justify their privileged status by invoking the shade of Socrates, they are invoking the ghost of a man their own intellectual forbears put to death.

Still the universities cling to the accoutrements of their old prestige, the prestige bought by Socrates and redeemed by the medieval Schoolmen. When a new faculty member takes his post, administrators carefully note that he was "appointed" rather than "hired," least anyone think the new professor is beholden to his administrative employers. In the old days of faculty collegiality the reference to "appointment" would have made sense, since all scholars shared equally in the governance of the institution, and no higher authority existed to supervise the "hiring" into a group of equals. Today that old nicety has little or no real meaning. With the complex demands of administrative overseers constantly in evidence, departments simply hire a scholar to fill a prescribed function. It makes no more sense to speak of U.C.L.A. "appointing" a professor than to speak of I.B.M. "appointing" an engineer.

The record of the modern university belies its highfallutin moral tone. As Isaac Bashevis Singer once said (in a very different context), "Sometimes, when you see the cook, the food doesn't seem very appetizing." So too with the schools. The repeated rhetoric is promising, the performance disappointing. Professors proclaim a glorious set of ideals, and then abuse those ideals constantly. If these people — these denizens of the new American leisure class — run the universities, then critics have every reason to worry.

The American people treat professors with great deference; the moral currency built up over the generations is still useful. But is this real respect, or simply a facade? Nietzsche would have suspected the latter. His own remarks about the scholar's social status are cynical and severe; he compares scholars with old maids — barren and solitary. "Indeed, one concedes to both, to the scholars and to the old maids, as it were by way of a compesation, that they are respectable — one stresses their respectability — and yet feels annoyed all over at having to make this concession."[12] In short, Nietzsche argues, we secretly wish they would do something more worthwhile and productive with their lives.

In the end we are left with two visions of the university. There is the rhetorical vision propounded by college publicists — a vision in which dedicated scholars subject themselves totally to the cause of knowledge. And there is the cynical vision propounded in this chapter — a vision in which venal academicians jealously guard their unearned privileges. The reality lies somewhere in between the two poles. Scholars by and large are not as hypocritical as this chapter might suggest, but neither are they as selfless as their own spokesmen would have us believe. Professors are like any other professionals: some are dedicated and ambitious, some slothful and incompetent. The point is that, like all other professionals, professors act consistently to preserve their own vested interests. Like doctors, lawyers, engineers, businessmen, and party politicians, academic workers are loath to surrender their spheres of influence, and quick to defend their perquisites against outside attackers.

Anyone seeking to reform the universities must begin with the understanding that scholars are imperfect beings, just like the rest of us. To protect ourselves against the excesses of academic rhetoric, we must be wary of the cold reality behind the rosy facade.

And do not be surprised, dear reader, if the academic community condemns this book.

CHAPTER THREE

The Multiversity

> A university anywhere can aim no higher than to be as British as possible for the sake of the undergraduates, as German as possible for the sake of the graduate and research personnel, as American as possible for the sake of the public at large — and as confused as possible for the sake of the preservation of the whole uneasy balance.
>
> *Clark Kerr*[1]

The university — the throne room of the imperial intellect — should be "as confused as possible." Surely, you say, this must be the ideal of some disaffected young firebrand, or some crusty old anarchist. Not so. Clark Kerr was one of the most prominent members of the American educational establishment. He was the president of the University of California (Berkeley) when he wrote the above statement, and he later served as head of the Carnegie Council on Higher Education. His book, *The Uses of the University,* is perhaps the most influential work of educational theory in the postwar era. All across the country colleges and universities exhibit the product of Kerr's ideal: confusion.

Not too long ago this confusion would have been impossible. Everyone knew, at least in outline form, what the universities sought to accomplish. Of course there were variations on the basic theme, but the universities existed in order to educate the country's elite. Most students came from privileged family backgrounds. The few exceptions were initiated into the ways of the elite during their college years, so that they graduated as full members of that class. There were no pressures to prepare students for the job market, since a diploma virtually assured the holder of a high place in society. Nor was there a need for occupational training: employers assumed that a college graduate would have an active and disciplined mind, and they would provide whatever particular training they considered necessary.

The liberal arts are the arts of the free man: today's educators repeat that formula as if it were an incantation, to ward off the reigning confusion. But in former days, when higher education was the province of the privileged few, the phrase had a broader meaning. The college student in those days enjoyed not only political freedom, but some measure of economic and social freedom as well. He could afford to spend four (or more) years cloistered in academe, studying things that would not advance his monetary interests.[2] He could afford the luxury of independent thinking, and the assumption that he would eventually become a leader in society. He could afford to detach himself from everyday affairs — his subordinates would handle them — and concentrate on weighty philosophical questions. To balance all these freedoms he had the heavy burden of social responsibility. He would be responsible for preserving and enriching his heritage, then for transmitting it to the leaders of the following generation.

Consequently, the liberal arts education had a fairly definite objective. Students were steeped in the best of their culture, so they would understand what they were called upon to preserve. They were introduced to philosophical analysis, so that they would, as rulers, appreciate the requirements of justice and the good society. Art and literature helped to refine their sensitivity, science to improve their understanding of nature, history to expand their horizons beyond the narrow confines of their own time and country. The particular formula varied from school to school and from age to age, but the underlying purpose remained constant. Only a few people could derive profit from the liberal arts, because only a few could comprise the elite.

In the twentieth century, the burgeoning forces of egalitarianism eroded that old understanding. Now more and more people saw in higher education a vehicle for social mobility, and demanded an opportunity to use it. At the same time, the increasing complexities of the industrial age required a growing corps of specially trained and educated workers, and general affluence furnished more people with the wherewithal to afford a college

training. Once the expansion began, the purposes of higher
education became somewhat muddled. Should the university
provide training for those who sought elite status, or only for
those who already enjoyed it? Or both? In any case, the perception of the university had changed. Once the emphasis had been
on culture and truth; now education experts spoke of training
and social mobility.

World War II and its aftermath completed the transition. The
G.I. Bill opened the doors of American colleges to thousands of
men who could not otherwise have attended. The postwar
"baby boom" presaged a dire need for teachers at all educational
levels, and the schools scrambled to comply. The federal government discovered the use of the university as a research consort,
and suddenly, sponsored scientific projects became a major
feature of life at the more prominent schools. For a full generation — until the close of the tumultuous 60s — higher education
enjoyed a period of dizzying growth. Everything involved seemed
caught in the expansion and proliferation: more students, more
schools, more teachers, more projects, and more diverse explan-
tions of the goals of the university.

Enter Clark Kerr, with his paean to confusion. Like so many
educationists of that time, Kerr could see no limit to the possible roles of the university. An individual school could choose
to promote students' intellectual and social maturation (the
British model), or concentrate on academic research (the Ger-
man model), or engage in social projects for the good of the surrounding community (the American model). All these roles
seemed too tempting to ignore, so Kerr and his supporters chose
to pursue all three (or more) goals simultaneously. Kerr went so
far as to coin a new word for the institution of higher education,
the "multiversity," and one institution happily served several
masters.[3]

Of course this new amalgam had its own peculiar problems.
For one thing, the different roles sometimes conflicted, so that
the ruling coalition was never far from collapse. When the conflict began, each side — in fact, everyone involved — had to be
ready to compromise. Kerr recognized the problem: "To make

the multiversity work really effectively, the moderates need to be in control of each power center and there needs to be an attitude of tolerance between and among the power centers, with few territorial ambitions."[4]

Which is fine; everyone can support moderation and tolerance. But what happens when the conflict is irreconcilable? What happens when, say, the university finds that it cannot fulfill its research ambitions without weakening its teaching staff? If all the officials insist on moderation and compromise, then no one will be happy; everyone will just be slightly less content with the new scheme of things. Compromise is the stuff of politics, but not of academics. Compromise and excellence do not coexist easily, and a university is nothing without a total commitment to excellence. Kerr's vision left no room for the unreconstructed idealist who seeks the truth single-mindedly, without regard for the costs or the consequences. The introduction of the multiversity, in short, was an attempt to avoid the ultimate question of the university goal. Ultimately, ineluctably, that nagging question was bound to reappear.

As long as the educational boom continued, the inevitable crisis lay dormant. A few personalities were ruffled, and many perceptive professors wrote of the decay of academic standards, but overall the outlook seemed rosy. This was a time, remember, when American society evinced an ebullient optimism on every social issue, believing in its ability to conquer any problem. The economy grew steadily, while the politicians talked of assaults on a New Frontier. Even in theology the trend (embodied in Harvey Cox's *The Secular City*) was toward a belief that we could create a sort of heaven on earth. At the time Vietnam and Watergate were simply geographical locations. Inside academe, the majority accepted the dominant mood. Each year the university could mete out budget increases to nearly every department, so that no one educational sector felt oppressed. The few dissenting cries were overwhelmed by the dominant optimism.

Then the bubble burst. Academic budgets stabilized, then contracted. Vietnam protestors contributed to a general radical critique that embraced the university itself. The artificial consensus that supported the multiversity evanesced. Writing in 1971, recalling that phenomenon, Robert Nisbet pointed out that the conflict was inevitable:

> I refer to . . . the university's roles of higher capitalist, chief of the research establishment, superhumanitarian, benign therapist, adjunct government, and loyal opposition. Each of these is doubtless a worthy role in society. What passes imagination, however, is any conception of their being harnessed together in a single institution that continues to insist upon its aristocratic or priestly virtue in the cause of dispassionate reason.[5]

Today educators are acutely aware of their limitations. Schools have enough difficulty satisfying any single constituency; they feel no need to take on new responsibilities. The costs of running a university are rising, while confidence and income drop. The college-age population is shrinking, and young professors find themselves unemployed, perhaps almost unemployable. And yet through it all one vestige of the multiversity remains intact: confusion. American colleges still refuse to limit themselves to any one role. Our universities still attempt, with rapidly diminishing success, to be all things to all men.

Think about it. Every college president warns incoming freshmen that the school cannot possibly fulfill all of their needs. So far, so good. But try to learn which roles the university *cannot* fulfill, and his tune changes immediately. Can the school provide excellence in undergraduate teaching? Of course, the administrator replies. Up-to-date research equipment? Exciting social opportunities? Certainly. Does the school emphasize teaching, or research? academic or social life? big-college diversity or small-college intimacy? With rare exceptions, the university officials will claim success on *all* these fronts. No one vision is put forth to the detriment of any other. The university is a neutral instrument, available for a variety of uses.

Historically, the university has been anything but neutral. The medieval universities flourished despite (or even because of) controversies that sometimes literally provoked bloodshed. These schools, from which today's universities descend as children, dedicated themselves to God and God's Truth — not subjects which brook compromises. The schools later discovered an interest in patriotic nationalism, and later still in combatting superstition with the cudgel of scientific knowledge. Still, the underlying search for truth was unabated.

Even in the relatively short history of higher education in America, the most dramatic successes have occurred under the aegis of subjective idealism, not neutrality. Charles Eliot scandalized the academic world when he introduced the elective system, but he revivified Harvard. Woodrow Wilson bullied and cajoled the Princeton faculty to accept his preceptorial approach, and Princeton's reputation blossomed. Robert Maynard Hutchins came to the University of Chicago an *enfant terrible,* and proceeded to alienate dozens of faculty members, but when he was done the strength of the school was unquestioned. When a school stands united in quest of one goal, its academic quality soon improves. Idealism breeds excellence.

Kerr's idea of the multiversity spread through academe like a spark through dry tinder. No wonder! The idea suits the interests of every educationist, professor and administrator alike. In the multiversity, no one feels any discipline or restraint. Each faculty member can do as he pleases, and the administration, looking on the resultant confusion, can pronounce it good. Is the course catalogue a hodgepodge of unrelated offerings? Fine. The multiversity seeks diversity. Are professors rushing out of the classroom to pursue research projects? Excellent. The multiversity encourages professors to explore new frontiers. Does each student have a different idea of what the college should do for him? Wonderful. The multiversity offers its services in support of any cause.

The neat, circular logic of the system makes everything possible. Now that the university will accept any goal, it will accept any program as well. How can any program earn a negative evaluation, when on one knows with any certainty what its purpose is? As long as the proponents know how to use the educationist argot, any program can earn the multiversity's approval and support. Professors can hire themselves and their departments out to the highest bidder for research contracts, students can demand credit for employment experience, adminis-

trators can enlarge their support staff. If the university does not
have a stated objective that justifies the program's existence, a
new objective can be invented. If the program fails to achieve
that objective, supporters can find some other goal that it *does*
achieve, and continue to justify it. Just when the cacophony of
conflicting programs reaches its highest pitch, the college can
proclaim success. Confusion! Just what the multiversity seeks!

In the multiversity, failure is nearly impossible. As the saying
goes, if the Edsel had been a college course. . . .

Actually, the reference to the Edsel debacle is quite appropriate. In that disastrous effort, the Ford automotive czars
designed a new car and then, working backwards, sought to
convince the public that the new car was just what we all had
been wanting. In the multiversity, the educationists first give
free rein to their own pet interests, and then summon up an
educational theory to justify the results. The multiversity has
existed for years before Clark Kerr wrote his book providing it
with a new name and a new respectability. Ever since the influx
of students after World War II had made education a growth
industry, academic leaders had been more intent on expansion
than on institutional cohesion. Especially after they discovered
the largesse of the federal government, administrators worked
to build more buildings, admit more students, train more teachers, hire more professors. Growth became its own reward.[6]
Educators boasted of the many new courses being offered, the
many new experiments being performed. Only a few lonely
critics raised objections, and they were quickly forgotten in the
general tumult.

As long as public support was plentiful — as long as federal
funds continue to flow, and record numbers of applicants clam-
ored for seats in the freshmen classes — educators had no reason
to question their ideas. Opportunities knocked, and the universities rushed to answer. Gradually, the lure of growth enticed
academe away from its ideals, until finally the ideals disappeared
and higher education became simply another sector of the
nation's economy. Kerr said that the multiversity was "held
together by administrative rules and powered by money."[7] So
much for the search for truth. Academe had methods and proce-

dures, but no underlying philosophy. The idea of the multiversity filled the void, creating a new ideal to match the universities' actual practices. For years the schools had acted as if growth and diversification were ends in themselves. Now a respectable theory made that presumption explicit.

While the multiversity pushed out simultaneously on all its frontiers, the home base was left unguarded. Teaching, the central mission of the university, lost its cachet. Try as they might, with language laboratories and closed-circuit television lectures, the education moguls could not make classroom teaching a growth industry. As soon as they entered the academic profession, young scholars learned that they could advance quickly by doing research, while their classroom efforts would pass unnoticed.

Once again, the university's resident theorists had a plausible argument to justify the new development. Good researchers, they argued, make good teachers; and no one could be a good teacher without keeping abreast of professional developments in his field. Moreover (the argument continued), a good teacher is the sort of person who never pauses in his own pursuit of truth, so he is naturally inclined toward research activities.

Undergraduates know better. Teaching takes a low priority at the multiversity, and students see the evidence. Professors avoid teaching introductory courses, leaving that set of responsibilities to their subordinates. Or, if they must teach freshmen, they do so with obvious disrelish. Senior professors cut back their office hours, using the extra time to work on their special projects. Dedicated teachers are turned down when they apply for tenure, while incompetent teachers advance quickly through the ranks on the strength of their research successes.

Actually, the argument that links good teaching with good research is quite thoroughly illogical. Yes, a good teacher always works to increase his own understanding of the subject, but broad understanding has little or nothing to do with specialized research. By the same token, arcane investigations have little or no impact on the introductory courses offered for freshmen. Perhaps there is some reason for political scientists to run computer analyses of local election results, but those analyses will

not help a lecturer to explain the basic structures of constitu-
tional government. And research fosters a frame of mind that is
almost diametrically opposed to the teacher's attitude. The
temperament of the ideal research scientist — solitary, careful,
and painstaking — is not conducive to lively lectures. Cardinal
Newman made the point clear:

> To discover and to teach are distinct functions; they are
> also distinct gifts, and are not commonly found united in
> the same person. He, too, who spends his day in dispensing
> his existing knowledge . . . is unlikely to have either leisure
> or energy to acquire new. The common sense of mankind
> has associated the search for truth with seclusion and
> quiet.[8]

But of course Cardinal Newman's ideas do not rule the multiversity. Far from it. The multiversity not only increased the
premium on scholarly research, but approved new uses of the
professor's time: consulting work with outside organizations,
contracts for industrial or governmental research, social work,
and so forth. During the Kennedy Administration, Harvard
became the model of the new engagement, with its professors
shuttling to and from Washington to give advice between classes.

Naturally, professors found that their outside activities generated more prestige than their teaching. (How many people know,
or care, whether or not Henry Kissinger was a good teacher?) So
they sought out new opportunities for consulting, advising, and
research. The multiversity became a clearinghouse for a diverse
collection of individual skills, all of them available to the highest
bidder.

Why should a teacher do research? Why should a researcher
teach? At one time the connection might have been obvious; the
universities were the primary suppliers of research skills. But
gradually other institutions began to emerge to do specified
research without the distractions of a student body. The development of "think tanks" in government and elsewhere presaged an
end for the university's research windfall. Robert Nisbet drew the
scenario:

> On some dread day — so might run the nightmare of any
> university president committed to the higher academic

capitalism — all congressional committees, industrial boards of directors, and foundation executives will realize at once that there are far cheaper and more efficient places to have their research done than in the academic guild that is the university. And, at the same time, all physicists, chemists, mathemeticians, biologists, and engineers, the ones, that is, that universities like to hold, will realize that by going to these new kinds of research center or institute they can have higher salaries for not having to share them with the Chaucerian scholar, freedom from the now-augmenting distractions of university existence, and, if things keep going the way they are, much higher status in the American social system.[9]

Ironically, the sort of research that carries the most prestige in academe is exactly the sort *least* likely to help make the researcher a better teacher. Government, industries, and foundations want immediate results for their investments, so the research centers on current problems. The researcher then marshalls facts about the problem at hand, and, inevitably, relays those facts on to his students. But by the time the student leaves school, the problem might have been solved, and the facts might have become obsolete. Students have no use for the information that comes to them from the frontiers of knowledge. Research marches on, and those frontiers move out, leaving the student with outdated facts. A successful teacher provides his students with knowledge that will endure, and with theories that outlive the results of a particular experiment. Research and teaching are simply not related. Of course there are exceptional individuals who combine both skills, but they are just that: exceptional. Their presence does not justify an otherwise untenable assumption that good research will breed good teaching, except in the minds of the people who train university professors.

Each young scholar, as he goes through his graduate training, researches one issue exhaustively for his dissertation. As he delves into this special field, he naturally grows more and more interested in it. Ordinarily, he retains that interest when he becomes a professor. If he can, he persuades his department to offer a course in that particular field, so that he can relay his knowledge on to undergraduate acolytes. Then another young scholar adds another specialized course to the departmental offerings, and another offers a third. Soon the entire course catalogue becomes a compendium of academic specialties, with only a few survey courses remaining to placate the academic generalists. Undergraduates take up specializations even before they reach their sophomore year. The curriculum is geared toward those who will continue on into graduate school in the same field. The college becomes Grad School Prep.

When they defend the burgeoning growth of the catalogue, educationists speak of the explosive growth of knowledge. But is knowledge itself growing at such a pace, or are scholars simply dividing their existing store of knowledge into smaller and smaller categories? Facts can be manipulated like a deck of cards — shuffled, dealt, and arranged in a staggering number of permutations — but they are still the same facts. New scholarly journals are introduced faster than the librarians can process them, but the articles they contain do not necessarily open new horizons for productive scholarship. In fact, the overabundance of professors seeking to publish their work leads to the publication of new journals whether or not they meet a real academic need. Scholars can poke into fields that have been justly neglected in the past, and dredge up information of no particular use to anyone outside the tight coteries of their academic specialty. The sickeningly familiar formula, Publish or Perish, encourages professors to pursue research even when it is obviously unrewarding, and to put forth their results even if they are undigested.

This dogged attitude toward research masks another, deeper problem in the university's approach. Theoretically, the function of the university as research institution is to unearth new truths, rather than to compile vast arrays of irrelevant facts. The goals of scholarly research should be to provide a better understanding of the world in which we live. And the discoveries which best fulfill that purpose are not specialized excursions on the frontiers of knowledge; they are broad-minded inquiries into everyday realities. In fact, the importance of an idea is almost directly proportional to the breadth of its scope. Einstein revolutionized physics not by confining himself to a narrow special realm, but by drawing up a theory to cover all of the relevant physical phenomena. The methodical plodding that constitutes research at most universities today does not aim at such revelations; at best, it can tidy up the loose ends that the truly innovative theories always leave.

Pure scientific research — research undertaken for the sheer joy of obtaining wisdom — is an enterprise far removed from the technical experiments that clutter most university laboratories. One aims at enlightenment, and features imagination; the other aims at immediate results, and features persistence. The former is an integral part of the search for truth, and thus a proper role of the university. The latter has no place in the liberal arts institution. The liberal arts university exists to stretch out the horizons of the mind, and imaginative people will gravitate toward such an institution. Competent technical researchers, admirable as they may be, have no particular reason to associate themselves with the liberal arts. And the liberal arts college has no reason to recruit them.

The compulsion toward research, combined with the university's constant drive to expand, leads to bizarre duplications of effort. Each university seeks to have its own electron accelerator, its own program in Near Eastern Languages, its own library subscriptions to all the exotic journals. Unless it has all the latest research equipment and all the most esoteric lines of study, the multiversity's potentialities will be limited. So schools often pass up the obvious opportunities to economize by cooperating with each other. The multiversity requires constant growth in all directions; any limitations, no matter how well justified, are repugnant.

When the time comes for scholars to publish their findings, the story is much the same. Most work takes aim at a tightly confined topic, appealing only to other specialists working in the field. Occasionally a maverick professor breaks out of the confining limits of his own specialty, and begins addressing broader issues, aiming to attract the general audience. When that happens, the popularizer quickly finds a wide following; people outside the university are anxious to learn when the material is presented in an approachable fashion. But often these popular versions are misleading, and sometimes they are nothing but pseudo-scientific claptrap. The general public is easily beguiled by such half-truths, because the real item is not usually available: most scholars are too wrapped up in their special fields to enter the public debate. Since the university is fragmented into narrow interest groups, the debate on general questions — questions that quickly enter the mainstream of contemporary thought — is artificially limited. Research specialists seek abstruse facts, but the general public (including most undergraduate students) only ponders sweeping theories. So the fragmentation of the multiversity actually defeats its own purpose; specialization makes nonsense more powerful, and the university fails to serve the public weal.

The evidence is everywhere around us today. Professional economists shoot holes in the theories of John Kenneth Galbraith, but since he combines his dubious economic formulas with broad social criticisms, his books are popular and influential. Carl Sagan concocts imaginative ideas about Creation, and because most other works on the subject are unreadable, the public reads his works respectfully. The best-selling books in college bookstores — the books students read for their own edification — are all too often examples of this genre. On a deeper level, undergraduates probe the bizarre mysticism of Carlos Castenada or the latest cultic guru because of the dearth of serious material about the spiritual life. The world outside academe, and undergraduates inside, look for broad theories — theories they can incorporate into their own world views — couched in lively prose. By failing to provide such theories, the universities forfeit their influence on public opinion.

Once, not very long ago, the universities proclaimed their dedication to the cause of truth, and let nothing distract them from that purpose. The multiversity, in its efforts to satisfy every demand, takes a considerably softer line. Some students come to college only in order to acquire a marketable skill, and so the multiversity takes pride in the fact that its graduates can earn higher salaries. Gradually, some institutions lose sight of all other goals. The liberal arts lose their primacy, and the college becomes a sort of elevated vocational school. Worse still, some educators begin to feel that no other educational goal is important save the training of students for high-paying positions. No less an authority than T.H. Bell, then U.S. Commissioner of Education and now Secretary of the U.S. Department of Education, argued for just that approach in 1975. "I feel that the college that devotes itself totally and unequivocally to the liberal arts is just kidding itself," Bell stated.[10]

But suppose the university did make vocational education its primary function. How could it achieve that goal? Society will need doctors and lawyers for the foreseeable future, but there are already medical and law schools to provide for that need. Electricians and plumbers are also necessary, but college training is not relevant to their skills. There are certain fields for which the university can provide some training — engineering and architecture stand out as examples — but in many other fields the university is simply incapable of the appropriate training. In fact, the college retards the process of vocational education, by keeping students removed from professional training for four years. If employment training is what the student wants, the university cannot ordinarily oblige.

Vocational training in itself is an unassailable idea. No one can fault students for wanting marketable skills, and no one can blame professional schools for supplying those skills. In fact, there are thousands of students in American colleges today who would be happier in professional schools than they are in the liberal arts. Students hoping to find high-paying jobs have remarkably little patience for philosophy and Elizabethan drama. Many of today's collegians are not adequately qualified — by talent or by inclination — for the liberal training.

If they chose, some colleges could concentrate exclusively on teaching students marketable skills, and leave the liberal arts to others. Then students, professors, and potential employers alike would be able to choose more knowledgeably. But once again the multiversity forbids such a solution. The liberal arts still retain a special privileged status, and the multiversity will not give up that fiefdom. So both the liberal arts program and the job-training program must suffer together, detracting from each other, to satisfy the educationists' demands.

The distinguishing characteristic of the multiversity is educational imperialism. Whenever and wherever an educational theorist sees prestige, he hurries to annex that prestige to the university. Government enjoys great prestige, so the multiversity becomes a partner with the government: doing research, consulting, advising, lobbying. Employment training provides an obvious benefit for society, so the multiversity advertises itself as a vocational school. The arts are popular, so the multiversity sets itself up as a patron. Wherever society sees a useful or elevating goal, the multiversity hastens to pursue it. Whenever society encounters a new problem, the multiversity promises to solve it. And whenever society enjoys an unexpected blessing, the multiversity quickly takes the credit.

At first the opportunities for growth seemed to be endless. Schools opened new departments in every conceivable field, eventually offering courses in such rigorous sciences as flycasting and horseshoeing. Students could earn degrees in Recreational Management and in Fashion Design. Next came industrial research projects, and soon the universities were furnishing technical solutions to the problems of American (and foreign) corporations. Universities dabbled in promotion of travel, and in entertainment. Intercollegiate sports, once a pleasant recreational outlet, became a mammoth national industry, bearing absolutely no marks of amateurism.[11]

At the same time they added new programs, universities sought a larger constituency of students. The multiversity propounded the notion that everyone should be entitled to a college education, and enrollments soared. Single-sex colleges saw the chance to expand by admitting students of the other sex, and coeducation became popular. (And some naive women believed that these universities were bowing to the demands of feminism.) Then the remaining single-sex institutions, fearing that they could lose students to their competitors, joined in the movement. A few other schools tested adult education programs, and soon the "continuing education" department was a regular feature of the university. The multiversity had broken down the barriers that reserved colleges for young adults, or for members of one sex. Extension courses, offering credit for work conducted off campus, broke down yet another barrier.

Naturally, the university kept its public relations staff (When did universities suddenly see the need for public relations staffs?) busy leading the cheers for each new advance of the multiversity's realm. Each new program generated headlines, and each new headline generated praise. Academe found a successful formula for growth; the universities advertised their ability to bring education into new realms, and everyone favors education, so everyone applauded the new crusades. In each program and each new experiment, the proponents of the multiversity announced another unqualified success. But the multiversity still always needed more funds, more students, more worlds to conquer.

The era of the multiversity was an era of growth. Higher education expanded at an unprecedented rate, and the sheer momentum of the expansion carried forward the good and bad programs together. University presidents managed their empires like business tycoons, seeking new areas for growth, new markets for their wares. Money, students, and public confidence were all in plentiful supply, so that new programs could be added constantly to the university's offerings. The university acquired more and more power, and demanded better facilities, more and better programs, more and better students. Any opportunity for growth proved seductive, and universities proved frankly promiscuous in their projects for growth. The multiversity made American colleges diverse, powerful, and (that word again) confused.

Now education has ceased to be a growth industry, and the days of the multiversity are numbered. Students no longer flock to the campus in larger numbers each year. Taxpayers grumble about the rising costs of maintaining the educational plant. The public has lost its optimism about the powers of the university. The universities have had their chance, and we have not noticeably approached utopia. Critics and friends alike have begun to see the limits the university must face, and to call upon the university to concentrate its efforts toward carefully defined ends. The growth mentality that begot the multiversity has disappeared.

But in the minds of professors and college administrators, the multiversity still lives on. Educationists still practice the higher capitalism, or educational imperialism. They still seek to insinuate the university into every corner of American society. America's colleges have tasted power, and they will not part with it voluntarily.

Still, the ideal of the multiversity is dead. Our colleges forfeited their old traditions in the quest for growth and power. Now the growth has ceased, the power is dwindling, and American universities are bereft of any guiding vision.

CHAPTER FOUR

Who Rules the Roost?

Why do you want to turn Yale education
over to a bunch of boobs?
Rev. Henry Sloane Coffin[1]

Who should run the college? Students? Professors? Administrators? Trustees? American universities are a welter of competing constituencies, each with its own distinct interests. What pleases the students does not necessarily please the deans, and faculty members do not always agree with overseers. Each one of these groups has characteristics that make it narrow-minded in its approach to university policy, and no single group embraces all the relevant viewpoints.

Maybe it was all much easier in Plato's Academy. As long as students deal individually with their teachers, the problems of defining educational policy are negligible. The contract between teacher and student is not a complicated one. Perhaps even today such a system would be attractive: let students choose their tutors individually, and contract with them on an individual basis. What a luxury! Then the academic process would not be tangled in a web of administrative irrelevances; only the subject itself would matter.

But today's colleges claim to be much more than a means of uniting students with teachers. They are institutions with a character and a mission greater than the sum of their parts. Professors may leave Harvard and go to Berkeley, but Harvard does not lose its personality, nor does Berkeley become more like Harvard. A school's atmosphere is, above all else, collegial. The institution has a continuity of its own, so that the university endures from generation to generation. True, there are changes.

Princeton today barely resembles the Princeton of, say, the 1940s, as many old grads mournfully attest. Nonetheless a Princeton degree means something distinct — something more than that the bearer passed certain specific courses taught by certain specific professors. American universities promise their students not simply a menu of individual course offerings, but a complete educational experience that incorporates life outside the classroom as well. Thus a Princeton degree certifies not only that the bearer fulfilled that school's course requirements, but also that he had passed through its extracurricular processes. It indicates, in short, that he is a Princeton Man.

So the task of those who formulate policy for the university is not simply to set up course requirements and issue reading lists. The larger task is to define the institution's total educational experience. What *is* a Princeton Man? What are the tests he must pass, and the processes he must undergo? Somehow, someone at every college must answer such questions.

Keep in mind, too, that the college cannot beg the question. Failure to choose a goal is every bit as confining as any choice could be. The multiversity, with its unlimited variety of educational roles, has a severely limited capacity to pursue any given one of those roles wholeheartedly.

Keep in mind, too, that colleges are centers of argumentation. Put any two students (or teachers, or administrators) together in one room and a debate will ensue: that is the recipe that colleges' promotional literature gives. All these arguments are wonderful methods of airing intellectual issues, but they are terrible impediments to the establishment of a consensus. Can anyone imagine that a college faculty would voluntarily, spontaneously agree on a curriculum? Or that the students would cheerfully accept such a curriculum once the faculty had proposed it? Of course not. The question is complicated, too, by the multifarious interests of the different parties. The school must have a means of settling such disputes. Which means, of course, that there must be some final authority.

So, again, who should run the university?

For the past decade or so, students have insisted that they should be included in all decision-making bodies of the university. During the upheavals of the late '60s students won appointments to diverse faculty committees; many universities set up cooperative governing bodies on which undergraduates and graduate students were fully represented. Even academic departments submitted to the demands, giving students a voice in the decisions about appointments and tenure. The students' argument, of course, was a simple one. They demanded to be treated as full partners in the educational enterprise, since they had as much at stake as the professors. They demanded, therefore, the right to determine their own educational fate.

As the '60s merged into the '70s, and campus life returned to what outsiders perceived as normal, the rise in student power became a major force for change within the university. Consider, for instance, the Afro-American Studies departments. Virtually all such departments are younger than the other academic departments within the university; most were formed (in response to student demands) in the period after 1968. Consequently, Afro-American Studies units, in their administrative forms and in their academic tone, accentuate the effects of the post-'60s educational policies. An additional factor, of course, is that hundreds of Afro-American departments were set up in direct reaction to undergraduate protests — often violent protests. At Harvard, for instance, during my own undergraduate career, the demand for the department arose as an offshoot of the protests over Vietnam. Somehow the six SDS demands that precipitated the 1969 Harvard Bust were transmuted into eight demands — the latter two being demands posed by black undergraduates — when the Afro-American Society joined the student strike. These demands, non-negotiable (as most demands were), stipulated not only that Harvard must create a black studies department, but also that students must be present at the creation, and thereafter. Harvard acceded to the demands, and now that department, like its counterparts at so many other colleges, features an unlikely administrative process in which undergraduates supervise their own teachers. Anyone who doubts the impact of this innovation need only compare Afro-American departments with, say, physics departments. The academic standards in physics are incalculaby more rigorous. And why not? Would undergraduates

presume to judge a scientist's knowledge of the physics of subatomic particles? Certainly not. But students in the black studies
departments do make that presumption — which is precisely why
the academic quality of those departments lags. The belief that a
second-year undergraduate is competent to judge the scholarly
credentials of an accomplished professor is sophomoric, as is
the pedestrian scholarship generated by that belief.

Students, after all, come to college as acknowledged inferiors.
If they were equal to their teachers they would have no need for
instruction. This does not mean that professors are necessarily
better human beings, nor even that they are necessarily more
intelligent. It does mean that professors have (or should have)
demonstrated their grasp of a certain discipline. Students may
eventually attain the same sort of grasp, but it is ludicrous to
pretend that they have already done so. No matter how much a
good teacher learns from his students, he keeps in mind that his
function is to convey a body of knowledge which he has and
they do not. And no matter how much the good teacher respects
his students and honors their opinions, he retains the final say in
all academic judgements. Democracy is impossible when the
parties are inherently unequal. When he enrolls in classes the
student thereby accepts an unequal condition. Or at least that is
how it should be.

In practice the situation is quite different. Students regularly
demand and occasionally receive representation on the bodies
that determine educational policy. Yet very few schools are so
open-minded on the subject that they allow truly equal representation. The more typical structure includes a minority of
student members, whose votes are easily overwhelmed, if need
be, by the majority of faculty and administrative members. So
when a conflict does arise, the students have just enough power
to raise a fuss, but not enough to carry the question. Three
possible results can occur, all of them undesirable. 1) The
majority can squelch the students' initiative, inevitably wounding
the very sensibilities that were nurtured by the creation of the
student-faculty panel. 2) The faculty members (or some of
them) can bow to the students' wishes. If the majority of the
nonstudent voters go along with student wishes, then student

representation was unnecessary; the measure would have passed without student votes. If a minority of the faculty representatives support the students, then the faculty majority will resent the compromising of its authority. (Indeed, many faculty members now refuse to participate on student-faculty bodies because participation would acknowledge the group's ability to override faculty decisions.) 3) The panel can find a compromise solution to the problem, leaving everyone partially satisfied with the result, and of course also partially dissatisfied. In this case, arguably the most frequent outcome of student-faculty deliberations on controversial subjects, the university compromises its ideals yet another time.

There are many lesser issues — student activities, undergraduate organizations, and so forth — that student governments can and do handle quite capably without any substantial intervention by the faculty. There are other issues that involve students and professors equally but do not call for an expert academic judgement; students deserve an equal voice in deciding such questions. (Questions about the mutual comfort of the college community would fall into this category. For example, given that the budget will allow the library to be open for 40 hours a week, which 40 hours should be chosen?) Even on serious educational issues, students will naturally have a special perspective which the faculty should not ignore; perhaps a nonvoting student presence on academic committees would be appropriate. But to give students the final authority is ridiculous.

The most frequent argument for student power involves the tenure process. Since a professor, to win tenure, must be judged as competent in both teaching and research, students regularly argue that they themselves should judge the candidate's teaching prowess. Obviously that claim has some validity; if a lecturer is consistently boring, his students will be the first to know and the last to forget. Students see failures where sympathetic colleagues might only see weaknesses. Student evaluations of teaching competence should be an integral part of the tenure process. And yet, on the other hand, there is a serious scholarly judgement involved here, and only professors should make it. A very dry lecturer might be dispensing pearls of wisdom to those who can stay alert, and a vibrant, exciting lecturer might be peddling academic nonsense. Students have a natural tendency to favor teachers whose courses are chummy and undemanding. They are not always equipped to distinguish between evanescent popularity and lasting intellectual attainment; that is the job of the faculty.

When students do have a voice in the tenure process, by the way, a curious fact emerges. Students, as a rule, don't care. During my stay at Princeton I watched the Dean of the Faculty labor to elicit students' comments on the faculty members who were coming up for tenure. He told everyone who would listen that he wanted to hear student opinions. He assured undergraduates that their voices would be heard and their confidentiality respected. He placed ads in the school newspaper asking for students to come forward. He virtually begged the student representatives to take advantage of the opportunity. Yet, when the campus press asked him to name the most troublesome aspect of the tenuring process, he annually replied that not enough input had been gathered. Students had the opportunity to speak their piece, and they neglected it. To make matters worse, every year students would complain bitterly about one or two tenure decisions — decisions they might have changed by answering the Dean's pleas in the first place.[2] The problem, of course, is that students have other things on their minds. They have their books to read, papers to write, parties to attend — and all this is as it should be. Students have plenty to do already, without the addition of administrative chores.

Therein lies one more argument against student participation in the highest university councils. Anyone acquainted with American colleges realizes that the students who dominate undergraduate assemblies are not truely representative of the undergraduate populace. The best students are absorbed in their work, while the campus politicoes undertake their maneuvers. To put it gently, student government officials are not the finest of undergraduate minds, any more than the U.S. Congress is the cream of the American intelligentsia. Yet if students did acquire substantial power, inevitably it would be the campus politicoes who would rise to the most powerful posts. In the case of the

U.S. Congress that result is not frightening; our country is a democracy, and one can never take the politics out of politics. But universities are not democracies, and politics has no place in academe.

One final note on the rise of student power. Recently a number of colleges have seen the rise of student unions. Now for years a Student Union was a meeting place where undergraduates shared coffee, newspapers, and ideas. No harm there. But now the new student unions propose to align all students as a power bloc to counter the weight of the faculty and administration. This development is as absurd as it is pernicious. When one begins to view the university as an ordinary business enterprise with buyers and sellers, raw materials and products, labor and management, then the entire educational process is distorted and degraded. (If I have compared academe to industry in other chapters, it has only been to highlight the uniqueness of the academic life.) And just for the sake of accuracy, if one were to make an economic analysis of the university, should students be the employers, and professors the employees? But of course the confusion here is a symptom of the real problem: schools are not and should not be run on ordinary business principles.

The absurdity of the student union effort is evident when push comes to shove, and the would-be labor leaders call a strike. When students go out on strike, they stop attending classes. And they stop doing their assignments, and they stop learning. Nothing else happens. The university might be a bit embarassed, but it certainly is not hurt financially. Professors still go about their research — they might well prefer to avoid the aggravation of teaching anyway — and administrators go about their house-keeping. Students, you see, have no bargaining power once they have paid up their tuition.

Their tuition. Eureka. If students really wanted to catch the university's attention — if they really wanted to demonstrate that the school was not fulfilling their expectations, they could drop out of classes and stop paying tution. For many students, at many schools, that might not be a bad idea.

Since academic decisions should be made by academic professionals, the university faculty has a large decision-making domain. As long as the tenure system endures, when a faculty member comes up for tenure the qualified judges must be his colleagues. So tenure decisions should be (and usually are) made by the departments. By the same token it is the department that must appoint new professors to fill available spots, design and approve course syllabi, match faculty members with their teaching assignments, and judge the competence of undergraduate performance in that discipline. The whole faculty as a body should (and usually does) set curricular requirements, approve new courses or new departments, and define the academic responsibilities of both teachers and students. In short, the faculty – either in departmental units or as a whole – has the unique competence to decide on questions involving specific academic judgements. The professors, after all, are the academic professionals.

Still, academic competence does not guarantee wisdom in all matters of university policy. The department should choose professors to fill openings in the department, but who should decide how many openings the budget permits? The faculty should set up the course requirements for undergraduates, but who should decide what sort of students the school should seek to attract? Who should decide whether or not to disband the football team, or eliminate an academic department? Or convert the school from a liberal arts institution into a technical college? Or participate in a government program? All these questions involve factors that cannot be judged on academic merits alone. So while faculty members will probably have strong opinions, they need not be correct.

Is this heresy? Particularly if one is a faculty member, one might say so. Every question of university policy is an academic question; everying that happens at the university has implications for educational policy. So should the decisions not rest with the academic specialists?

And I answer: No, they should not.

Academic specialists are precisely that: specialists. A faculty member today is not versed in all academic lore; he is merely qualified to serve in one particular department. Perhaps he has taken a few courses in the Department of Education (notoriously one of the weakest departments at most schools), but he is not a professional educator. He is a professional biologist, or classicists, or economist. His credentials indicate his special competence in those specific academic disciplines; they say nothing about his common sense, or lack thereof, nor do they indicate that he has a special reservoir of wisdom. Like most sterotypes, the image of the absent-minded professor has a touch of validity. So we ask our professors to teach us, but not to run our lives for us. They are learned, but not necessarily wise; erudite but not necessarily sensitive. A biologist knows the nutritional needs of the plants and animals he studies, but not necessarily of the human soul.

In addition to their natural human limitations, professors also have particular debilitating weaknesses which limit their ability to govern the university wisely. Each department, and each faculty member, has special vested interests. Occasionally those special interests color the faculty's perception of an issue. Philosophy teachers tend to think — and who would want it otherwise? — that philosophy is the most important of all scholarly disciplines. Perhaps it is, but what of the psychologists who make the same claim? And the geologists? Since the university must allocate its financial and intellectual resources among the different disciplines, such biased judgements can be at least very inconvenient.

Then too, faculty members have interests as a group. Like every other professional group, professors will normally seek to maximize their own comfort, and minimize the power of those who supervise them. When a proposed curriculum reform would exact more work from the faculty, the professoriate will naturally have its reservations about that plan. Conversely, any attempts to lighten the faculty workload will find a receptive audience. But clearly such initiatives might not promote the best interests of the school as a whole.

Again, my personal experiences confirm my argument. As an undergraduate I sat on a committee pondering curricular reforms. Our proposals, when they were completed, were to be transmitted to the faculty for approval. Invariably, when we considered a change that would have imposed new obligations on the faculty, our professor-advisers counselled us to drop the sugges-

tion; it would never stand a chance.[3] Ironically, ten years later
Harvard passed a comprehensive proposal for curriculum reform
— and the most prevalent criticism of the measure has been that
the mishmash of special interests deterred the faculty from
inaugurating a truly encompassing reform.[4] During my undergraduate career the interests of the individual faculty members
were arrayed against the proposals for reform; more recently it
was the interests of the departments that blocked the more
ambitious proposals. In both cases the result was a compromise.
One more compromise of educational ideals.

Each case is instructive, revealing faculty prejudices. The first
involved prerogatives enjoyed by all faculty members. In 1970
Ernest May, the Dean of the College, issued an invitation for all
undergraduates to join in an effort to propose curricular reforms.
Of course that year was not a good one for systematic thought;
the most violent disruptions of the era diverted campu attention
away from other worthy issues, and curriculum reform was one
such victim. Dean May's laudable initiative generated a hodgepodge of proposals, demands, and amateur educational theories.
The effort soon sputtered and died; all but a few trivial proposals
were stillborn. But one particular proposal, moderate and work-
able, died an unnatural death.

All Harvard upperclassmen live in one of several residential
units known as the "Houses." (There were ten such Houses in
1970; more have been added subsequently.) These Houses, in
theory, are educational units in themselves; they have associated
faculty, libraries, lecture and concert series, and an occasional
House seminar that bears full academic credit. But the theory
diverges from the practice. Most of the faculty members affili-
ated with Houses — and every Harvard professor is assigned to
one — had little or nothing to do with the life of the House
system. Those of us involved in the curriculum reform committees suggested that the House system was a prime candidate
for reform. As long as each member of the faculty was assigned
to a House, we asked, why not take steps to see that he honored
that assignment? Why not require him to at least eat lunch there
one day a week, or put it a certain number of appearances in
the course of the academic year? The suggestion seemed to be

moderate reform incarnate; it called for nothing not already proclaimed as university policy. We only suggested that the faculty members fulfill a task to which, on paper at least, they were already assigned. And the educational benefits were equally clear; the presence of faculty members in the dining halls would have done wonders for the level of intelligent conversation. Faculty members could not oppose the measure on economic grounds, since their meals were subsidized by the college. (Harvard's dormitory food is notoriously awful, but I doubt the faculty would have defended its reluctance on culinary grounds.) But the suggested reform would have impinged, however slightly, on the freedom of faculty members. And so it was squelched. The faculty never even considered the proposal.

Several years later a new Dean of the College, Henry Rosovsky, issued a new call for reconsideration of the curriculum. The times had changed, and Rosovsky proved an unusually able organizer; this time the curriculum reform movement blossomed. After long and thoughtful deliberations the relevant faculty committee determined that Harvard should embrace an entirely new approach to the liberal arts. The faculty set about the task of redefining the necessities of a liberal education. And then, just when the crucial question of course requirements was pending, the departments balked. No department would admit that a student could be considered educated without having taken at least one of its courses. In principle the faculty agreed that students should share some common core of knowledge, but when the time came to define that common core, every department advanced the interests of its own discipline. Eventually Rosovsky's efforts bore fruit, but the result was less impressive than it could have been. Harvard did take a step toward a common-core curriculum, but the chosen approach was an incremental reform, not a regeneration of the entire curricular concept. Instead of discarding all course requirements, and rebuilding the curriculum in accordance with its new understanding, the faculty has chosen to revise and improve the existing requirements.[5] There is a new attention to basic education at Harvard today, but surely not a new approach or a new beginning.

If Harvard's faculty is indecisive in its approach to educational policies, so are the faculties of other colleges. Consequently, the administration finds itself in an unwonted pivotal role. The faculty decides matters incompletely, leaving the deans to interpret their vague directives. And the more confused the faculty directives become, the wider is the discretion that redounds upon the administration. At the multiversity, with its vague and diffuse lines of authority, the power of the administrators — President, Provost, and Deans — becomes overweening. When the university is not committed to a set of ideals, the administrators sit atop an impressive array of intellectual forces without a clearly defined purpose. What do they do with these forces? Well, of course, it depends on the character of the administrators.

The crucial point is that administrators exercise their power by default. They are not generally chosen for their ability to settle lofty academic questions; more likely they are culled out of the faculty because they — unlike most of their colleagues — evince some ability for an interest in bureaucratic paperwork. The intended task of an administrator is, self-evidently, to administer policies — not to propound them. And the skills essential for effective paperwork, or effective delegation of authority, or (what is an increasingly important administrative function) effective fundraising — these are not skills associated with the scholarly wisdom necessary to define the university's ultimate ideal.

Administrators, too, have their own vested interests. They want to minimize conflict within the university, since all conflicts eventually interfere with the smooth workings of the administrative mechanism. A problem avoided, from the administrators' point of view, is a problem solved; a temporary solution is superior to a general turmoil. But minimizing conflict sometimes means minimizing debate, and nothing could be more inimical to the idea of the university. Sometimes a temporary solution masks a more serious problem that saps the vigor of an academic institution. Once again, the compromise solution is not the ideal.

In huge academic plants like the ones that dominate American higher education, administrators have dozens of duties that relate only indirectly to the school's primary teaching function. They must raise funds from wealthy donors, parley with government officials, and manage all the business affairs (real estate, personnel, maintenance, portfolio management) that accrue to a large institution. They must cajole their subordinates to cooperate with one another. Before long, administrators at large universities lose their distinctive academic stamp and become indistinguishable from administrators of other complex organizations. Small wonder, then, that so many university officials go on to work in administrative capacities for government agencies, or philanthropic foundations.

Administrators at the multiversity are not only frighteningly powerful, but also amply equipped to maintain their power. Unlike students, they do not leave the university after four years, but remain to consolidate their position. Unlike faculty members they do not have to attend to an already busy schedule of course assignments. They have the unique opportunity to influence all other members of the university community, since they control the flow of information. They can form close alliances with other constituencies, since they alone have occasion to interact with every other group in the university community: students, faculty, alumni, trustees, employees, donors, government officials, etc. In a system dominated by ideas and personal relationships, university administrators control the flow of ideas from group to group, and enjoy the broadest available range of personal contacts.

So eventually we come to Plato's question: Who will guard the guardians? Who will supervise the administrators? Faculty members and students are not suited to the task, since they have interested, limited viewpoints. If the faculty supervises the curriculum, and the administration coordinates the educational program, then the remaining task is the most comprehensive one. The final echelon of university governance must be the one that determines the broad academic goals of the institution.

Ironically, most American colleges do have such an ultimate board of arbiters: the university's trustees. The purpose of the trustees is to serve as the link between the academic world and the community at large — to assess the university with the disinterested view of the intelligent layman, and to judge what sort of university would be most beneficial to the community at large. Trustees are removed from the everyday functions of the school, so they have no vested interests. They are free to solicit information from any group on or off campus, to bring their own special talents to bear on questions of academic policy — in short, to see academic questions in the broad view that begets informed, prudent decisions. And trustees have the legal power to effect whatever policies they find necessary. If the trustees of Yale decided to give the school to the state of Connecticut, as William Buckley observes, nothing could stop them.[6] So there is, after all, a body with the competence and the power necessary to settle the final policy issues.

Where is the irony? The irony lies in the fact that university trustees almost never use their authority.

For all their vaunted power and prestige, university boards of trustees almost invariably defer to the college administration. Technically the trustees still decide all major policy issues, but in fact the administration proposes a solution and the trustees enact it; trustees have become little more than a rubber stamp for the decisions of the very people they are meant to supervise.

Even is they were disposed to use their authority, the trustees would face substantial barriers. First, like other groups within the university, they rely on the administration for their information. They cannot conduct independent investigations without openly questioning the competence of the incumbent university officials, so they accept the information they receive. The university's president sets the agenda, defines the problems, and suggests solutions, leaving the trustees with little room for independent analysis.

Trustees are men and women of consequence, and they do not readily surrender their power. Every now and then a board of trustees asserts its independence and authority by rejecting an administrative proposal. (In the late '60s, for instance, many trustee panels refused to abolish campus ROTC programs despite the recommendations of the faculty and administration.) But by and large, the trustees prefer to leave questions of educational policy in the hands of the professional educators.

Which would make sense, if "professional educators" existed. They do not.

The creation of boards of trustees illustrates a peculiarly American conception of the university's role. Since we think of school as servants of the whole society, we appoint a special body to supervise college policy. Perhaps the department of English can assess the needs of future English teachers, but the trustees are empowered to assess the more general needs of future citizens. The faculty as a whole has an obvious expertise in the preparation of future professors, but American society expects the university to train future legislators, bankers, businessmen, ministers, doctors, and so on across the entire range of professions and occupations. Trustees are men and women who have distinguished themselves in some of these different professions. They have their own special insights and particular expertise to lend to the formulation of educational policy. In order to fulfill all of the functions society sets for it, the university needs this eclectic input. Trustees provide the wide range of viewpoints that, taken together, produce a comprehensive picture of the university's needs and goals.

Does this mean that the trustees should involve themselves in every phase of university governance? Certainly not. Only the professors have the appropriate academic credentials; only they should determine the content of courses. If the faculty judges a student to be qualified for graduation, the trustees have no business withholding the diploma (although at many schools they are legally empowered to do so). Trustees, by the very nature of their role, spend only a small fraction of their time on campus. They should leave everyday tasks to others, and since they are themselves busy men, they certainly will. Specialists have the most intimate knowledge of the particular factors involved in minute decisions. But when it comes to the broad philosophical questions of the institution's goals and purposes, the trustees should not devolve their duties.

Trustees should work harder. They should air all the possible arguments for and against university policies, solicit all the possible expert opinions, and deliberate the outcome exhaustively. They should not hesitate to disagree with one another and with other members of the university. They should argue, battle, and decide. And, having decided, they should make certain that their decisions are accurately observed within the university faculty and administration.

The workload should not be too onerous; universities rarely face questions of ultimate purpose, and ordinarily the trustees could confine their activities to simply supervision — making sure that the university was running on an even keel. Because of the way boards of trustees operate today, appointment is a great honor but a small responsibility. Trustees are distinguished but indistinguishable. The honorific nature of their posts need not change, but the task should be something more than symbolic.

Many ambitious trustees unfortunately misinterpret their role in providing a new perspective on university problems. If they are businessmen they subject all academic programs to a cost-benefit analysis, eager to find the bottom line; if they are public servants they ponder the public-policy implications of every potential decision. By taking such approaches they *do* interfere with the academic assessment of academic questions, and they merely confuse the picture by adding one more specialized viewpoint to an already cluttered field. The liberal arts do not show a profit or loss, nor do they promote a healthy balance of payments. The special input which the university seeks from its trustees (or, rather, should seek) is the opinion of a distinguished laymen on the subject of education. Trustees should not be full-time businessmen who lend their talents to university business affairs, because the university already has employees to handle those problems. Trustees should be part-time educational theorists who bring a fresh new perspective to that work.

Trustees, in their turn, are responsible to the people who appoint them: the voters (indirectly) in the case of public schools, or the school's alumni in the case of private schools. So trustee elections should not just emphasize the public accomplishments of the candidates, however impressive they may be. A trustee should be selected on the basis of his ability as an educational theorist. The voters who appoint trustees should receive ample information about the candidate's views on education, his ideas on which the university could and should be: his campaign platform. Then the alumni and the voters — the people whose contributions support the university — could choose the institution's governors.

But wait. There are those who feel very strongly that the voters and alumni should not decide college policies. When William Buckley made the case for alumni control in *God and Man at Yale,* the outraged reaction was deafening. Rev. Henry Sloane Coffin (see the quotation at the front of this chapter) was only one of many people who decried the abilities of the alumni. When I myself made a similar proposal to a local New Jersey journalist, he asked, "Wouldn't you be letting a bunch of Babbitts run Princeton?"

My answer is, I think, the same as Buckley's. Are Yale alumni really "a bunch of boobs?" Are Princeton alumni "a bunch of Babbitts?" If so, neither school is worth saving.

Alumni are the college's final, finest product. If after four years at Yale the typical alumnus is still a boob, then Yale education produces boobs. (As a Harvard graduate I am perfectly willing to entertain that possibility.) And if that is the case, then it seems fitting and natural that the school should be run by boobs. The point is that alumni, having absorbed all the school can provide — or at least enough to gain them the certification of a degree — deserve the respect of the institution that certified them. If Yale does not accept a Yale degree as indicative of intellectual competence, then who will? Alumni are merely students once removed. If undergraduates deserve a voice in university governance, then so do alumni. In fact alumni are even more worthy of that voice, since they have completed their undergraduate journey and arrived (theoretically) at full communion with the university's goals.

The mentality that shudders at the thought of alumni participation in university governance is the same mentality that effectively emasculates alumni opinion. This mentality dictates that alumni should be seen — at football games and fundraising dinners — but not heard. Then, having consigned the poor fellows to the role of cheerleaders and tub-thumpers, the college officials discover with shock that they are boobs; they have never discussed Aristotle during the football halftimes, nor pontificated about Chaucer during the boozy reunions. Having eliminated them from all but the mindless phases of university existence, the officials then note with disdain that alumni act mindlessly.

The elitist attitude that demeans the intelligence of everyone stationed outside the university's walls is a complex and instructive phenomenon, and one which I shall pursue at some length in a later chapter. For now, suffice it to say that the educationists dismiss alumni opinion not because alumni are stupid, but because the message alumni will give is contrary to the message educationists hope to hear. The academic elite has a view it hopes to advance, and if by virtue of its position it can claim immunity from criticism of that view — if it can convince the outside world that its view arises not from a basic political judgement but from a special esoteric insight — then it will do so. So alumni and taxpayers, and the wealthy men and women who donate funds to universities, are told to keep their distance. You may contribute your money, they are told — in fact you *must* contribute your money — but keep your ideas to yourself.

If they knew more about the basic attitudes fostered by contemporary academe, businessmen would disapprove strongly. But this too is a subject for a later chapter. Businessmen actually know relatively little about the schools to which they contribute, precisely because those schools insist on treating them like boobs. But if they did know, and if they did disapprove, and withdrew their funding, wouldn't that be an infringement on academic freedom?

Absolutely not. By any moral reckoning, those who contribute to a college deserve some indication of how their funds will be used. Colleges are not different from all other charities: they must demonstrate that contributions are used wisely, and their appeals for funds must inform donors accurately about how gifts will be spent.

Now suppose that when the college provides donors with such

accurate information, the donors decide to hold back their grants. Supposed that the monied interests decide, *en masse,* that educationists are misusing their charitable contributions. (The supposition, by the way, is not at all absurd. It could happen.) Then, again, by any moral reckoning, the schools should either amend their ways or else abjure their right to such donations.

So then what about the schools which could not find any donors (or taxpayers) to support them. Well, they could solve the problem easily. By closing their doors.

CHAPTER FIVE

Paying the Piper

Why is affirmative action so ineffective, despite the furor it arouses? Simply because its shotgun approach hits the just and the unjust alike. For example, the University of Michigan had to spend $35,000 just to collect statistics for 'affirmative action.' For all practical purposes, that is the same as being assessed a $35,000 fine without either a charge or proof of anything.

Thomas Sowell[1]

The year was 1953, the location Trenton, New Jersey. Harold Dodds, the President of Princeton University, addressed the State Supreme Court:

There are educators that dream of a day of expansive federal grants-in-aid to both public state-supported and private institutions, and that this aid is to be divorced from all political control or accountability whatsoever. This dream I conceive to be both vain and immoral. It is vain because it will never be realized, for he who pays the piper calls the tune. It is immoral, because it is the duty of the governmental authority which raises the taxes and spends the taxpayers' money to see that it is used in accordance with the will of the legislature . . . Thus, both as a practical matter and as an ethical matter, the tax-sustained university will ways be, and should always be, subject to political control.[2]

Today virtually every major American university is in the thrall of the federal dollar, and Dodds' words have the ring of truth. Yet the major research universities need huge infusions of funds. Ordinary citizens cannot provide the support necessary to finance a new cyclotron, or endow a new professional chair, or build a new library. Such massive support can come from only two possible sources: the government, or large corporations. The universities face a simple choice: federal money, corporate money, or, for all practical purposes, no money.

When President Dodds made his statement to the New Jersey court, he was acting as a witness in support of A.P. Smith Manufacturing Company. A.P. Smith, a New Jersey concern, had favored Princeton with a small ($1500) corporate grant, and a group of rebellious stockholders had sued to block the gift. In its defense, the company argued that a gift to Princeton was in the best corporate interests. Princeton not only agreed, but added that corporate philanthropy gave the university its only chance to avoid reliance on federal support. The court upheld the company's position, and Princeton received its gift. But as William Buckley has observed, "the price of victory was academic freedom as commonly understood."[3]

The key words here are "as commonly understood." The A.P. Smith decision did no violence to the doctrine of academic freedom itself; it did undermine the universities' public interpolations of that doctrine. In 1953 Princeton and A.P. Smith won their case by emphasizing two arguments that they would never dare advance today.

First, they argued that the private university provides active indirect support for the business corporation. This is the argument that convinced a Superior Court judge. "The proofs before me are abundant," he ruled, "that Princeton emphasizes by precept and indoctrination, the principles which are very vital to the preservation of our own democratic system of business and government."[4] In other words, the company convinced the court that its contribution to Princeton was an investment, not a pure gift; in return, the company expected Princeton to support the free enterprise system. Nothing wrong there: a university can support free enterprise and still honor the search for truth. But how many universities today would admit, as Princeton admitted — no, as Princeton boasted — in 1953 that they (to use the judge's words again) "built respect for, and adherence to, a system of free enterprise?"

Second, Princeton argued that corporate support enabled the

university to avoid dependence on government finance. Today Princeton is thoroughly dependent on the government: more than two-fifths of the university's operating budget comes from the public coffers. And Princeton is no exception; American universities rely heavily on government support. Columbia's President William McGill put it succinctly when he admitted that his own university is "only trivially different in this respect from the University of Michigan."[5] How many universities today would admit that their reliance on government support entails a diminution of their academic freedom?

But those are the questions universities would have to ask themselves, if the A.P. Smith case were somehow resurrected. Does the college actively support the free enterprise system? Is the college still independent from the political control of the federal government? For the overwhelming majority of our colleges and universities, the answer to each question would be No. Which leads to a third, knottier question. Can the universities continue, in good conscience, to accept corporate funds? In order to do so, they would have to demonstrate that the corporate funds were being used to further the interests of the stockholders. And so we would be back to the condition of the A.P. Smith case.

At least one of McGill's predecessors at Columbia would have recognized the dangers of massive federal support for the universities. In a speech given just before he left the White House — a speech made famous by the introduction of the term "military-industrial complex" into the American lexicon — President Eisenhower warned, "The prospect of domination of the nation's scholars by federal government, project allocation, and the power of money is ever present, and is gravely to be regarded."[6]

As Eisenhower recognized, blunt repression and bookburning are not the only threats to academic freedom; the seductive powers of money can be equally destructive. Enticed by federal grants, universities can undertake research projects without sufficient scholarly justification. Incompetent teachers can be hired and retained because they attract grant support. Worst of all, individual scholars can ignore their academic mission — the search for truth — in order to fulfill the terms of a pressing government contract. The basic ethical conflict is irresolvable: the university wants scholarly justification for research projects, and the government wants political justification. When the two conflict, as they so often do, the attractions of the federal dollar can overwhelm the university's moral armament.

On this level, at least, the threat to academic freedom is a subtle one. Princeton's President William Bowen was a lowly economics teacher in 1962 when he analyzed the problem:

> The real danger is not that the university will be unable to pay its bills, but that the dependence on outside support will deprive the university of a measure of its independence . . . The university today is far more dependent on the good sense of Congressmen and representatives of government agencies than was the case prior to World War II.[7]

What reasonably prudent educator would voluntarily rely on the good sense of politicians in the academic sphere? Professors are famous for jealously guarding their turf, and anyone (outside government) who begins interfering with scholarly judgements is immediately accused of tampering with the values of academic freedom. Yet despite their protestations, the universities have been remarkably docile in the face of government intervention. Through the affirmative action program, the Department of Health, Education and Welfare (HEW) has demanded and received a voice in universities' hiring and admissions policies. The appointments of faculty members and the admissions of students — two utterly crucial areas that define the university's academic life — have been shuffled into the political realm.

Of course the universities have squirmed. Each year a bevy of prominent academic leaders troops into Washington to tell Congressional committees of their concern for the independence of academic judgements. They are worried, but they are conciliatory; they still want the money. Administrators have evolved an arabesque definition of hiring practices, so that when HEW demands the hiring of a certain quota of minority teachers, the university insists that the number is a "goal" rather than a "quota." The educationists do not want people to worry about government control; that might compromise the schools' ability to extract more favors from Uncle Sam. So HEW has had its way.

Consider the absurd, overweening strictures of HEW's affirmative action program. A college cannot simply appoint new faculty members on the basis of individual competence. The university must draw up a master plan, detailing its hiring plans for several years into the future. Each anticipated opening on the faculty must be listed, and each departmental turnover. Along with this hiring schedule, the university must submit its projected compliance with the affirmative action guidelines. Thus, a certain percentage of the anticipated openings must be reserved for women, a certain percentage for blacks, a certain percentage for Eskimos, and so on.

Quite frequently, the required minority scholars are simply not available; there are no qualified candidates to match HEW's ethnic preferences. Until very recently, relatively few blacks entered the academic professions, and so there is a shortage of black Ph.D. recipients to fill the faculty openings. But the HEW officials to whom the plan is submitted have no interest in such niceties; they merely want the quotas filled. So the university surrenders its power to choose the members of its own faculty. A federal bureaucrat — who has no experience in higher education, and no understanding of the university's special needs — can veto the hiring plans of a great university.

Even if HEW does eventually accept the school's hiring plans, the preparation of those plans entails an enormous expense of administrative time and money. The college officials must plow through personnel records, estimate faculty turnover for periods of five years or more, and prepare massive documents for the bureaucrat's inspection. Often the plan must be edited and revised two or three times before the federal overlord pronounces it satisfactory. Particularly for the smaller, independent colleges, it becomes an onerous task merely to keep up with all the paperwork required by federal regulations. (Affirmative action is only the most expensive and notorious of the many overlapping federal requirements.) *Change* magazine, after surveying American colleges, estimated that American colleges spend more money on federal paperwork than they receive from all voluntary contributions.[8]

Think of it. Just to keep the bureaucrats happy, the universities spend all the funds they receive from all other contributions. Alumni gifts, corporate grants, foundation awards — all these together only match the cost of *compliance* with federal programs.

Or look at the same statistic from another point of view. Any nongovernmental grant to the university could be seen as a contribution to pay the overhead for the government programs. Imagine, then, the size of the government's share in the university's finances! Alumni could cut off their support; corporations could restrict their grants; foundations could do their own research; and still the universities would survive the financial loss. But if the government pulled out of the academic world, the economy of the higher education industry would immediately collapse.

No wonder, then, that the universities treat HEW with such deference and understanding. If the university depends on federal grants to support its budget, and if HEW can cut off all government aid to the school, then naturally the school's administrators will do everything in their power to keep the bureaucrats happy. Even if an HEW ukase tramples on the principles of academic freedom, the administrators will handle the matter gingerly. After all, the bureaucrat whom they offend today might be the one who judges their hiring plans tomorrow; the universities must be diplomatic. Academic freedom is not the only issue at stake in the universities' negotiations with HEW. Many universities must keep in mind that they are fighting for their own economic survival. Under such straitened circumstances, administrators are not likely to give due regard to abstract ideals like independence and academic freedom.

A few courageous schools, however, have bucked the tide and challenged HEW's power to intervene in scholarly affairs. The two heroes of the struggle have been two small, private midwestern colleges: Hillsdale College in Michigan and Rockford College in Illinois. Each school has steadfastly refused to accept money from the federal government. But HEW insists that even this independence is not enough; as long as a single student pays his tuition with funds from a federal scholarship, the school must obey the federal regulations. Both Hillsdale and Rockford have balked, insisting that their independence must be preserved. Thus far, the ensuing struggle has been inconclusive.

But why was it only a pair of small midwestern colleges that challenged HEW? Why did the large, prestigious private schools not join in the effort, or at least express their solidarity with their smaller brethen? They too are theoretically independent, and their administrators constantly warn of the necessity to preserve the independent sphere. Why then were they silent?

Evidently, the largest and most prestigious colleges in our country are cowed by HEW. They will not challenge the power of the bureaucracy, nor will they support the braver schools that do take up that challenge. Whatever HEW proposes, the universities will reluctantly but quietly accept.

Consequently, the universities' reliance on the government's good sense is abject. After years of paying the educational piper, the federal government has begun in earnest to call the tune. At first the government sought to root out all vestiges of discrimination. Then HEW went a step further and required the schools to make amends for society's past injustices. All this without regard for educational concerns. What will the government ask next? Will HEW begin distributing a set of guidelines for the curriculum? Will the federal government issue a reading list for all students? Once the federal government presence is established — once the universities have allowed the government to encroach on their decisions — all things are possible. In 1975 Yale's President Kingman Brewster threw up his hands and admitted that "use of the leverage of the government dollar to accomplish objectives which have nothing to do with the purposes for which the dollar is given has become dangerously fashionable."[9]

At least half of the argument that won the A.P. Smith case is accurate, then. Reliance on federal funding does detract from the autonomy of a private university. What of the other half of the argument? Can a corporate contribution be justified on the grounds that private universities support the free enterprise system?

Unfortunately, no. Analyzing a recent poll of American collegians, George Gallup reported that "a strong anti-business mood prevails in most of our colleges and universities." Moreover, Gallup continued:

> This survey presents cogent evidence that the four years that typical students spent in typical colleges and universities tend to disillusion them about their country and to increase their alienation with its institutions.[10]

Now there is a sharp reversal from the logic of the New Jersey court. American universities do not preserve free enterprise, nor do they strengthen it. On the contrary. American higher education leads students *away* from faith in the economic system.

Alert businessmen have recognized the universities' hostility for many years. After all, *God and Man at Yale* had depicted the problem in detail a generation ago. Until recently, however, the business community's response had been guarded. Then in the last few years, as the problem became both acute and apparent, many prominent businessmen have enjoined their colleagues to scrutinize schools carefully before making educational contributions. The corporation, David Packard pointed out, should not support academic programs that denigrate the free enterprise system. Soon William Simon had joined him in making that argument. Then Henry Ford. They ask, in effect, "Why should corporations contribute to the subversion of their own best interests?"[11] Irving Kristol gave them a compelling answer in a *Wall Street Journal* editorial: "Businessmen or corporations do not have any obligation to give money to institutions whose views or attitude they disapprove of. It's absurd to suggest otherwise — yet this absurdity is consistently set forth in the name of 'academic freedom.'"[12]

Alas, Kristol is right on both points. It is an absurd argument. Yet the universities have used it. The educational establishment, alarmed by this spate of criticism, has limbered up its powerful public-relations machinery and charged that selective contribution would imperil academic freedom. Why? Because a university should not be beholden to corporate donors. So, the scholars continue, the universities cannot accept a grant from any corporation that seeks to advance its own views. Every grant must be certifiably free of compromising conditions. No strings can be attached.

The universities' argument has an obvious superficial strength, and two less obvious but damning flaws. Its strength lies in its rejection of political pressures. No university should appoint a professor on political grounds; that would sacrifice the institution's dignity and autonomy. Corporate donors cannot expect the colleges to violate their principles. So any corporate donors who ask the university to compel adherence to the prevailing corporate interests deserve the rejection they receive.

The first weakness of that argument, however, is that the universities have *already* bowed to political pressures — the pressures of the federal government. Scholars *are* appointed for political reasons, and HEW meddling *has* cut down the range of the universities' autonomy. Academe has lost its innocence. There was a time when the universities could have upheld their unsullied honor, but that was long ago: before they succumbed to the seductive powers of the federal dollar. Now it is much too late.

The second weakness lies in the disingenuous assumption that all selective corporate contributions would involve heavy-handed censorship on the university. Why should that be so? Even the crudest corporate operative should realize that he could not impose a set of industrial dogmas to be put forth in the curriculum. At best he could help support research in areas he found interesting, and encourage scholars who dealt with corporate interests objectively. Keep in mind, too, that most large corporations today give unrestricted grants to colleges, to be spent at the discretion of the faculty. It is likely that such generous and understanding donors would suddenly take the part of Torquemada, rooting out any professors who refused to sing the company song? Hardly.

The rationale for selective corporate philanthropy is modest and simple. The corporations simply want a fair treatment from the academy. Colleges often boast that they expose their students to every point of view. But there is one viewpoint that collegians rarely hear. You guessed it. "Lack of knowledge of the free market system is shocking," revealed George Gallup after his 1975 survey of American undergraduates. "College juniors and seniors have a more distorted idea of the profits of business than high school juniors and seniors."[13]

In the course of their college education, then, students become *less* knowledgeable about corporate enterprise. Now the question jumps into focus: should corporate donors assist in this mis-education of college students? The answer is obvious.

The overwhelming campus bias against business interests suggests to some people that academicians have conspired to subvert the corporations. But one should not jump too quickly to that conclusion. Rather, the overwhelmingly liberal profes-soriate chooses to research, examine, and teach other questions, criticizing the business viewpoint but allowing other views to escape unscathed. Professors are not generally hostile to the corporate world; they are just not interested in hearing the corporate view. But the result is the same. Universities not only instill a congenital mistrust for business in their students, but also neglect to present the countervailing facts.

The irony of the situation is that the universities take so little interest in the institutions that made their existence possible. Without individual private wealth, independent schools would never have been possible. Without substantial corporate generos-ity, the standard of academic life would be far less comfortable. Without the spectacular economic welfare that the free enter-prise system has fostered, a college education would still be a luxury. And without a society in which the power of the govern-ment was checked by the power of other private institutions — such as corporations — the schools would be totally defenseless against government pressures. And yet the schools persistently battle against private wealth, against the free market, and against their corporate beneficiaries. Despite the fact that private univer-sities are obviously an elite institution, the academic fashion opposes all forms of elitism. Thus Senator Daniel Moynihan, no anti-intellectual, was moved to declare that "the elite universities are opposed in principle to the social arrangements which make their existence possible."[14]

All American universities accept the notion that students should be exposed to the broadest possible range of views. Why then should they not be exposed to the claims of corporate enterprise? Hundreds of corporate executives are appointed annually to serve as the trustees of private universities. If they are capable of assessing the needs of these universities — as trustees are charged to do — are they not capable of guiding corporate donations wisely? Why should a large corporation make a donation to, say, Stanford instead of Rockford? Very few shareholders will have graduates from either school. To justify the contribution in the eyes of the shareholders, the corporate management must demonstrate that the contribution will be used to serve the corporate interest. Corporations do not have a *right* to be selective in their gifts to educational institutions. It is a moral obligation.

What could the colleges be expected to do to advance the corporate interests? Obviously, they could not be expected to advertise the company's products (although of course the publicity stemming from the company's gift might generate some incidental advertising benefits). But the company's interests would be served by a school that produced well trained graduates: graduates whose notions about business profits had not been distorted during their undergraduate years. Better yet, the school might undertake projects to examine the virtues of the marketplace, and the vices of government regulations. Different industrial firms might be interested in supporting different sorts of basic scientific research; law firms might subsidize law schools, and engineering firms engineering schools. As long as the university gave the corporate world a fair hearing, the company's interests would be served. After that, the corporate management would be left to decide how exactly to allocate the available corporate grants. That — no more — is the nature of selective donation.

Selective contribution does not mean abandonment of the country's universities. Corporations can aim their gifts carefully, so that they support the academic programs that serve their interests best. They can contribute to one department within the university, or even to one professorial chair within the department. They could choose to support the colleges that refuse government funds, thus setting up academic monuments to the strength of the free enterprise system and of pluralism. Most important of all, they could consider each educational donation carefully. Today's students, as the educators so often remind us, will mold tomorrow's opinions. American corporations have an obligation to guarantee that those students gain adequate exposure to the arguments of free enterprise and its advocates.[15]

Private universities should have an ample area of agreement with private enterprises. Government regulation threatens the continued health of the corporations, just as it threatens the continued independence of the private universities. The universities can safeguard corporate interests by producing scholars and leaders who have a responsible and objective understanding of the corporate sphere. And corporations can ensure the future of private education by supporting the schools that uphold their independence. In the face of a growing governmental presence in society, every private institution should seek out the company of other mediating institutions, to check the power of the federal bureaucracy.

The universities would prefer that all financial gifts arrive without strings attached. But, as one prominent defender of free enterprise has said, there's no such thing as a free lunch. Businessmen who do not demand results from their investments go broke; politicians who do not satisfy their constituents lose elections. Every contribution to a college comes with some strings attached. The responsibility of the colleges is to select those donors whose gifts entail the least risk for academic freedom. If a corporate donor demands fealty to the corporate view, then his gift should be rejected. If the federal sponsor demands a voice in university hiring policy, then his grant should be declined. But if the terms of the grant are acceptable, and the gift poses no threat to unfettered scholarship, then the danger is chimerical.

CHAPTER SIX

The Admissions Lottery

> Every innovation that reduces the pressure
> on colleges and universities to accommodate
> all, including those who are not interested
> or able — and that reinforces an element of
> choice on the part of the individual — is
> desirable.
>
> *Assembly on University Goals and Governance,*
> *American Academy of Arts and Sciences*[1]

Organizations acquire their own internal momentum as they grow. The stern logic of the bureaucratic apparatus takes its toll, and individuals bow to the organization's demands. Ralph Waldo Emerson bewailed the tendency a century ago when he wrote that "Things are in the saddle,/ And ride mankind." Modern literature abounds with references to the ineffable power of the organization. And educational organizations are no different. When Herman Hesse wrote his novel about a young man's schooling, he chose the suggestive title *Beneath the Wheel.*

Since they have so thoroughly forsaken their ideals, the universities have no defense against their own grinding organizational imperatives. A slight push sets the bureaucratic machinery in gear, and inertia takes over. The machinery rumbles on, overriding the needs of teachers and students. Nowhere is this more evident than in the process by which the schools choose their students: the annual admissions lottery.

Admissions competition has made more than its share of headlines during the last decade. The decline of standards, the legitimacy of standardized tests, the brutal competition, computerization, preferential treatment, affirmative action — all these subjects have provoked heated protests and denials, essays and editorials. Our intelligentsia has labored mightily over the question: how should institutions choose their students?

Virtually no one has worried about the companion question: how should students choose their institutions?

The needs of the institution are fairly obvious; they are embodied in the reports prepared by the Admissions Office. The institution seeks to attract more and better students every year. "More and better" is defined by the available statistical categories. Each class should, if possible, have more impressive high school records than the class preceding it. Admissions officers will search for special indications of talent: artistic, political, and especially athletic. The institution wants to be able to assemble what is known as a "good class profile," listing statistics and awards to indicate that the incoming class is the best ever.

What the institution does *not* want is also fairly obvious. The institution does not want complications in the recruiting and admissions process. From the organization's point of view, the object of the game is to enroll the best students possible; whether the students will be happy at the college or not, and whether the students have an accurate idea about the college's resources or not — these questions do not appear on the organizational performance chart. So from the institution's vantage point, the competition for good students is unrestricted. The admissions office is constantly tempted to paint a rosy picture of campus life for the potential applicants, to exaggerate the college's virtues and to downplay or even ignore its vices. The admissions literature therefore portrays the college as a place of unblemished beauty where anyone and everyone can be happy.

Consequently, admissions literature from very different colleges bears a striking resemblance. Just replace the proper names, and one pamphlet could describe another college with equal accuracy. Each college boasts of a competent and dedicated faculty, an idyllic pastoral campus (or the other variation, an exciting urban campus), and a total commitment to the welfare of the undergraduates. Even photographs of campus scenes are unoriginal, as a rule. Every pamphlet seems to feature one shot of a professor at the blackboard, another of a seminar meeting on the campus lawn, another of a couple (their backs to the camera) strolling from the classroom. Often these pamphlets are downright misleading. When I last noticed, the Uni-

versity of Chicago advertised the proximity of beaches on Lake
Michigan; this despite the facts that a) Lake Michigan at that
point is much too rough for water sports, b) the weather in
Chicago during the school year is not conducive to beach out-
ings, and c) the crime rate in the area is so high that a visit
to the beach is a swashbuckling adventure.

Usually, however, the deception is much more subtle. Schools
do not so much dissemble as tiptoe around the unpleasant issues.
The University of Chicago, in most of its admissions literature,
says relatively little about crime on campus, and what it does
say is couched in vague, ambiguous language. But at least Chicago
says something. Many urban schools make absolutely no reference to the students' physical safety, leaving the freshmen to
learn about that problem when they hear the disquieting rumors
during their first week on campus. By the same token, Harvard
speaks glowingly of its illustrious faculty members, but the
pamphlets never mention that those illustrious professors disdain
all contact with undergraduates. Princeton makes much ado
about its facilities for minority students, but glides over the
pronounced racial separation on campus. All of these omissions
leave the pamphlets technically accurate; they say nothing
untrue, but they do not accurately inform potential students
about the college.

Since the admissions literature is so uniform, college-bound
high school seniors are at a loss for a means of judging colleges.
From what the pamphlets say, Harvard seems very much like the
University of Michigan, or Notre Dame, or for that matter Ripon
College. They all provide the same basic reportoire of courses,
the same bland dining hall food, the same undergraudate social
life. Everyone knows, deep down, that these schools are very
different, but where do the differences lie, and how do they
affect the typical undergraduate? If the potential applicant
comes from a family of limited means, he cannot afford to visit
every campus and see for himself.

More to the point, how does the applicant know anything
about the all-important attitude the college embodies? The
course catalogue merely lists departmental offerings; it does not
mention that the department is dominated by one school of

thought, or that the courses do not include coverage of a certain analytical theme within the discipline. The catalogue invariably points out the strongest departments; less often the weakest. Every college halfheartedly advertises its educational theories, but those theories are expressed in language so vague that only another educational theorist could catch the nuances that make all the difference. High school students are not educational theorists; they do not have the familiarity necessary to read between the lines and judge the various departments, or to recognize the professors' analytical slants just by reading through the course descriptions. Most likely, the applicant has not given much thought to the sort of educational approaches he wants. The literature does not help him decide.

High school guidance counselors, if and when they are competent (and that is rarely) can provide their charges with a few good questions about college plans. Does the student prefer a large university or a small college? an urban or rural campus? close to home or far away? Most students have responses ready for these questions. But after that, the going is slow. Most students have no further ideas about the sort of school they want to attend, and very few counselors can evoke the sort of thinking that would lead students on the road to a carefully considered conclusion. So high school students rely on the schools' reputations — not always an accurate measurement, by any means — and on their own ability to gain admission.

The colleges themselves *could* help students immeasurably by viewing their admissions literature as an educational device. They could explain the school's educational theories and outlooks in detail, using language that an intelligent layman could understand fully. They could describe their strengths and, yes, even their weaknesses; universities, after all, are supposed to be places where unpleasant truths can be aired. They could compare their academic approach with those of other schools, showing the aims it fulfills and the aims it ignores. Every educational theory, and every academic approach, has its own characteristic advantages — its particular competence and its failings. The admissions brochure could provide the applicant with a thumbnail guide to educational theory, thereby preparing him for his choice.

But the institutional needs of the university include no such reform of the admissions literature. If the students have high grades, the bureaucracy is happy; the institution has no vested interest in seeing students choose wisely.

So high school seniors, barely past adolescence, make a decision that will govern their lives for four or more years, a decision that may cost them and their parents as much as $75,000, a decision that will profoundly influence their adult life — on the basis of hearsay evidence and vague impressions.

Ironically, the potential students who choose their colleges most wisely are prize athletes. These young men (and, now, women), who are not known for their overwhelming intellects, have ample opportunity to survey each campus and ponder each school's offerings. Coaches and athletic recruiters do what ordinary admissions officers rarely do: they describe the university's programs in detail, and tell how the sports program differs from the programs offered at other schools. The prize football player visits each school competing for his services, talks to the coach personally, visits with team members, and goes on the next campus for the same tour. After a season of such visits, the athlete becomes adept at making judgements about different schools; he begins to see subtle differences that he did not notice on his first visits. Eventually he compares the schools' offers (which often can be assigned a straight cash value) and makes his choice. In athletic recruiting the institution's objectives are not the same as in the normal admissions process. The school seeks to capture certain key individuals, rather than to construct an impressive cross-section or class profile. So in sports recruiting the admissions process is a learning process, the students are regarded as individuals, and the results are gratifying to all concerned.

Of course, some coaches and athletic recruiters lie to their recruits, and many more convey a highly inaccurate picture by selectively avoiding embarrassing questions. But the same things happen constantly, unpublicized, to ordinary students.

It goes without saying that the above paragraphs do not mean that I approve of the athletic recruiting process. High-powered bidding wars for athletes are appropriate to professional sports, not to the liberal arts. Athletic recruiting today has stopped even pretending to justify itself on educational grounds. (As I write this chapter, a basketball star from Virginia is keeping dozens of college coaches in suspense while he decides which school's scholarship offer he will accept. The coaches involved are speculating that this young giant could bring them a national championship. The youngster himself has said that he will only attend college for two years before joining the professional ranks. No one even pretends that this prize recruit will ever finish his college education.)[2] Colleges exploit athletes unmercifully, and athletes exploit colleges. But that is not the issue here. My point is that, for better or worse, most recruited athletes know what they are doing when they finally choose their school.

Before I go any further, let me explain some of the mechanics of the admissions process.

First, for the better colleges, there are more than enough students to go around. Some small and undistinguished schools have trouble filling their freshmen classes, and resort to the strange tack of hiring advertising firms to entice applicants. But the older, established schools have no such problem. On the contrary, the better colleges choose their students from an applicant pool that contains many more qualified candidates than the school can possibly accommodate. In 1974 Princeton undertook a study of its applicant pool, and concluded that for every student admitted, there was another qualified student rejected; that is, Princeton could admit twice as many applicants without compromising its standards.[3] Yet Princeton, like most of its counterparts, tries constantly to *enlarge* the applicant pool. Admissions officers consider themselves recruiters as well as selectors, and they do their best to convince outstanding students to apply to their institutions. The admissions process would be simplified if the applicant pool could be shrunk, so that students applied only if they were interested in the unique strengths of one particular college. Admissions officers, too, would have an easier life if the students selected their college, as well as having the college select them. But the prevailing trend is in the opposite direction; admissions officers make life difficult for themselves and for the people they serve. Colleges work to enlarge the number of applicants even when the number is already too large to accommodate. They strive in effect, to increase the number of applicants that they can reject.

A constantly growing applicant pool, you see, helps the institution in its efforts to construct a class profile. Perhaps in a pool of five thousand students the school can find five hundred bright and dedicated enough to succeed academically. But is the pool grows to encompass *ten* thousand students the school can pick and choose among the bright students, capturing prospects who, in addition to performing adequately in the classroom, can also play the trombone in the school orchestra, or quarterback the football team. If the recruiting net spreads out to snare students from a wider geographical area, the school can boast about its new diversity. Whatever qualities the institution desires, a larger applicant pool will help it find them.

Second, the admissions process is risky, as everyone concerned will readily acknowledge. When the qualified applicants outnumber the available places, the admissions office must begin to make some very uncertain distinctions, inventing means of telling the difference among students even when very little quantitative difference exists. Most applicant pools quickly break down into three categories. There are the sure-fire applicants, whose qualifications are so outstanding that the admissions office has no choice but to accept them. There are the immediate losers, whose credentials simply do not meet the minimum standards. And in between there are the candidates who are qualified, but not dramatically so — who have the necessary qualities, but do not stand out from their fellow applicants. These students are capable of managing the academic work, and yet they are not so outstanding that the college is forced to accept them. Unfortunately for the admissions officers, the middle category is by far the largest.

So the admissions officers must invent ways to make distinctions. Officers search through the applications for some signs of individuality, so that they can consider the person behind the academic credentials. They look for intangible qualities that might help or hinder the student in his college life: maturity, dedication, leadership. They notice carefully whether or not his record shows gradual improvement through the years. If other candidates from the same school have been admitted in previous years, the admissions staff checks their performance. Finally, as the day of decision draws near, the staff begins to fill the last remaining seats in the class by sifting out the least interesting applications.

Admissions officers are human, and they make difficult judgements constantly; they often err. Sometimes they select a student because they perceive a special quality that will help him overcome his problems, but that special quality is a mirage, and the student is an academic flop. Sometimes a skillfully designed application can fool the admissions staff, and the student's weaknesses are overlooked. Most often, however, the admissions officers make an educated guess about the student's ability, and the guess proves wrong. In many cases the admissions staff realizes the risk it is taking, but takes it willingly in the hope that the student will vindicate such confidence. They are right at least as often as they are wrong; some of the most successful college students start out as "high risk" admits.

Once the students are admitted, however, the admissions office fades out of the picture. Admissions officials have very little opportunity to assess their results. Of course they see the students' grade averages, and they are aware of their outright failures. Dedicated staffers maintain some contacts with under-graduates, too, to keep track of their progress. But in general they can only learn about a student's academic performance or nonperformance by means of grades. The office does not know if the student is unhappy, or if he has gained some special benefits from the school that do not show on his grade reports, or if his personal development matches his academic achievement. So when the next class of applicants arrives, the admissions office has no more information by which to gauge the importance of these intangible factors.

Finally, one should realize that admissions officials are not academicians themselves; they are not qualified to make sophisticated scholarly judgements, nor are they conversant with educational theories. Most admissions officers are cheerful, capable, but not philosophical. Many are graduates of the school they serve, who remain there out of devotion to the college. They are, to be blunt, very fallible people. The admissions office allows the faculty to decide its policy, and staff members implement that policy without seeking to enlarge their own discretion. The whole process, then, is one step removed from the process that sets admissions policy. The people who actually select students are not those who decide how students should be selected.

Because of this divided responsibility, faculty councils set admission policy. But remember, the faculty is composed of specialists, not generalists, and faculty members do not spend much time meeting with high school seniors. The primary interest of any faculty member is his own academic discipline, not the overall composition of the student body. As long as an adequate supply of undergraduate students keeps flowing into their departments, most professors are not attuned to the needs of the larger selection process. Collegiate admissions policies are neither original nor profound.

Nor even logical. Today the most prevalent idea governing the recruiting and admissions process is the search for diversity in the student body. Diversity: the word itself has the impact of a talisman. Schools aim to enroll students from every background — social, economic, racial, geographical, and even national. The colleges proclaim their willingness and their ability to teach students regardless of their backgrounds, and to create a miniature cultural melting pot on the campus. Actually, this hunt for diversity provides more benefits to the institution than to the individual students. Students from different backgrounds have different educational needs, and different orientations; not every school can provide for every need. But from the institution's point of view, diversity means an improvement in the all-important class profile. Whether or not they have the ability to accommodate the students, the colleges can trumpet their success in attracting them.

The ultimate statement of this ideal came when a few colleges — notably the City University of New York — instituted a policy of Open Admissions. Here the schools accepted all applicants, regardless of the applicants' backgrounds, desires, abilities, and needs. The multiversity proudly announced that it could serve all needs, no matter what those needs might be.[4] Eventually cooler heads prevailed, and the trend toward Open Admissions is now on the wane. But the quest for diversity continues unabated, with the schools boasting that they can serve the academic needs of every conceivable student.

No university can serve all comers equally well. Different students bring different needs and different skills with them. The institution cannot provide for one without sacrificing its ability to serve others; it cannot be all things to all men (and women). Some freshmen soon find themselves forced into an educational program that does not suit their needs or their talents. If the university admitted its limitations, it could counsel students to seek their education elsewhere unless they found the appropriate programs. But the contemporary multiversity never admits such limitations; the university forces every student onto the same Procustean bed, insisting that what the institution provides is what the student wants. The admissions process, in its unthinking quest for diversity, makes a lively parallel to the Caucus Race in *Alice in Wonderland:* everyone starts at a different place, everyone runs in the same circles, and then everyone is pronounced a winner.

Among all the questions that affect college admissions policy, one stands out as the most controversial: the question of discrimination in admissions.

Now one preliminary observation is necessary: the admissions process is inherently discriminatory. The duty of the admissions officer is to discriminate. Colleges discriminate against stupid people regularly, and everyone (well, almost everyone) agrees that they should do so. The real question is not whether or not schools should discriminate, but on what grounds they should discriminate.

Our society considers discrimination on the basis of race to be unjustifiable and immoral; discrimination on the basis of sex is much the same. Fine. But other areas of discrimination are still controversial. Is it legitimate for a school to prefer young students, thereby discriminating against the elderly? Should schools make a special effort to enroll students from faraway places, thereby discriminating against whoever lives in the vicinity of the campus? These questions are much more complicated, because they involve educational judgements. The school might decide that its purpose is to train future leaders, in which case elderly applicants would be rightly disqualified. Or the school might aim to create a cosmopolitan atmosphere on campus, making geographical preferences an educational necessity. Then the argument shifts to the realm of educational theory: should a college set out to train future leaders, or to attain a cosmopolitan ambiance? These are questions of educational theory, not of civil rights.

The universities could — if they wanted — offer a perfectly valid reason for favoring underprivileged students in the admissions process. A youngster who overcomes his socio-economic handicaps and distinguishes himself in school shows both talent and determination; he is probably a stronger candidate then a wealthier counterpart with similar credentials. But American universities today do not use that argument. American universities, viewing themselves as the executors of the public will, claim that they must give preference to minority students in order to promote the social welfare of the nation.

That argument is a fraud.

First, the university does not exist to promote the social welfare — at least that is not its primary *raison d'etre*. Governments promote the social welfare; universities are meant to educate students. If the appropriate legislature sees some social need, then that legislature has ample authority to pass laws pursuant to that need. Yet the universities have taken it upon themselves to decide what particular social situation is desirable, to decide what sequence of steps should be taken to remedy that situation, and to take those steps on their own initiative: all without regard for the proper democratic forms.

Second, the university assumes that by admitting their annual quota of minority students they can advance the cause of the nation's underprivileged people. No so. Minority students have no obligation to return home after graduation and work with children in their old neighborhood; they may choose to join the middle class in its suburban existence, and the universities cannot prevent them from doing so. Preferential treatment therefore helps the very people who are most likely to escape from the clutches of poverty — the ambitious and talented young people — without any guarantee that the less talented poor will enjoy any benefit whatsoever.

Third, and most important, a blanket preference for all minority students does not promote the cause of the underprivileged. It promotes the cause of the people who are admitted under the quota; no others. Not all black people (or Hispanic people) are underprivileged; not all underprivileged people are black. Yet the reigning admissions systems give special preference to every black or Hispanic applicant, regardless of his or her socio-economic background.

This, of course, is reverse discrimination, and the U.S. Supreme Court found it to be invidious discrimination in the case of Alan Bakke. Any system that judges people solely by the color of their skin or the sound of the surname is repugnant to our ideals. And dangerous, because preferential treatment for one group inevitably implies discrimination against another. Once the system allows discrimination, no safeguards remain to protect any group against discriminatory treatment. If the political climate changes, any group could find itself suffering from discrimination.

The current affirmative action programs are an insult to black and other minority applicants. Any such applicants who do gain admission are tainted by the presumption that they would not have been accepted but for their skin color. If the admissions office paid more attention to individual students, that suspicion could easily be allayed. The admissions office could judge each applicant personally, comparing his credentials with his background to see how far he had progressed and how much talent he had shown. But the modern university has no interest in such a process; it would not affect the class profile. As long as the statistics show that a certain number of minority students has been admitted, the institution's conscience is salved. The minority students who are admitted under this system need not be needy, or deserving, but the statistic remains all the same, and the university can claim proudly that it is dedicated to equal opportunity and social justice.

Equal opportunity — now there is an interesting phrase! How can any institution offer equal opportunities to everyone? Students come to the university equipped with different talents and different backgrounds, which make them unequal in their ability to take advantage of the institution's programs. To say that every student at a university has an equal opportunity is like saying that everyone has an equal opportunity to run a four-minute mile. There is no legal barrier to prevent anyone from running a four-minute mile, but only an athlete in peak condition can take advantage of the opportunity. Similarly, there may be nothing in the university's regulations saying that a student cannot enjoy the full benefit of college education, but if he is not prepared for the curriculum, or not interested in what the university has to offer, the opportunity means nothing.

Every individual has different educational strengths and weaknesses, different interests and different dislikes. If every university made a conscious effort to pursue some goals whole-heartedly, admitting that, in the process, it would forfeit its chance to pursue other goals — then students could match their talents to the university's offerings accurately. A student who sought only to prepare for medical school could attend a university that advertised a no-frills premedical program, while a student who wanted to study the liberal arts could find a college dedicated exclusively to that pursuit. Then equal opportunity would be a reality rather than a slogan, and students could rest assured that their talents would be appreciated and developed.

Instead, contemporary American universities entice all sort of students onto campus without any assurance that those students will fit into the college's programs. This superficial approach solves no problems; it creates several. Students learn too late that they cannot take advantage of the college, and they become hostile, unreceptive to whatever attempts the university does make. Their classmates become resentful in their turn, and the campus is divided into different competing groups: those who feel comfortable with the existing programs and those who militate for change. (Often the division is along racial lines — the very thing that "equal opportunity" programs set out to correct.) Since no consensus exists about the goals of the university, the community cannot unite for any one purpose. Positive academic discipline — teamwork — is impossible.

By reining in their ambitions, and concentrating on certain limited objectives, the universities could make the most of their limited resources. Perhaps a school could be a mediocre multiversity, with every sort of academic department and professional school; or else it could dedicate all its efforts toward undergraduate teaching, and be a first-rate liberal arts college. Another school might decide to confine itself to the teaching of engineers. Quite a few colleges have already gone so far as to say that they best preserve their excellence by confining themselves to the instruction of women alone. And why not? If the university specializes in a particular sort of education — or education aimed at a particular sort of people — then it should be far more successful in that mission than the university that pursues every conceivable goal with equal ambition.

Would such schools be discriminatory? Absolutely. But not in a way that should offend any group within our society. Engineering schools do not discriminate against nonengineers, but no one complains, and no one should. Students who want to be in the company of other engineers can head for that school, and others can prudently stay away. Is there any reason why liberal arts colleges could not do the same?

In the last analysis, an ideal admissions process would ask only two questions about every applicant. First, could the applicant do something to benefit the school? Second, could the school do something to benefit the applicant? Unless the answer to both questions was "yes," the candidate would be rejected, no matter what his credentials were. The admissions office might recommend other schools for his consideration, but the applicant would not be admitted unless his skills matched the university's particular offerings. And from the student's point of view, choosing a college should be a little bit like choosing a husband or wife. There are good colleges and bad colleges, just as there are good husbands and bad husbands. But no husband, and no college, is right for everyone.

CHAPTER SEVEN

Grading and Discipline

> Accordingly, it should be the aim of an ideally constructed education that the discipline should be the voluntary issue of free choice, and that the freedom should gain an enrichment of possibility as the issue of discipline.
>
> *Afred North Whitehead*[1]

When Harvard's would-be curriculum reformers first gathered for work in the spring of 1970, the first topic for discussion was the abolition of grades. Selfish? Yes, of course, at least in part. Every student can relate to the odious possibility of a failed exam, or a mediocre grade in an important course. Then, too, 1970 was the height of the political season, and grading bore the taint of the Establishment. Did grades not convey the approval of the powers that be, and were those powers not evil and oppressive? Did grades not introduce inequalities of condition, and should all people not be equal?

The argument against grades, however, was (and is) much stronger than those selfish arguments, or those political arguments. Even from a dispassionate point of view, the abuses of the grading system were (and are) apparent and real. We idealists saw students cramming for exams, grubbing for grades, regurgitating information mindlessly. There was no excitement, no real search for truth, here. The mindless struggle for grades spawned the most evident flaws of our educational environs. Any curricular reform, we reasoned, would have to include a reform of the grading system. Somehow, by changing the motivating force that impelled students to study, perhaps the university could encourage creativity and discourage drudgery. It was, once again, an argument born of idealism.

Education is, or at least should be, an enterprise driven by idealism, so the arguments against grading should carry some weight. Surely all is not well in the premedical courses when competing undergraduates sabotage each other's experiments and hide library books so that their grades will compare more favorably with their classmates'. Surely there is little educational benefit in the cutthroat competition which becomes more and more prevalent among pre-professional undergraduates.

Grades, in fact, furnish only a very rough indication of a student's grasp of his field. Some students possess the enviable ability to cram facts into their memories on the night before an examination; they can spew out the result well enough to pass, and retain none of their expertise two days later. Others can grasp the relevant facts necessary to pass the course, without bothering to understand the analysis underlying those facts. In either case, the student can receive a satisfactory grade — perhaps even a superior grade, if he has mastered the arts of dissembling. But in neither case does the grade betoken any lasting grasp of the field.

Nor are grades a particularly accurate instrument by which to compare students, if that is the desired purpose. What sort of a comparison is it, when all students are divided up into five categories: A, B, C, D, and F? Even with the appended pluses and minuses, these grades show a very cavalier disregard for individual variations. Obviously not all "B" papers are alike; some are brilliant but flawed, while others show well researched banality. Nor are all "A" pieces equally worthy. If a freshman philosophy student refutes Kant's transcendental critique, he has thereby shown his consuming genius. But he receives an A just like the ones given to his less brilliant classmates; the transcript shows no distinctions among them. And what of the difference between one class and another? When it comes time to compute grade averages, an A in Organic Chemistry (notoriously among the more taxing courses at every university) counts for no more than an A in the most elementary sociology course. So students often seek a "gut" course, in which they will learn almost nothing, for the sake of their scholastic standing. Someone who finds four "guts" each term can amass an imposing collection of high grades, without ever bothering to exert himself.

The common academic practice of "grading on a curve" highlights the inaccuracy of grading as a means of comparison. Professors (generally at the behest of deans and/or department chairmen) usually aim to distribute the possible grades evenly in each of their classes. Thus a more-or-less predetermined percentage of students will fail every course, while another predetermined percentage will receive A's. The grading curve erases many potentially informative distinctions among students. Is it not at least possible that all students in one class would master the field? And still more conceivable that every student would fall short? But the ubiquitous curve masks that result. Even if one course produces undifferentiated failures, and another produces uniform successes, the grade distribution of the two classes will look the same.

Suppose, for the sake of argument, that one class did in fact enjoy a spectacular success, and another did fail utterly. Assuming that the college's students were blessed with roughly comparable intellectual skills, wouldn't that result say more about the teachers than about the pupils? The same holds true even in less dramatic circumstances: grades show the teacher's prowess, as well as the student's achievement. But the teacher is not being judged; his performance is not appraised on the basis of students' grades. So a student can suffer for his mentor's failings. Incompetent instructors issue inaccurate grades, and inaccurate grades protect incompetent instructors.

Enterprising — but not necessarily worthy — students can beat the grading system consistently. A student with special verbal gifts can manage to cover up his ignorance, and inflate his ordinary observations. Every class has its masters of the art: students who, in class presentations or in essays, can say nothing whatsoever and still sound profound. A very dull term paper, properly padded, becomes an imposing opus. Why use one word, when three or four would do the trick? And if the three- or four-word formulation sounds more obscure, so much the better; obscurity might be interpreted as profound.

Every student occasionally will try to "snow" the teacher with a flurry of impressive-sounding facts and ideas. And every teacher has his weaknesses; students learn to guess what sort of approach will play into the teacher's predilections. For example, any accomplished college student knows that one tested ploy to impress the professor (and to camouflage his own lack of knowledge) is to respond to a question by patiently explaining that, really, the question misses the point. The *really* important question is . . . (here our hero names a question that he can answer comfortably). Then the wily student proceeds to rattle off the few facts he has mastered.

All these means of beating the system involve subtlety, but not outright dishonesty. There are more nefarious methods. Some students — not many, but some — buy their grades with monetary or sexual favors. (And the subjective grading system gives corrupt professors the opportunity to elicit such bribes.) Others cynically dance attendance on the teacher until the grades are in, plying the time-worn trade of the teacher's pet. Still others, like the most vicious premedical competitors, boost their standing by undermining their classmates. And of course some simply plagiarize their work. The catalog of dirty tricks is nearly as inexhaustible as the one used in politics. And as colleges increase the level of competition, and anxiety builds among the undergraduates, the pressure increases on students of weaker character. One cannot view the breakdown of innumerable collegiate honor codes, or the cheating scandals in the military academies, without noticing how tempting cheating must be to an unscrupulous student.

After all these procedural objections have been weighed, one substantive argument against grades still stands out as unusually cogent: letter grades are insulting to the student. Consider the earnest, honest undergraduate who has devoted his energies completely to scholarly pursuits, avoiding all the grade-grubbing gambits. (Such a student would be hard to find, by the way; everyone occasionally succumbs to temptation.) Suppose such a student spends most of the academic term in research for one paper; he labors mightily, and turns in what he considers a fine piece of work. Then the paper comes back to him with a single letter on it. Let us say his grade is a B. No explanation, no cirticisms, no suggestions for possible improvements; just B. As anyone who has experienced that phenomenon can testify, the result is severely deflating. The student will not be as enthusiastic about preparing his next paper; perhaps he will grow cynical and join the ranks of those who tell the professor whatever he wants to hear. In any case, he has received virtually no reward for his efforts.

Letter grades make life too easy for the grader. In graduate school, I once received a paper back from my professor marked with the words, "Good paper. B." There were only two other marks on the entire eight-page paper: the professor had twice corrected my spelling. In each instance, my spelling had been correct, and his correction was wrong. Obviously this professor had been reading my paper after his third martini of the evening, or while his mind was fixed somewhere else. But the grade was final, however carelessly he had awarded it. And if a graduate student received such little attention, imagine how the same professor must have treated lowly undergraduates! I could go on. One Harvard sociologist told me that I had "successfully succeeded" in making an argument. How much effort had he devoted to reading my paper, or to writing that critique?

Such instances, fortunately, are not too common. Most teachers do provide students with some criticisms of their work, and the best teachers give ample indication of how the work could be improved. When that happens, the student enjoys a tremendous educational benefit from the assignment, even if his grade does not show it. But the grade has nothing to do with the benefit involved. In fact, the grading system, by allowing lazy teachers to neglect that critique, makes that particular educational experience less common. In other words, grades can actually hamper the process by which a student learns from his own successes and mistakes.

Do I deny the usefulness of grades altogether, then? Not quite. A failing grade does say something about the student's performance — something everyone involved should want to know. (Especially today, when grade inflation has made failure a task much more difficult than success.) The difference between an A paper and a B paper is subtle; teachers constantly make mistakes in trying to discern between the two. But failure is something any competent teacher can distinguish. Either the student has grasped the subject or he has not. And if he has not, then his record should indicate his failure.

But this one redeeming feature does not justify the primacy of grading in American colleges, much less the variety of grades available: A, B, C, D, each with pluses and minuses attached. A student knows the material or he does not. The difference can be expressed quite adequately with only two categories.

The difference between competence and failure should be clear to any teacher when he grades the student's performance on any assignment. Some students might demonstrate a thorough insight into the subject, while others might have a shaky grasp. But the ones who fail stand out; they cannot even begin to answer the questions. More likely than not, they do not even understand the questions.

Colleges could prune out failing students by any number of means. They could test every student at the end of every course, as most American colleges do today. Or, if they had some common conception of what students should study as they approached their degree, they could provide comprehensive examinations at the end of each academic year. British universities take the process one step further, testing students only when they have completed their degree program. If the students have a reasonably clear idea of what is expected, then the testing could come at any given point in the progression toward a bachelor's degree.

Yes, such tests would make students nervous. All tests make students nervous. But this system should be no worse than the system that pervades academe today. For most students the anxiety could be much less intense, since the test would only measure minimum competence. The A, B, and even the C students could relax somewhat, knowing full well that they would pass. Only the borderline cases would have to worry. And they should.

Grades do indeed measure something. Any comparison between honor-roll students and their plodding classmates reveals a clear dichotomy. As a group, the successful grade-getters will be substantially more successful in other areas of achievement as well. They will be brighter and more diligent; they will command higher salaries in the corporate or professional world. But the value of that comparison is limited. Talented and dedicated people will find ways to prosper in almost any system. The fact that they find a way to secure high grades in school should come as no surprise.

But what is it that grades measure? Are students rewarded for intellectual attainment, or for recognizing the rules of the grading game? For philosophical profundity, or for paying obeisance to academic conventions? The truth probably lies somewhere in between these two poles. There are some straight-A students with unmistakable intellectual talents, and others whose leading characteristic is the ability to play along with the academic game. The university treats them all with equal affection. In the last analysis, the most serious defect in the prevalent system is not that it fails to compare students, nor even that it cannot measure their performance. The most serious defect is that the system judges students on irrelevant grounds.

The solution seems ludicrously simple: abolish grades. Alas, the argument against that solution is also formidable. If grades provide an escape route for lazy teachers, their absence indulges lazy students. In the many colleges where students may take a few courses on a Pass-Fail basis, professors remark some steady deterioration in performance among those who choose the Pass-Fail option. (Of course, this might be explained in part by the fact that students choose to receive grades in their strongest subjects, while taking the Pass-Fail route in their weaker courses. Thus the inferior performance of Pass-Fail students might indicate that they are outside their primary field of interest.) Knowing that he can slide through without effort, the student is naturally tempted to do so. Grades furnish the carrot and stick of motivation. Perhaps the truly dedicated students do not profit by receiving grades, but their weaker counterparts do. Like most other educational policies, grades are aimed to benefit not the best students — who will learn regardless of the school's weaknesses — nor the worst students — who will not learn, no matter what the inducements — but the majority in the middle. Grades provide the added impetus and the necessary feedback to urge students toward extra effort — the extra incremental effort that will make the difference between satisfactory plodding and true educational enlightenment. Caught on the horns of this dilemma, many educators have called for some sort of compromise. Perhaps a student's transcript should contain some other form of written evaluation. But most such proposals suffer from all the weaknesses of letter grades without adding any new advantages. A system based on "Honors-Average-Satisfactory-Failure" is different from one based on "A-B-C-D-F" only in that it omits one classification — hardly a major reform. And a system in which teachers enter a short comment onto the transcript easily deteriorates into one in which teachers devise code-words to approximate the same categories: "excellent" translates as A, "good" as B, and so on, just as the transcript explains now.

Here, if I may, I shall propose a third possibility — one which was proposed by Harvard's student reformers of 1970, and, I think, unjustly ignored. Why not expand the student's transcript into something like a comprehensive academic file? Colleges already maintain files on their students, including diverse documents about the individuals' personal traits and administrative standing. Why should his academic records be confined to one or two pages?

Obviously they should not. And there lies a remedy. The student could submit into this file one representative work from each of his courses, together with the teacher's evaluative comments on that work. Teachers could designate in advance the work to be included in the transcript, or they could allow students to choose. In either case, the teacher could indicate failure if he thought the work unsatisfactory, or issue a special commendation if the work was unusually meritorious. Otherwise, the student's work and the professor's evaluation, taken together, would constitute the student's "grade" for that course.

The system would have several important benefits. Knowing that their critiques were destined for the university's permanent files, professors would have an incentive to elaborate, thereby furnishing students with a useful indication of their strengths and weaknesses. (At the same time, the professor's critiques would also give his superiors some indication of his competence as a teacher.) To anyone intimately connected with the student's progress, the representative piece would provide much more information than a single mark on a transcript could convey. Students would still have an incentive to work diligently, since the fruits of their labor would go into the permanent record. But they would also enjoy a new incentive to take risks — to dispute the teacher's dogmas, or to undertake a novel approach to some academic problem. Knowing that the teacher could not dismiss their creative efforts completely — knowing that anyone perusing the files could form his own independent opinion about the merits of the work — the student would be less tempted to parrot the teacher's line. The many advantages of academic gamesmanship would pale, and students would be free to do their best work regardless of competitive niceties.

Such a system would assure the student that his grade was not an insult. It would provide him with the guarantee that his teacher was being evaluated along with himself. The entire school, particularly the faculty, would therefore have an interest in discharging bad teachers before their evaluative comments embarrassed the university. In short, the system would not only perform a motivating function, but also add a twofold educational benefit, encouraging creativity in students and diligence in teachers. It would become itself an educational instrument (which the current grading system is not), precisely because it involves the attention of the entire university community. It would answer the stipulation of Afred North Whitehead: "I suggest that no system of external tests which aims primarily at individual scholars can result in anything but educational waste."[2]

Why then did Harvard not adopt this system? And why do other colleges remain aloof? Because, like most other radical departures from standard procedures, the system would encounter tremendous opposition from people with vested interests.

The opposition to change, in this case as in most others, would come from people who have a special stake in the present system. Not professors, who merely hand in their evaluations and move on to prepare for the next semester. Not students, who have no reason to cherish one form of transcript over another.

Unless, of course, they want to impress graduate school admissions officers.

Ah, there it is. The group that has an interest in preserving the current grading system is the group that reads through thousands of college students' transcripts every year. Students must aim to please the people who preside over postgraduate admissions, so they in turn develop a stake in the shorthand system. So the opposition to the file system of evaluation rests not on any educational values — grading is not viewed as an educational tool — but on the preferences of people outside the college community.

One cannot blame graduate admissions officers for their preference. It is easier — much easier — to run through a list of single-letter grades than it would be to peruse an entire series of papers and examinations. The admissions committee in many cases would be incompetent to judge the merits of work done in some undergraduates courses. Admissions officers would be forced to expand dramatically if the change took effect, in order to cover the mushrooming workload. They would require the (reluctant) assistance of professors from other departments, to help judge the applicant's work in fields outside his proposed graduate specialty. There can be no doubt that this system would inconvenience graduate and professional schools' admissions committees.

So what?

Should a college retain an inferior grading system, merely to placate outsiders? Yes, the college does have some responsibility to help its graduates enter the best possible postgraduate schools, but it also has a more immediate responsibility to safeguard and nourish the educational climate at the undergraduate level. The purpose of the college is to educate its students, not to serve as a processing plant for postgraduate institutions. Colleges are not and should not be preparatory schools for graduate students.

And would not the additional emphasis on graduate school admissions decisions bring some educational benefits of its own? In the course of their more comprehensive evaluations, admissions committees would learn much more about their applicants. They would have a better opportunity to cull out the unimaginative, to detect signs of real creativity, and ultimately to select the students best suited to their programs. Some schools might assign a high value to traits other schools would despise — traits which letter grades cannot possibly indicate. A law school, for instance, would look askance at an applicant whose imagination continually distracted him from the subject; not so a creative writing program. Any school should be able to discern when a student had shown dramatic improvement during his college career, thereby serving notice that he was able to meet the more demanding standards of the graduate curriculum. Conversely, the schools would be forewarned by examining the work of students whose work did not substantially improve, indicating either sloth or incapacity for futher learning. Perhaps most importantly, admissions officers could determine whether or not a student's individual approach meshed with the particular strengths and slants of the graduate program.

Eventually, perhaps some schools will test a grading system similar to the one I have described. However, the experimental colleges, the schools most likely to make the effort, are the schools least likely to succeed in this experiment. If a small college with no special reputation embraces the plan, graduate schools can simply refuse to assess the students' transcripts. Or the admissions committee can force the students to provide a briefer transcript — one with the equivalent of letter grades. Eventually, students planning graduate training will press the college to change back to the letter grades, and the experiment will collapse. As long as the reform is confined to small colleges, the power of the graduate schools will be overwhelming.

But suppose a large prestigious college — or, better yet, a group of large prestigious colleges — adopted the new system. Graduate schools could not simply refuse to accept applications from the Big Ten universities, or the Ivy League. In order to maintain the size and quality of their graduate enrollment, the schools would be forced to cooperate. Graduate instructors, bent on attracting the best possible students, would rebel against any obstruction. In short order, the universities would alter their graduate application procedures, making it possible for smaller colleges to join the grading reform.

A few other arguments against the reform would still remain, but none is compelling. Would the new system be less efficient as a means of comparing classmates? Perhaps so, but there is no educational value in such comparisons. If Student X has grasped the course material, that graps is unaffected by the fact that Student Y has an even better grasp, or that Student Z has no grasp at all. Do letter grades induce better performance by goading students to compete against each other? It seems unlikely, except insofar as students seek a competitive advantage in the struggle for postgraduate placement. And if it is true, it is an unfortunate source of motivation. A much more attractive source of motivation would be the student's desire to answer the criticisms of his last paper. Does the prospect of a high letter grade promote special effort? Yes, but the prospect of a special commendation would do the same, and perhaps more; in the latter case, the student would retain not only the professor's kind words, but also the detailed and inevitably flattering explanation of the grader's enthusiasm, etched forever in the student's records.

Finally one might argue that letter grades furnish a convenient means by which professors can maintain classroom discipline. The teacher can compel participation in discussions by telling his students that they are being graded on their contributions in the classroom. He can penalize the lazy students, whether or not that student knows the material. He can motivate the plodding student by assuring him that a well researched paper, no matter how dull, will be favorably received. Since his evaluations are rarely questioned (especially if they are favorable), and still more rarely overruled, he can protect his control over his classroom empire. He can force students to pay attention no matter how boring and pedestrian he may become, and to put effort into every assignment no matter how routine and unrewarding it may be. If this is the most desirable means of discipline available at today's universities, then the disciplinary system, even more than the grading system, is ripe for reform.

American colleges today should need no elaborate disciplinary machinery. Students apply to colleges; colleges do not apply to students. When a student drops out of school, there are others waiting to take his place. The more selective schools turn down several applicants for every one they accept. The school should be in a strong position, then, to select and maintain an enrollment of students who are willing to work assiduously. Attendance at college is a privilege. Even in private schools, and even among nonscholarship students at those schools, tuition covers only a fraction of the total cost of educating a student. If and when a student displays unwillingness to work, or to cooperate with the rules of the institution, he should be asked to leave. Dead weight in the classroom harms everyone concerned; the school would do much better to replace the lazy student with one who has something to contribute.

Seminars, which represent an increasingly popular mode of undergraduate instruction, illustrate the need for a positive disciplinary requirement. In a seminar, each student must contribute to the classroom discussion, or he detracts from the value of his classmates' educational experience. If he keeps his thoughts to himself, or comes to class unprepared, or does a shoddy job in preparing his own presentations, then he effectually sabotages the course. Such a slacker is wasting not only his own time, effort, and tuition money, but also his classmates'. In every real and conceivable sense, the college community cannot afford his presence.

Academic discipline, of course, must be detached from social discipline. A student may work earnestly during the day, then indulge his baser tastes at night. The latter, too, are potentially destructive to the college as a community, but American colleges seem better equipped to control them. A normal policing mechanism, coupled with a dollop of avuncular understanding that, after all, boys will be boys, should suffice to handle that problem. Social discipline is a matter of constraints; it is a negative discipline that stipulates what a student may and may not do. As such, it involves no distinctively academic ideal: only the ideal of social order, which is common to all societies. After all, the reasons to frown upon drunken rampages on campus are the same as the reasons to frown upon drunken rampages on city streets.

There is one important exception to the above generalization.

When social disorders impinge on the academic freedom of the college community, they become a serious and distinctively academic problem. Disruptive political demonstrations, intimidation of speakers, and destruction of educational resources would fall into this category. Here the enforcement of discipline does indeed call for a strict adherence to the underlying academic ideals. And here, as my first chapter suggests, American colleges have failed to enforce that ideal. Whether it is to prompt students to maximum effort, or to deter them from disrupting the efforts of others, American colleges require a new understanding of the purposes of academic discipline.

Until very recently both academic and social discipline were invested in one authority: the college's dean. Acting as surrogate father as well as university official, the dean could issue any sort of instructions and/or ukases, and students would obey. A grudging consensus gave the dean authority to tell students when they must work harder, or cut their hair, or end their parties. The dean's decisions could be appealed, but his power was unquestioned. His decisions could be capricious, of course, and his judgements could be arbitrary, but his personal involvement gave students an understanding of their responsibilities to the college. That understanding was vague, but it worked to solidify the institution.

Discipline was undeniably strict. The poet Allen Ginsberg was thrown out of Columbia College — not warned, not suspended, but summarily ejected — for scrawling an obscenity on his dormitory window. Surely that was a draconian punishment, particularly by today's relaxed standards. But one cannot overlook the fact that the incident occurred during the "Golden Era" of Columbia's undergraduate program. This same personal discipline which allowed a strict punishment for Ginsberg simultaneously supported an unusually active and vibrant liberal arts community. Nor is there any contradiction here. Ginsberg was punished not so much for the obscenity itself as for his failure to participate actively in that community. By assuring participation, and spirited participation at that, Columbia was assuring the quality and intensity of the undergraduate academic experience.

By the late '60s, the consensus underlying such disciplinary

systems had fractured, and ironically Columbia was the scene of
the earliest and worst campus riot. With the collapse of academic
ideals, students began questioning and eventually rejecting the
legitimacy of the dean's authority. And eventually colleges
acceded to student demands, creating new judicial bodies to
replace the deans' paternal rule. The campus regulations were
expanded to cover the areas formerly within the dean's personal
discretion. The legal structure of the university came to resemble
the legal structure of the government itself, with detailed penal
codes, bureaucratic regulatory bodies, and repeated calls for due
process of law.

But universities are not like states, and university discipline
when ideally enforced bears little resemblance to ordinary law.
In civil law the citizen has the presumed right to undertake any
activity not specifically proscribed by statute. The university,
in contrast, cannot possibly list all the actions which would be
detrimental to the scholarly enterprise. In civil law, the goal is
to preserve order: a negative goal. In the university, the aim is to
facilitate and encourage cooperation among members of the
community: a positive goal. Thus university discipline, properly
understood, is not preventive but prescriptive. Since effort and
cooperation cannot be measured accurately, the university cannot catalogue desired actions or offensive attitudes. The university dean is like an athletic coach: although he cannot precisely
define teamwork and "hustle," he must exhort his charges to
practice these virtues, and reprimand them when they do not.
The imposition of elaborate rules defining academic discipline
is as misguided and as debilitating as the imposition of rules
defining "hustle" on a football field. Neither team can be en-
capsulated in a simplistic description; each demands different
responses to different situations. But every football player knows
what "hustle" is, and every student should know what academic
discipline is. The football coach makes subjective decisions about
individuals, but the players' understanding supports his authority. By the same token, the old-style deans made subjective
judgements in disciplinary cases, but the consensus of the student
body supported their authority. Those deans, for all their failings, worked far more effectively than the current formalistic

system in promulgating a consistent vision of the community's responsibilities.

Let me illustrate my point with a dramatic example from my own experience. While I was a student at the University of Chicago, two freshmen began threatening to kill a classmate who had somehow earned their enmity. The threats were not serious, but the purported victim took them seriously, and indeed the bullies intended that he should. Eventually the relevant deans were assembled, and informed of this continuing crisis in the residence hall. (One would think, after the episode with Leopold and Loeb, that the University of Chicago would be particularly sensitive to such threats.) The deans caucused, debated, and temporized. There was a problem: the University had no rule against threatened murder. Eventually, after repeated and diverse provocations, the two offenders were required to leave the dormitory, but not the school. No formal disciplinary action was undertaken, and the two continued in good standing.

Now anyone with a child's understanding of academic discipline knows that threatened murder inhibits the action of the college learning community. But as long as the college limits its disciplinary action to proscriptive rules, even the child's understanding cannot be put into effect. Needless to say, the same misguided presumption works in less dramatic cases. At Harvard, I met a student who played pinball for four or five hours on an average day. Of course it was a harmless form of recreation, and yet it did serve to deprive the college community of the use of his talents. He broke no rules, although he did skip classes to indulge his habit. By dint of unusual mental talent, he still maintained extremely high grades. His classmates never received the benefits of his ideas; he was busy in the recreation room. So in that sense he robbed the college, by denying his own contribution. Yet he left Harvard with a prestigious scholarship for graduate study. Clearly, he had more to contribute; and a stronger, positive sense of academic discipline would have elicited something more from him.

What do pinball and threatened murder have in common? They are both activities that disrupt the smooth operation of the university as a community. A student who is threatened cannot concentrate on his studies; a student whose classmate skips discussion sessions cannot hear all the ideas he should be able to hear. And of course both activities are destructive to campus morale, since they demonstrate to students that some of their classmates are flouting the university's ideals. A strong college dean, supported by a consensual understanding of the need for scholarly teamwork, would call a quick halt to either of these vices. His decision would be subjective, of course; the school's regulations could not possibly contain specific provisions against such bizarre behavior. But without such subjective decisions, academic discipline is emasculated.

Since the ideal academic discipline is a subjective standard, little more can be said about its specific dimensions. The college must incorporate this discipline into the very fabric of the university. Students — and professors as well — should be informed in unmistakable terms that they are members of a team, and will be expected to contribute their best effort to the cooperative endeavor. They must realize that it is not enough simply to fulfill course requirements and attend mandatory meetings and observe a few minimal standards of conduct. They must realize that their active, spirited participation in the campus community is wanted, and indeed demanded. As long as they remain within the university, they should expect to govern themselves in accordance with its dictates. Every individual member of the community must dedicate himself to the communal goal: pursuing the truth.

Given that dedication, and even allowing for occasional lapses on the part of every individual, the university will be guaranteed a lively and stimulating intellectual environment. In a sense, the establishment of this dedication, this positive academic discipline, is more important than the curriculum itself. Dedicated scholars will teach and learn regardless of the curricular agenda, just as surely as halfhearted pupils leave their intellectual curiosity behind when they leave their classroom desks. Cardinal Newman assessed the situation accurately. The company of intelligent and dedicated young men, he said, is the most educational aspect of the university. Given a theoretical choice, he preferred a university without teachers to one without such students. Where true cooperative academic discipline is established, the curriculum cannot fail.

CHAPTER EIGHT

The Cult of Dissent

> Yale, like every other major college, is graduating scores of bright young men who are practitioners of the 'politics of despair.' These young men despise the American economic and social system.
>
> *Stewart Alsop*[1]

American colleges have set themselves apart from the rest of our society. The social attitudes on campus, the moral and political views held by teachers and by students: all are radically different from the values of American society in general. Academe has become a virtual counterculture. We have seen the evidence persistently: in the academic revolts of the '60s; in the recurrent use of a double standard of rhetoric that protects radicals and punishes conservatives; in the perverse attempts to exclude alumni and businessmen from active roles in university governance. Ideas that seem radical in society at large are accepted into the academic mainstream.

Yet American society remains strangely complacent about this cultural stranger in our midst. We have been taught all along that universities are seedbeds for all sorts of new ideas. We assume that students will have the independence to decide crucial questions for themselves. We feel confident that the current student generation will mellow with age — will learn to respect our cultural heritage. On all three counts we are mistaken. The academic marketplace is severely controlled, and not all ideas flourish equally. Students hear only one side of most social and political problems, and their decisions are ill informed. And the current generation of collegians has not learned to appreciate the strengths of our culture. On the contrary, they have been taught to disdain that culture.

Education is a process, not a product. Schools, as we all agree, should teach students *how* to think, not *what* to think. The student should hone his intellectual abilities so that he can approach and resolve serious questions by himself. But the dichotomy is not a simple one; training and indoctrination are not altogether different, at least not at first glance. Intelligent people differ not only in how they resolve certain questions, but also in how they approach them. As another timeworn dictum asserts, the identification of the problem is the first step of the solution. Or, to put it differently, the answer itself depends on the way in which the question is phrased. When confronted with a problem, should one react with pure logic or pure emotion? A cost-benefit analysis or a moral ordering? A creative impulse or an appeal to authority? Each of these responses could be appropriate in some situations; none is always productive. Academic training should refine the student's use of each method, but it should also teach him how to choose the approach that is appropriate to the problem at hand.

Since education is not like chess, different institutions emphasize different ultimate objectives. (Even in chess there are different tactical approaches, but at least everyone agrees that the final goal is checkmate.) Whether the college concentrates on piety or efficiency, dialectics or pragmatism, the institutional personality will develop accordingly. As time passes that personality undergoes various changes, but still every college retains its own peculiar flavor. What separates Notre Dame from Berkeley is an intellectual climate: an intangible characteristic way of thinking. In my own experience I have found that a school's stereotyped reputation generally reflects the underlying reality of its intellectual climate. Harvard's detachment, Princeton's bonhomie, Chicago's bookishness — all real enough traits on a superficial level — are the outward evidence of an inner orientation. The school's distinctive atmosphere translates itself into a prevalent social and academic attitude.

To state the argument more directly, a school affects the way its students think and act. A Notre Dame graduate is not quite the same person that he would be if he had attended Berkeley. The implication should be clear. Colleges, in teaching people how to think, also inevitably form their characters. Colleges have an almost frightening power, then; forming the character of a generation involves an incalculably stronger influence than mere political indoctrination would command. The most memorable description of that influence comes from no less a student of power than Napoleon: "Give me an army and I will rule the country; make me a teacher and I shall rule the world."

The process of education is powerful in part because its results are not readily perceptible. The student is merely trained to address certain questions in certain ways; the practical effects occur much later in his life. C.S. Lewis explains, "It is not a theory they put in his mind, but an assumption, which ten years hence, its origin forgotten and its presence unconscious, will condition him to take one side in a controversy which he has never recognized as a controversy at all."[2]

A generation ago William F. Buckley Jr. shocked the educational establishment with his book *God and Man at Yale*. His theme, which earned him sensational controversy and widespread condemnation, was that Yale disdained Christianity and free enterprise. At the time that charge seemed brash, provocative. This young man was charging that Yale indoctrinated its students, nourished the values of agnosticism and socialism. Educators reacted with lockstep outrage, issuing denials and denunciations.

Today Buckley's charges appear as ludicrous as the educators said they were a generation ago. But for a different reason. They are quaint; they are too obvious. One reads *God and Man at Yale* today and murmurs, "But of course; how could this surprise anyone?"

Today everyone who has any understanding of university life knows that American campuses are hotbeds of political and social dissent. In 1972, while America at large was voting overwhelmingly for Richard Nixon, the Princeton faculty supported George McGovern by the lopsided margin of 88 to 12 percent.[3] The *Harvard Crimson* poll that year showed Nixon running approximately even with Mickey Mouse; McGovern's main opposition in that survey came from the splinter candidates of the extreme Left. This, remember, was before the Watergate scandal blossomed.

Once again, the years have not mellowed campus opinions. If anything, college students have become more obdurate in their political views. Positions and attitudes that generated excitement and controversy a decade ago are now routinely accepted. Anyone who doubts that conclusion need only strike up a political discussion on campus. Or, if he is living in a college community, the skeptic should ride a bus to a nearby town — one with no substantial academic population — and overhear political debates in a local barbershop.

The predominant political and social liberalism among students is mirrored (or is it caused) by the liberalism of faculty members. Two sociologists, Seymour Martin Lipset and Everett Carll Ladd, conducted an exhaustive poll of university professors in 1976 and produced striking conclusions. "It is clear from our data that faculty members constitute a massive force in favor of liberal domestic, pacificist, anti-militarist, and Democratic policies. The influence of academe is even greater than the ideological preferences of the majority imply, since the most politically active among them are to the left of the profession as a whole."[4]

The Ladd-Lipset findings demonstrated more than the ideological imbalance of the American professoriate. A breakdown of results yielded the crucial information that professors in the social sciences and humanities are decidedly more liberal than their colleagues in the natural sciences, and professors at prestigious universities are more liberal than their colleagues at less competitive colleges. So the effects of this imbalance are magnified fourfold. Conservative professors in the sciences have little occasion to deliver political pronouncements in the classrooms, whereas social scientists can inject every lecture with political beliefs. And since the most influential opinion-makers of the next generation go to the most prestigious colleges, they fall into the hands of the most liberal teaching corps. Since other colleges recruit their faculty members from the most prestigious universities, the obvious inference is that the next generation of college teachers — and especially those in the social sciences and humanities — will themselves be students of liberal professors.

Now and then the universities make a halfhearted effort to

alleviate this political bias. When a campus seminar features seven or eight speakers addressing a political topic, the organizers scrupulously include one lonely conservative, "for balance." As often as not, the allegedly conservative speaker is really quite middle-of-the-road by ordinary political standards. And of course his speech in overwhelmed by the numerous opposing presentations. Still the organizers can righteously point to his presence as an illustration of their willingness to hear and air all views.

A similar ploy involves the recruitment of a token conservative so inarticulate, so extreme, or so personally repugnant in his manner that his presence actually enhances the liberal argument. If students see a bloated, supercilious reactionary arguing against an urbane progressive, they naturally assume that the reactionary's stance has no intellectual merit whatsoever. The conservative is seen as an extremist, and so the ideological spectrum is warped again, with students seeing nothing to separate moderate traditionalists from raving reactionaries.

As an innocent sophomore, I ventured to enroll in a course on political and social philosophy, not realizing that the instructor (like most of the enrolled students) was a member of the radical Maoist Progressive Labor Party. The reading list for that term comprised a Who's Who of Communist theorists: Marx, Engels, Lenin, Karl Kautsky, Trotsky, Rosa Luxembourg, Mao. (That's right: Mao, in a philosophy course.) Then, in the final weeks of the semester, just before we took on Herbert Marcuse, we read one conservative thinker: Karl Popper. (As it happened, the instructor joined with students in the ritual anti-Vietnam strike halfway through the semester, so I never did hear him exorcize the conservative demon.) Now Karl Popper is a brilliant scholar and thinker, but his views are certainly not the mainline of the conservative tradition. And his writing is formidably academic, certainly not accessible to the unprepared undergraduate reader. There are literally dozens of other thinkers who counter the Communist line differently, and more effectively, from the undergraduate's point of view. But in this course, the instructor's presentation was not meant to ensure ideological balance. This professor was preaching revolution. His purpose was to present students with a blunt choice: accept Popper's argument or Marx's; there is no other alternative.

Does all this skullduggery sound a bit too Machiavellian? I should hasten to add that most academic institutions, and most professors, do not purposely set up such invidious comparisons. Most schools do relish visits by responsible conservative spokesmen. Still, most professors do follow their own ideological instincts. They may earnestly try to achieve a balanced presentation, but their personal feelings tug constantly in the opposite direction. They present opposing ideas out of a sense of duty, but they present their own ideas out of a sense of conviction. If they are painstakingly fair, they pause occasionally to explore "the other side." But then, with a sigh of relief, they go back to preaching their own beliefs.

Confronted with the overwhelming evidence of ideological imbalance, university administrators wrap themselves in robes of innocence, proclaiming that professors never, never attempt to promulgate their own political attitudes. Professors merely convey the subject matter, the educationists say; their personal beliefs have nothing to do with their scholarly abilities. Perhaps professors are indeed very liberal, but they leave their political attitudes out of their classroom presentations. And anyway, even if they did try to indoctrinate their classes, the students would be able to separate scholarly wheat from subjective chaff. Princeton's President William Bowen delivered a typical response of this kind when conversative alumni pressed the question. Bowen averred that a) Princeton students are too bright and independent to be easily swayed and b) a professor's personal political views are so divorced from his scholarly work that he, Bowen, could not honestly guess how many faculty members were Democrats, how many Republicans.[5]

Nonsense.

As Bowen knows, the problem is not a matter of party politics. The danger provoked by ideological imbalance is not that professors will begin acting as ward bosses for the local politicos, or delivering campaign speeches in the classroom. The danger is that students will be exposed to a one-sided view of the world, a view heavily founded in the same presumptions that inform liberal politicians. Professors do not inculcate their specific views on issues of public policy. Rather, they convey something of their overall approach to intellectual questions: their *Weltanschauung*. Since students are exposed almost exclusively to the same attitudes, they come to equate that *Weltanschauung* with intelligence itself. So when students follow their teachers down the liberal political path, they do so for the reason Lewis explains: they act upon the basis of an unexamined presumption, acquired somewhere in their schooling.

If all this seems unduly complicated, perhaps there is a simple refutation of the educationists' argument. The fact is that Bowen and his allies rely on a preposterous argument when they say that teachers do not influence their students. How else do students learn, if not by absorbing the material their instructor gives them? To claim that instructors do not sway students is to admit the futility of education. If one scholar can coax students toward a love for Shakespeare, another can coax them toward devotion to Marx. (I can name the scholar who taught me to love Plato, and the one who taught me to love Josquin de Prez; I can cite the book — on a course reading list — that awakened my interest in St. Thomas Aquinas.) Professors are not only sources of knowledge, but also role models for their young charges. In their actions and their attitudes, just as much as their lectures, they serve as examples. Any scholar who cannot influence students has no business in a classroom, and any pupil who does not seek to be influenced has no business in college.

So the school takes on a *Weltanschauung* of its own, one which contradicts several of the most basic tenents of American society. Students leave the college with new perspectives, or with old prejudices strongly reinforced. As Buckley predicted in 1952, students leave the university with a headful of notions contrary to our traditional beliefs in God and country. The frightening result is that students whose philosophy is agnostic become ministers; students who scorn patriotism become national political leaders; students who despise the market economy become businessmen. Perhaps their attitudes change along the way, and then again perhaps not. Even if they do modify their political and social and religious beliefs, they still labor with that old set of unexamined assumptions. Surely they are not habituated to their new roles as society's leaders. They have been trained to be society's gadflies.

An interesting sidelight to this issue has been the gradual progress of intellectual chickens coming home to roost. For years the universities have been preaching the virtues of governmental supervision in virtually every sector of American society. Now, in the past few years, bureaucrats trained in that manner of thinking have begun asserting control over the universities themselves. Of course academe has been uneasy with these new impositions, and suddenly found arguments against government intervention in the life of private institutions. The arguments are all quite cogent, and yet one wonders. Why did the professoriate never raise these arguments in the past?

The universities certainly have no reason to affect surprise that their own cherished ideas are coming back to haunt them in bureaucratic form. Because a large and growing proportion of American citizens pass through colleges, the attitudes promulgated there creep into every corner of society. Moreover, the most important and influential posts in society usually are occupied by graduates of the better colleges and universities. (Remember? The ones with the most liberal faculty members.) College graduates monopolize the mass media, publishing houses, political parties and pressure groups, foundations, the arts, lobbying organizations, clergy, corporate hierarchies, bar associations, and of course schools at all levels. College graduates form the network that generates the society's ideas, and influences society's opinions. Their beliefs are doubly and triply important, since they become, willy-nilly, the beliefs of the entire nation. When this opinion-generating elite becomes disaffected from society's basic ideological underpinnings, the consequences are unavoidably traumatic.

The economist Joseph Schumpeter predicted those consequences forty years ago in *Capitalism, Socialism, and Democracy,* a book of chilling prophetic powers. Schumpeter theorized that the capitalist system would produce an affluent yet disaffected intellectual class, and that society would soon find itself bereft of defenders to counter the intellectuals' fulminations. The intellectuals would call for increasing government supervision, thereby foisting their own ideas off on society through the mediating efforts of the regulators. The net result would be the demise of free enterprise and the replacement of capitalism by socialism. Thus far the course of American history has conformed to Schumpeter's expectations.[6]

The relative virtues and vices of capitalism and socialism are not at issue here. The fundamental issue is the ideological waywardness of the intellectual establishment, and its deleterious effects of American culture. As the universities churn out graduates who neither understand nor appreciate our cultural heritage — of which capitalism is one facet — and as these graduates proceed to positions of influence, that entire heritage is jeopardized. Failing to appreciate the meaning of traditions, the new opinion-makers confuse the purpose of societal institutions, thereby robbing them of their full strength. A culture cannot long hold onto institutions whose purposes are distorted. So the institutions begin to falter, and society's leaders begin to misuse them still further. And while critics recognize the problem, they do not understand the cause. So the intellectuals continue to deride the institutions and traditions, even after they have lost sight of their proper place and usage. The process is cunning and pernicious: first the institution is misused, and then, when it fails as a consequence of misuse, critics blame the institution rather than the misuse. Worst of all, this adversary relationship generates a profound skepticism of all institutions — a creeping cynicism that infects society's morale and morality. I leave the reader to provide illustrations, in the full certainty that anyone unable to do so has rejected my thesis several chapters ago.

Those who value tradition — for simplicity's sake I shall call them conservatives, although the ideological breakdown is considerably more complex — have a tendency to see conspiratorial overtones in the universities' ideological imbalance. Their charges are buoyed up by the occasional political persecutions that do mar campus life, but they miss the fundamental point. Reputable scholars do not intentionally exclude viewpoints that differ from their own, and the American professoriate is much too fragmented to conjoin in any such conspiracy. Academe does have a very palpable bias, but it is implicit rather than official, a function more of ignorance than of premeditation. The exclusion of traditional and conservative points of view results from the professors' naive inability to see merit in the conservative or traditionalist position.

Every scholar, when he chooses his field of specialization, picks a range of topics that he considers important. It would be too much to say that he ignores all other topics, but surely his interest in them is secondary. Naturally his perception of the important topics is governed by his own *Weltanschauung*; the way he perceives the world and orders his priorities affects the way he approaches his scholarly duties. Men with differing fundamental values embrace differing views of which questions are most important. An atheist might consider the question of liturgical ritual as thoroughly irrelevant, while to a priest that same question is pivotal. The choice of topics, then, is the first step in defining one's academic approach. And, as I noted earlier, the first step toward an answer lies in the definition of the question.

At the same time, the choice of topic also defines the character of schools and departments within schools. When the faculty meets to design course syllabi, the professors will quickly assert the importance of the issues they themselves address, and of companion issues. They tend to overlook issues that fall outside their own ken. In like manner, when the department meets to consider appointing new professor or granting tenured posts, the faculty members took with special favor on colleagues whose research answers the questions they themselves consider most important. Thus professors who dissent from the reigning academic orthodoxy face double jeopardy in their efforts to gain appointment or promotion. Even before they submit their scholarly credentials for inspection, they must convince their potential employers that their work is relevant to the purposes of the department. More than that; they must somehow alert the department to the very fact that they exist.

For illustration, consider an economics department dominated by liberal professors. (The imagination should not boggle; most university departments do answer to that description.) If the professors hold the accepted liberal verities, they focus their attention on several key areas: government fiscal policy, for example. They read certain journals, to the exclusion of others, correspond with certain colleagues who share their methodological approaches, and in general derive their knowledge of the professional community from within the confines of their own restricted views. They would not normally consider hiring an economist of, say, the Austrian school, because they would not have heard of him; that school addresses different questions, which do not particularly interest liberal economists. They would not ordinarily worry about the absence of courses dealing with free-market processes, because liberal economists do not spend their time pondering market remedies to economic problems. Moreover, they would not ordinarily find themselves attracted by the academic potential of a young scholar who approached the subject from a libertarian angle, because they do not believe that such an approach yields the best scholarly results. (If they did think so, they themselves would adopt that approach.) Such a department would gravitate toward the abundant supply of bright young scholars whose approach coincides with the one already dominant in the department. The reasons are all perfectly reasonable, but the effect is the same as the effect of intentional repression: a curtailment of ideological diversity.

Economics, needless to say, is not the only discipline thus divided along methodological lines. In every scholarly subject area there are countless modes of inquiry, and when a scholar chooses one he implicitly decides that the others are less productive, or at least less interesting. Consequently, when a department is dominated by one methodological approach, the domination reinforces itself steadily over the years. Thus certain departments at certain universities acquire a very distinctive reputation within the field. When the methodological approach coincides with an ideological framework, and when that ideological framework envelopes the entire university — indeed the entirety of academe — then the effect is as pervasive as any conspiracy could be. More innocent, perhaps, but for that very reason more threatening.

If indoctrination is the desired end, the subtler approach is always more effective. Students *are* clever enough to recognize bias when it announces its presence. If the professor assails one point of view ferociously in every lecture, the students can surely assume that his perspective is not neutral. But what if he never so much as mentions that point of view? A student, unfamiliar with the range of scholarly viewpoints, has no way of knowing how much his teacher has left untouched. The economist who ridicules Milton Friedman in every lecture runs a risk: students might venture over to the library and scout out Friedman's books to see what causes all the fuss. Then, of course, Friedman's arguments might work their spell, and the instructor's bias would be repulsed. But if that same instructor simply ignores Friedman altogether, many of his students will never have reason to know that such a man exists, so the teacher's arguments will meet with no competition. Ideological imbalance is not usually manifested in evident bias; the quiet, superficially objective approach is every bit as effective.

Objectivity, then, is a two-edged sword. Even before he begins his lectures, the professor makes a subjective decision about what subjects they will include; he subjectively determines what he will be objective *about.*

When they are mentioned together, the term "objective" and the title "scholar" should sound an odd jarring note. The detrivation of the word "professor" is obvious: he is one who "professes" something. How can one "profess" objectively?

Scholars today answer that question by introducing the so-called fact-value distinction. They claim that one can separate a man's beliefs from his command over scientific facts — that one can categorize some judgements as factual, therefore objective, and others as judgements of values, and therefore subjective. Objective scholarship, they go on to say, refrains from discussion of values, and concentrates instead on the facts of the matter.

So far, so good (if we ignore the question of how a scholar can "profess" facts; the academic scene is littered with words and titles bereft of their original meaning). But the refusal to consider values leads quickly to the canard called "value-free" scholarship. Whether or not he discusses his values, the scholar certainly must have them, and they must infect and color his scholarship. Is he dealing exclusively with facts? Still, remember that he has chosen which facts he will seek, and he has assigned an interpretation to those facts. Every fact-finding mission betrays the human prejudices and subjective instincts of the participants.

In some fields, the notion of value-free scholarship seems transparently impossible. Those who study English literature generally agree that Shakespeare is the greatest of all dramatists. How do they reach that judgement? Certainly there are no "facts" that prove Shakespeare's greatness. Yes, there is the fact that his plays are read and performed everywhere today. But if someone contrived to sell millions of copies of plays written by mediocre playwrights, would that "fact" make them somehow Shakespeare's equals? Of course not. Scholars in the humanities constantly make value judgements. That is the pith of their profession.

In the hard sciences, value judgements comprise a smaller part of the scholar's work. Nevertheless, in his choice of subject and his selection of facts, every scientist makes judgements that no "facts" will sustain. Scholarship can never be value-free.

Scholarship can, however, be value-less. And often it is. Scholars assiduously avoid giving any place to subjective values, no matter how widely accepted those values might be. The time-honored beliefs of Western civilization count for nothing in this calculus; if they cannot be supported by hard "facts," they can be dismissed immediately, along with any other frivolous ideas and myths. So modern academe throws out all the authority of old precepts. Cherished old beliefs have no special place; they are given the same status as any new idea, to be tested and debated, discussed and attacked, in the marketplace of ideas. Does society believe that marital partners should be faithful? Never mind; that is a value judgement. Is there any scientific evidence on the subject?

- Thus the scholars place every traditional value under the microscope, searching for some signs of unsupported belief. It is as if community health officials, in their efforts to root out dangerous foods, began finding fault with mothers' milk. Which, come to think of it, they have.

Once this eerie split between facts and values takes full effect, the principle of marital fidelity has no advantage over the call for random adultery. What is the difference, scientifically speaking? Each new idea receives a full hearing. In fact the old ideas have something of a disadvantage: they have survived for so long that the stoic intellectuals begin *assuming* that they are based in some dark prejudice. Society was propounding the ethic of marital fidelity countless centuries ago, when people believed in ghosts; who knows, in the land of disembodied facts, whether the two beliefs are on a par?

The academic world seeks out new ideas that expose old prejudices, always looking to increase the power of the imperial intellect. If reason cannot support our deepest beliefs, those beliefs must be tossed aside. If there are prejudices still slumbering unrecognized in the human psyche, the value-free approach demands that they must be unearthed and discarded. Any idea that challenges old beliefs, then, has a special merit of its own: it might expose an unexamined value. So whatever is shocking tales on added importance; whatever comforting, less.

The "objective" scholarship, then, asks us to part with all our cultural predilections — to surrender all our comfortable old ideas and replace them with more suitable new ones. Above all, to recognize the puissant supremacy of mind over matter on all fronts and all occasions. A provocative thought is better than a consoling one; an argument that grates on our sensibilities is inherently good. Our tastes — that is, what we like — mean nothing. They must change. The contemporary art world is imbued with this strange aesthetic. We should learn, we are told, to love the things we hate, on the assumption that our instincts are likely to mislead us.

So now we have an outpouring of new ideas and new approaches, many of them bizarre, even offensive, by our old standards. The intellectual equivalent of what economists call Gresham's Law ("Bad money drives out good") takes control with a vengeance. Strange new ideas upset us, so we must ex-

amine them carefully. But the old ideas, which fit so neatly into
our lives, must be suspected. Academic journals provide room
for every new theory, multiplying the range of scholarly enterprises as fast as the printing industry can oblige. The mass media,
with their insatiable appetite for news, report every little epiphe-
nomenon, every new arrival on the intellectual marketplace. A
scholar seeking to build a wide reputation looks to the fringes of
academic respectability; he will not draw any attention by
improving slightly on a long-held hypothesis.

Inexorably the value-free culture assaults our established
beliefs and our traditional institutions. The new ideas have
special privileges. Our entire culture is cast in jeopardy, for what
is culture but a collection of old beliefs: a system of values?
The scholarship that turns its back on values ends by abandoning
the founding strengths of society itself. Academe becomes a
society with values unto itself — a counterculture.

The counterculture does not accept its status happily. Scholars
inveigh against the unexamined prejudices that govern the non-
academic world, piously invoking the need for an open mind.
The scholarly community becomes a special class, with a very
definite air of moral superiority. Thus many social commenta-
tors have referred to the "New Class," or the "knowledge sector," whose members take it upon themselves to prescribe for
all society's ills. The primary tactical weapon of this new class is
that selfsame pious belief — the value (that word again!) the
sustains their scholarship — in the need for an open mind.

As it happens, the need for an open mind was effectively
circumscribed nearly a century ago by G.K. Chesterton. The
reason for having an open mind, Chesterton said, was the same
as the reason for having an open mouth: in order to be able to
snap it shut when something good enters it. Good ideas, like
good food, merit careful tasting and digestion. The relentless
pursuit of new truths renders us unable to savor the ones we have
already found, and allow them to nourish further insights and
values. An open mind is a means toward an end. It is not, or at
least should not be, an end in itself.

A society cannot long survive without its own culture — its
own set of accepted values and truths. The culture provides the

founding ideas upon which the society builds; it is the adhesive that binds the societal fabric. Culture has many manifestations, many different interpretations. And it changes constantly. Contrary to the simplistic view of those who bewail cultural prejudices, society's ideas and ideals change constantly, often dramatically. A culture is a fluid force. At any given time, it means different things to different classes of people, and its forces gradually change to accept new ideas, incorporating them within the old stream. Anyone who expects to live contented within society and contribute to its growth must understand the society's culture — must appreciate the values that guide society's actions and responses.

Appreciation for culture, respect for culture, understanding of the role of tradition — these are precisely the things which the academic counterculture undermines. Today's college students have only a vague idea of how to remedy society's ills because they have only a vague idea of how our society operates. They have a meager understanding of our trations and institutions, and so they have a meager chance of using those traditions and institutions efficaciously. The ideological imbalance of the American academy threatens society at a fundamental level. Once the culture is destroyed — once the values are subverted and rejected — the society has no binding force. Alienation becomes the rule rather than the exception. The problem assumes a frightening immediacy as our society passes on the reins of leadership to the current, alienated student generation.

What is to be done? Universities need not limit faculty membership to button-down, Rotary Club members of the cultural mainstream. They need not — must not — impose political tests on professorial applicants. But they must seek out and appoint professors who can provide students with a sound appreciation for their cultural heritage. Since American academe today is so heavily overbalanced in the opposite direction, colleges must actively recruit scholars who know and appreciate the workings of our cultural heritage and our traditional institutions. The key, again, is not specific political beliefs, but rather *Weltanschauung,* or overall world views. In order to inculcate an appreciation for our heritage, the professors must appreciate it themselves.

Professors who teach courses on Shakespeare invariably love his plays; that is why they have chosen that line of study. Professors specializing in ancient philosophy invariably find great merit in premodern thought. One does not spend a career in pursuit of knowledge unless one finds that particular knowledge important, So by setting up a professorial chair in a given field, or embarking on a new study project, the university assures itself that the field will be treated seriously. The professor may be controversial; he may upset standard notions that guide research in his field; he may evince any sort of political views; but he will treat the field with some respect.

When the university seeks such devoted scholars, it does not compromise the professor's academic freedom. The university does not demand that the scholar hold any given attitude toward the subject in question. But the subject will receive the attention it deserves. That is all the university knows, and all it needs to know.

Our universities today strive mightily for diversity. We have seen how they struggle to include students of every ethnic stripe. Why should they not take equal pains to ensure diversity in the faculty's ideology? Are not a scholar's ideas as important — in the life of the mind — as the color of his skin? The evident bias of the existing professoriate enforces a strict limitation on campus debate, and every university should abhor such limitations. Conservative professors, professors who reject the ubiquitous academic liberalism, are today unusually provocative and therefore unusually valuable. If an "affirmative action" program is justified anywhere in the university, it is justified in the search for talented traditionalist scholars. Such scholars abound in some academic circles; the conservative intellectual movement is extremely vibrant in American life today. A determined effort could promptly produce a spectacular rise in the level and scope of campus debate.

But wait. Some readers are nervous. Why should the universities take such pains to protect the old ideas? Aren't the universities the seedbeds of unpopular notions? Isn't it the function of the university to challenge all accepted truisms, and subject them to stern analysis?

Quite so. And on campus today, the pat assumptions and accepted truisms are those of ritualistic liberalism; the unpopular views are the ones espoused by traditionalists. Anyone who doubts this need only listen to a speech delivered on a college campus by an articulate conservative. Do his ideas not sound extraordinarily new? Does the undergraduate audience not appear shocked? Then the pat assumptions are being shaken, and his views deserve a fuller hearing.

Given the extent of faculty imbalance, the potential donor has every reason to channel his educational gifts carefully. If his contributions are earmarked for general use, the faculty will continue its one-sided quest. If on the other hand he specified a particular use, he can singlehandedly break the liberal stranglehold and broaden the range of debate at the institution of his choice.

One witty observer, confronting the same question from the opposite perspective, argued that one should never assume that only a Marxist can teach Marxism. That, Geoffrey Wagner pointed out, was like saying that only a plant can teach botany. True enough; and it follows that one need not be a conservative to teach traditional values. As long as the professor understands his subject, and approaches it with a high regard, his personal preferences are irrelevant.

And yet, the need for a balanced faculty is evident.

Suppose plants could speak. Wouldn't they have a great deal to teach us about their lives — about botany?

CHAPTER NINE

On Giants' Shoulders

We are in danger to lose our identity and
become infantile in every generation.

Woodrow Wilson[1]

The cheerleaders are not all on the football field.

At every university I have known, one minor administrative official possesses a nostalgia so torrential, a loyalty so fanatical, that he never tires of chanting the institution's praises. Always a consummate raconteur and avid collector of university trivia, he lets nothing deflect him from those purposes. His fond attachment makes him blind to all criticisms fo the university — to his way of thinking, whatever is, is good.

At Princeton this role was faithfully filled by a charming eccentric, the late Reverend Doctor Freddy Fox. Always quick with a quip, Rev. Fox told questioners that "my religion is Princeton, and my denomination is Class of '39." And when a persistent interviewer sought his reaction to charges of ideological imbalance on campus, he replied with Olympian equanimity that such imbalance was wholly to be expected. Because, Dr. Fox patiently explained, Princeton is a liberal institution.

If Freddy Fox could not distinguish between an institution committed to liberalism and an institution committed to the liberal arts, virtually everyone else can. In modern political parlance the term "liberal" has dozens of conflicting interpretations. But the meaning of the term "liberal arts" is universally accepted. The liberal arts are the arts of liberty; a liberal arts institution is one which prepares the student to enjoy a life of freedom.

Freedom from what? Again there is general agreement. Freedom from ignorance and from the tyranny of crude ideologies. The liberal arts enable people to see beyond the confines of everyday life, and to grasp ideas more enduring than the latest intellectual fashions. One learns to think for oneself.

Too often educators repeat the phrase, now hopelessly trite, that we must study the past in order to avoid repeating it. That argument is true, but superficial; the study of our heritage has a much more profound purpose. Matthew Arnold expressed that purpose beautifully when he defined culture as:

> . . . a pursuit of our total perfection by means of getting to know, on all matters which most concern us, the best which has been thought and said in the world; and through this knowledge, turning a stream of fresh and free thought upon our stock notions and habits, which we now follow staunchly but mechanically, vainly imagining that there is a virtue in following them staunchly which makes up for the mischief of following them mechanically.[2]

Liberal arts training provides the graduate with an understanding and appreciation for our culture. He lives according to a rich vision informed not by a string of halfbaked assumptions and vague ideas, but by an accurate perception of how our past has conditioned our present. He understands the cultural framework that supports our thinking and our social customs. So he sees the present in its larger context — as the latest development in a cultural process that has been unfolding for hundreds of years. The historical perspective gives a new importance to our actions today, making them part and parcel with the growth of Western civilization. What we do today gives meaning to the lives of our forefathers, and sets the stage for our children. That is why Alfred North Whitehead adjured his readers to treat the present with great dignity, for it is hallowed ground.

Anyone can muddle through life from day to day, blissfully unaware of the cultural context in which he operates. But such a person lives in a world foreshortened by his own ignorance. His is a poor, bleak world; Socrates goes so far as to say that the unexamined life is not worth living. And such ignorance cannot be remedied by mere information. As the great Oxford don C.S. Lewis points out, ignorance can come under different guises. The first stage of ignorance, as Lewis illustrates it, comes when one has no idea whatsoever as to how bread is made. The second stage of ignorance — no improvement, really — comes when one believes that the sole, ultimate source of bread is the baker.[3] Information by itself does not allay ignorance.

The liberally educated man may often lack information, but he is never ignorant in the sense described above. If he needs to know more about a particular subject, he knows how to undertake his research: he knows where to find the best information. Obversely, when he comes across a new set of facts, he knows how to evaluate them and place them in context. He recognizes intellectual fads for what they are; having become acquainted with the works of truly creative thinkers, he knows how to recognize an impostor. He knows which new ideas demand utmost seriousness, and which merely embellish old theories. (The liberally educated reader, for instance, knows how very little this book can add to the understanding furnished in Cardinal Newman's *The Idea of the University,* or C.S. Lewis' own *The Abolition of Man.*)

Maybe the old adage is accurate, and there is no subsitute for experience. But liberal education is the closest approximation. We cannot share the experiences of our forebears, but we can learn from them and from their ideas. Education provides a shortcut to experience. By claiming our intellectual patrimony we can become wise beyond our years — no matter how old we are.

As yet another old adage runs, tall men cast long shadows. It would be too much to say that the great men of the past have done our thinking for us, but it is certainly true that they have formed our habits of thought. Copernicus taught that the earth circles the sun, and so we instinctively work on the basis of that belief, although very few of us have ever performed the experiments necessary to confirm the Copernican theory. Harvey taught that blood circulates in the body, and we accept that explanation without opening our own veins to check. We constantly use machines and implements — radios, cars, computers, even electric lights — which function according to scientific principles we do not fully understand.

In much the same way, even outside the scientific and technical realm, our society operates on the basis of inherited wisdom.

Our customs, tastes, and political structures have been handed down to us from previous generations, and we accept them. Of course many social critics and political activists do attempt to change all these inherited notions, and over the course of time our culture does shed certain ideas and take up new ones. (The scientific world also discards old theories to assimilate more elegant ones.) But whether we accept them or reject them, we must come to grips with these inherited notions. They dictate how we think; we cannot escape their influence.

What can happen, however, is that we can misinterpret and thereby misunderstand the old ideas. Received wisdom is never authentic; there is always some distortion in the second- and third-hand transmission. To make matters still more complicated, men of genius devoted most of their lives to formulating those old ideas; we cannot expect to grasp them completely in a short time. In the end, unless we set out on the impossible task of checking every cultural assumption for ourselves, we must accept some wisdom from authority. Our best hope, under these circumstances, is that the authoritative version will be reasonably accurate — that the ideas we hear ascribed to Aristotle and Rousseau really are close approximations of what those men thought and wrote. If the distortion is too great, we find ourselves living in a world whose patterns of thought have been formed by Aristotle and Rousseau, yet ignorant of the basis for those patterns. We become, in short, strangers within our own culture.

Culture envelopes us. It teaches us how to think, and act, and feel. Without its support we are confused, lost, alienated. If we were to lose our cultural heritage we would become infantile, as Wilson warned; we would have to begin anew on the Herculean task of explaining the world and defining our relationship with it. Or if we consciously reject our culture, then we begin thinking in terms and patterns that no one else understands: in other words, we become functionally insane. Nietzsche illustrates the latter phenomenon. After studying Western thought intensively, he rejected it all, and died a madman. How many others today suffer the ravages of the same intellectual disease (although most of them, taking the matter much less seriously, avoid the full measure of Nietzsche's fate)? How many people, and particularly well educated young people, look upon their culture as something alien to them? Alienation splits the victim's personality down the middle: he must live in the everyday world according to principles and mores he cannot intellectually accept. Schizophrenia becomes an occupational hazard of modern thought; alienation is a virtual badge signifying intellectual stature. And much of the blame lies in the inadequate and/or mistaken apprehension of our culture.

Does this mean that we must accept our culture as it is? Absolutely not. We may change it as much as we see fit. A culture is not a static entity; it is a process in itself, within which change takes place constantly. Each generation adds its own interpretations and elaborations of the culture it inherits, so that over time the evolution of a given culture becomes very noticeable indeed. We tend today to think of Greek culture as a monolithic whole; I feel sure the residents of Athens did not see it that way. A few hundred years hence, historians will place our own cultural epoch in one category or another, lumping it together with other societies we now perceive as quite completely foreign to us. Culture is a flow of ideas, attitudes, and opinions, with a shadowy past and an indefinite future.

Our cultural heritage is not a straightjacket, then. We can overthrow the opinions of our forefathers when they prove useless or pernicious. The important point is that we must grapple with those ideas; if we reject tradition, we must make it clear why we are doing so. Otherwise we disrupt the continuity of cultural development. We can channel the cultural flow into whatever new directions we choose, but we cannot afford to lose all the power and depth of that stream. Culture is transmitted from generation to generation, and if any one age squanders that precious resource, the loss impoverishes all future inheritors. A sound liberal education enables us to preserve and even enrich our heritage, thereby fulfilling an obligation to our children.

And to our forefathers as well. When we strive to learn from the past, we keep alive the wisdom of our forebears. We invite the great thinkers of bygone eras to share our councils. And why not? Their advice is always handy; they lend a new perspective to our discussions. But there is another consideration, too. Just as we have obligations to preserve our culture for oncoming generations, we also have some obligation to respect the vision of our elders and ancestors. G.K. Chesterton justified this respect for tradition with one of his characteristically lively figures of speech:

> Tradition may be defined as an extension of the franchise. Tradition means giving votes to the most obscure of all classes, our ancestors. It is the democracy of the dead. Tradition refuses to submit to the small and arrogant obligarchy of those who merely happen to be walking about. All democrats object to men being disqualified by accident of birth; tradition objects to men being disqualified by accident of death. Democracy tells us not to neglect a good man's opinion, even if he is our groom; tradition asks us not to neglect a good man's opinion, even if he is our father.[4]

If we owe so much to tradition, and to our ancestry, how much more do we owe to the particular men of genius — artists, poets, and philosophers — who provide our greatest cultural achievements? These intellectual titans provide us with a breadth of view that we could never manage by ourselves; their insights enable us to think on a level we could never attain alone. One more old aphorism expresses the point: if we see far, it is because we are standing on the shoulders of giants. Interestingly enough, the origin of that phrase is unclear. Isaac Newton used it; Bernard of Chartres used it; Lucan used it; its lineage seems to be endless. The feeling — of indebtedness to the great men of the past — is a universal theme of intellectual history, and the same image recurs again and again, acknowledging that debt.

We are like pygmies, and the great thinkers and artists are giants. The metaphor requires a little salutary humility, but it does make sense. One or two such giants may exist in the world today, but the rest of us, confronted with the awesome accomplishment of a Mozart or an Einstein, can only gape. There are fine dramatists in every generation, and then there is Shakespeare; excellent philosophers, and then there is St. Thomas Aquinas. These men enrich our culture by seeing new dimensions of truth and beauty — dimensions which ordinary men, even hard-working intelligent men, simply cannot see. But once the new horizons are opened to view, we can stand atop the giants' shoulders and survey them.

Too often, today, scholars put a perverse new twist on the giants-and-pygmies metaphor, claiming that we can now see *further* than our greatest forebears. The great men have done the groundwork, and supplied us with the foundations, scholars say. Now we can build up our own intellectual structures, soaring over the heights tradition achieved. We can see further, the theory runs, because after all we are standing on the giant's shoulders — our eyes are now sweeping a broader horizon than their's.

One simple question should suffice to dismiss that preposterous interpretation. How does a pygmy mount a giant's shoulders?

The answer should be obvious. The pygmy can clamber up only if the giant invites him, and he can see only as far — and for only as long — as the giant allows.

Fortunately, our cultural giants do want us to climb aboard. Mozart does want people to hear his music, Shakespeare to attend his plays, Einstein to understand his cosmology, St. Thomas to acknowledge the truth. The great thinkers provide us with books, and experiments, and works of art by which we can grasp some of their insights. This does not mean we become geniuses of equivalent stature. (I listen to Mozart's music constantly, but I still have no talent as a composer.) We can only scan the vistas afforded by our lofty perch. Then we must dismount; we have our own lives to live, and we must make do with whatever quick insights the great man's vision provides us. Still, by studying those great works we do stretch our minds, and grasp new ideas, and attain a more comprehensive understanding of the world. We may not always have the giant's vision, but at least we know that there is a world out there beyond our own more limited horizons.

Our acquaintance with the great men expands our appreciation of true widsom. Now only one more step remains, and it should be the simplest step in the process of liberal education:

we must know which men to study. We must — to belabor the metaphor — learn to recognize the giants.

Incredibly enough, American universities today have trouble identifying the great men whose works must be studied by anyone who hopes to appreciate our cultural heritage. Only a handful of institutions (St. John's College in Annapolis, Maryland, is the outstanding example) forthrightly list the indispensable luminaries. At most other schools the student is free to choose his own plan of studies, adhering only to some vague distribution requirements; the college does not stipulate that there are some things a student *must* know, some works he *must* study, before he can consider himself liberally educated. As a result, students are free to indulge their educational whims, and the "liberal arts" quotient of the curriculum becomes a sort of academic tea-tasting. Students dally with one topic, then pass on to another, without any real effort to come to terms with their cultural heritage.

The results can be devastating and dismaying. I myself once encountered a Harvard sociology instructor, with a Ph.D. from that same school, who had never even heard of St. Thomas Aquinas — never heard of the man whose synthesis of Hellenic and Christian thought virtually defines the scope of Western civilization. At Cornell University in 1974, things had reached such a pass that two professors wrote, in a public letter to the institution's President,

> If we prove to you that an Arts and Sciences student can now receive a B.A. degree at Cornell, and thus be presumed to have acquired a liberal education, without having been required to read a line of Plato, the Bible, Shakespeare, Marx, or Einstein, would you consider this to be evidence that there is a crisis in education at Cornell?[5]

The President never publicly responded, but Professors Werner Dannhauser and L. Pearce Williams had already made their point. Think of it: a graduate of Cornell — supposedly one of our nation's finest liberal institutions — innocent of these crucial works! How could he begin to understand philosophy, when all Western philosophy, in Alfred North Whitehead's phrase, is a footnote to Plato? How could he appreciate any poetry without a passing knowledge of Shakespeare — and beyond Shakespeare with Homer — from whom so many poetic images are derived? And the Bible is not only a blueprint for salvation (as if that were not enough), but the single work that has sparked the most serious thought throughout human history. This hypothetical Cornell graduate would be unable to appreciate the essentials of our culture. With or without a diploma, he would be hopelessly ignorant, and likely to remain in that condition.

Not too long ago, such an educational travesty would have been unthinkable. Schools required a minimal competence from their students, and certainly from their graduates. Columbia issued a blunt statement during the heyday of general education: "There is a certain minimum . . . intellectual and spiritual tradition that a man must experience and understand if he is to be called educated."[6]

What is the antithesis of liberal education? Presumably conservative education — conservative in the worst sense of that term. It would be an education that renders the student complacent, unimaginative, and pliant in his acceptance of political demagoguery and economic blandishments. The sort of education that not only fails to enlighten the student, but fails to inform him that he is unenlightened.

Our universities today provide just such a "conservative" education. Liberal arts graduates are bright and facile with ideas, but their intellectual grasp is tenuous. They are prepared to manipulate ideas, but not to take them seriously. Lionel Trilling remarked the tendency in his own students at Columbia, and admitted,

> To some of us who teach and who think of our students as the creators of the intellectual life of the future, there comes a kind of despair. It does not come because our students fail to respond to ideas, rather because they respond to ideas with a happy vagueness, a delighted glibness, a joyous sense of power in the use of received or receivable generalizations, a grateful wonder at how easy it is to formulate and judge, how little resistance language offers to their intentions.[7]

Is there some study that constitutes a liberal, as opposed to a "conservative" general education? Princeton's august Committee on the Future of the College pondered that question, then solemnly announced that it must be answered, intoning that when a college sets out to define its curriculum, it must forsake "educational agnosticism" and profess its educational objectives. But the Princeton Committee did *not* answer the question, and did *not* renounce its agnosticism. The Committee confessed that in order to prescribe a minimum common core of study, it would first have to define the crucial features of the Western intellectual tradition — and *the Committee could not do that.* Instead, the Committee placidly recommended that Princeton adhere to its existing policy, requiring each student to study the natural sciences, social sciences, literature, and humanities for one year apiece.[8]

The Princeton solution, which many other colleges also employ in one form or another, guarantees that the student will not concentrate his studies exclusively in any one area. That is all it guarantees. Surely such a requirement does not introduce students to the greatest products of Western thought and culture. A Princeton student could choose unchallenging courses in each of the required fields, and emerge as ignorant as his hypothetical Cornell counterpart. But Princeton officials, with their usual aplomb, professed confidence in their general education requirements. A few years later, as Harvard undertook a reform of virtually identical requirements. Princeton officials ignored the results of the Harvard study. Princeton did not need any such reform, they announced, because Princeton had never gone astray. Princeton could not move "back to basics" because Princeton had never deserted the basics.

For every school with distribution requirements as lax as Princeton's, there is another with even vaguer prescriptions. Colleges require a course in this or that field, but very few schools define a common core of knowledge that is intrinsic to a sound liberal education. Harvard has taken to devising such a common core, but the anticipated result is not likely to change the contemporary educational scene. Harvard's new curriculum will feature — as the University of Chicago, among others, already features — a limited number of "common core" courses from which the student may select. The Harvard reform is certainly a step in the right direction, but it is only a step, and it only directly affects one university.

(As I write this chapter, Harvard has announced the courses to be included in the "common core" curriculum. There shall be 55 such courses at first, with the number eventually rising toward 100. Of these the student must choose eight. Simple mathematics shows the problem: most students still will not have studied the same subjects, and there will be no well defined common core of knowledge which all undergraduates must master. And although most of the 55 courses listed suggest a broad interdisciplinary focus, others are quite limited. Courses such as "Weimar Culture" and "The Literature of the Spanish-Speaking Peoples from 1898 to the Present" offer a poor substitute for a comprehensive survey of Western thought.)

Many American colleges now feature survey courses that allegedly cover the topic of "Western Civilization" in one year, or even one semester. These courses sweep through intellectual and political history at a dizzy pace, touching on Plato for one hour, Virgil for twenty minutes, and the entire Medieval era for one class session (if that). Rome wasn't built in a day, but it is studied for considerably less time. In a course such as this, the student has no chance to attain real understanding. He must slap a label on each philosopher, devise a crude notion about each poet, and rush on to catch up with the whirlwind tour. If he is so fortunate as to have an interesting lecturer as his guide, he emerges from the course with a vague sense of the broad cultural sweep that has left us where we are today. If he has a less exciting teacher (and teachers in such survey courses are notoriously dull), he concludes the course with nothing but antipathy for the study of past civilizations.

When general education is treated as a burden, to be dismissed as soon as possible, students naturally shrink away from the required courses. And just as naturally, students will always seek to have as few requirements as possible. In a completely elective curriculum, those who want to study Western civilization are always free to do so on their own. But if the university seeks to develop some common core of understanding, it must impose minimum standards for all students. Survey courses and minimal distribution requirements, encouraging the students to dispatch their cultural obligations promptly, cannot fulfill the mission.

In any attempt to provide students with a general education, some sort of survey course is inevitable — there simply isn't time, in a four-year interval, to probe deeply into every intellectual nook and cranny. But there is a world of difference between the reckless pace of a shoddy survey and the calmer tone of a serious introduction. Similarly, there is no simple way to judge a school's general education program by reading the list of course requirements; the teachers' approach is all-important. At Harvard, during my stay, the course load required to fulfill all general education requirements was roughly equivalent to the "common core" obligation at the University of Chicago. Yet at the former school the program was an utter failure, while at the latter it was a four-star success.

At Harvard, undergraduates viewed the "general education" requirement with the same attitude we took to the swimming test: it was a burdensom duty to be discharged as quickly and painlessly as possible. Once we met our quota, we could relax in the knowledge that we would never encounter the same material again, except perhaps by choice. The course offerings in the "Gen Ed" department were so diverse that no future instructors could possibly assume that we had all mastered a common core.

At Chicago, on the other hand, the prevailing attitude still reflected the influence of President Hutchins and his affinity for the Great Books. Students looked upon their common core courses as the heart and soul of their undergraduate education; the specialized courses that followed were almost an afterthought. The course offerings in this field were strictly limited, and one elective course paralleled the other. Thus professors could (and did) assume that upperclassmen all knew something about, say, the philosophical significance of the Reformation. A student could crack a joke based on Aristotlean categories, and draw a laugh from his lunchtime companions. Perhaps the campus is too self-conscious in its devotion to the intellectual tradition — certainly the nervous reference to the "life of the mind" become cloying after a while — but the success of the common core program makes the University of Chicago the most vigorous academic environment I have encountered.

The prevailing trend in American universities leads in an entirely different direction: away from general education, toward even greater diversification of the curriculum. Academic departments proliferate, generating new courses by the dozens for each year's edition of the school's catalogue. Straining under the centrifugal force of these new courses and departments, the college cedes control of the curriculum to the several departments. The college as a whole no longer has a corporate idea of what the student must study; each individual department devises its own rules. And as the departments look inward into the needs of their own disciplines, they lose sight of the broader educational goals confronting the liberal arts institution. Harvard's effort for a more radical curricular reform, aborted by the conflicting interests of different departments, amply illustrated the point. When the reform was first bruited about, crusaders suggested that the "common core" courses should be limited in number and compulsory for all students. But soon the departmental interests were aired: shouldn't there be a course offered is Psychology? in Physics? in Engineering? By the time all the competing departments had been satisfied, the course list had been expanded from two or three common core offerings to embrace eighty or ninety diverse topics.

In a university dominated by academic departments, scholarly generalists have neither prestige nor security. Any intellectual endeavors that do not fit neatly into departmental pigeonholes are suspect; the reigning departments have neither the incentive nor, often, the breadth of scope that would enable them to read and evaluate the work of outsiders. Maverick scholars (who should provide the lifeblood of intellectual controversy) find it difficult to arrange a hearing for their views. The successful generalist, who could teach basic courses well but has no research abilities or ambitions, finds his path into the professoriate blocked by departmental chauvinists. Academe does not want professors who understand the basic heritage that constitutes the liberal arts. Academe wants specialists, to pursue the endless quest for new facts on the frontiers of knowledge. A scholar whose only expertise involves arcane and exotic tidbits stands a far better chance of gaining the university's approval.

The process of academic training aggravates the problems created by specialization. In order to become a professor, the graduate student does research in his special field, culminating in a doctoral dissertation. He passes some general examination along the way to his Ph.D., but he is never tested on his knowledge of the intellectual world outside his academic discipline. Nor is he tested on his teaching ability. Thus the absurd situation arises in which the young faculty aspirant receives his credential to teach without ever having indicated any ability to teach. His graduate work may include a seminar or two on classroom presentation, and of course he will have delivered a few papers to his fellow graduate students. But nothing in his training has prepared him to address and inspire undergraduates from outside his scholarly covey. Or even to try. The department is acutely conscious of his ability to add to the academic lore, but very little aware of the possibility that his esoteric research might have nothing to do with the needs of undergraduate learners.

Consequently, many professors are dry and ineffective lecturers. But the poverty of their classroom style is exaggerated by the material they convey. They have been trained to address topics that interest their advanced colleagues, and they often have trouble placing themselves in the position of a novice student. They often neglect the crucial ingredient that any successful teacher knows; they forget that students need a context in which to place the course material, and an explanation of its importance. To the specialist, the material is important for its own sake, and no hortatory introduction is necessary. So teachers present the facts in great lump sums, devoid of any motivating preface. And since teachers adopt such an approach, they naturally attract similar personalities into the academic profession, so that the scholarly world abounds with professors who are caught up in their own interest, unable or unwilling to explain that interest to their students.

The second generation of specialists becomes a corps of deadly boring teachers, and their research work is deadlier still. Why should they search for provocative new insights? New insights would require new visions, and new visions might lead them out of the disciplinary mainstream. No such risk is necessary; in fact, graduate departments discourage students from pursuing radical approaches. Better to play it safe, and garner the Ph.D. uneventfully prior to any attempts to overthrow the governing prejudices of the profession. Better to reshuffle the same old set of facts, or research an area so abstruse that no one else has thought to take interest in it. The requirement that a Ph.D dissertation should represent an *original* contribution to knowledge is universally disregarded. As long as the work is not actually plagiarized, and as long as it represents a considerable scholarly effort, it can be as mundane or as trivial as the student's pride will allow. And the student's pride is a small obstacle indeed; every academic topic seems interesting to the one who pursues it. Looking at the work through the prism of the specialization, scholars see facets of novelty, imagination, and interest in the minutiae they study. A more normal perspective of the same work shows unrelieved boredom.

In his provocative (and suggestively titled) book, *Ideas Have Consequences,* Richard Weaver devotes an entire chapter to the proliferation of academic specialties. Entitling the chapter "Fragmentation and Obsession," Weaver launches a withering attack on contemporary academic training:

> The modern knower may be compared to an inebriate who, as he senses his loss of balance, endeavors to save himself by fixing tenaciously upon certain details and thus afford the familiar exhibition of positiveness and arbitrariness. With the world around him beginning to heave, he grasps at something that will come within a limited perception.[9]

Imagine a society full of social inebriates. Perhaps it would be an exaggeration to call it a "society"; each individual would be too preoccupied with his own tenuous focus to bother with the others around him. So it is with the university faculty. Each professor, wrapped up in his own special field, finds it increasingly difficult to discuss academic issues with colleagues outside his own discipline. Physicists and historians find that they have little to discuss beyond the usual social chitchat and the nuts and bolts of university machinery. Attendance at faculty meetings dwindles to a mere handful of professors, most of them primarily interested in protecting or advancing their own pet theories.

Faculty politics, then, becomes a series of disjointed disputes over questions unrelated to real liberal education. Various factions strive for power, but none of the leading contenders concentrates on any definable academic doctrine, much less on any advancement of the common understanding. Professors never tire of telling their students that all knowledge is inter-related, and yet very few professors care enough about that interrelation to work with people outside their special fields. The faculty, far from being a community cooperatively searching for truth, becomes simply a body of governance for the conduct of university affairs. Scholars leave their academic sensitivities behind them when they enter their faculty meetings.

Robert Maynard Hutchins had foreseen the problem.

> Unless students and professors (and particularly pro-fessors) have a common intellectual training, a university must remain a series of disparate schools and departments, united by nothing except the fact that they have the same president and board of trustees. Professors cannot talk to one another, at least not about anything important. They cannot hope to understand one another.[10]

Recognizing the sterility of academic specialization, some would-be reformers call for an increased attention to interdisci-plinary studies. The idea is fine, but the practice falls far short of the desired goal. Many interdisciplinary programs simply meld two existing departments, creating a hybrid specialty with parameters of its own. Other programs do genuinely attempt to break down the barriers that separate departments, but the resistance is too strong. Each scholar comes to the interdisci-plinary project with different ideas on such crucial issues as what should be studied and how it should be evaluated; the program must respond either by establishing a new, recognized specialty, or by abandoning its scholarly standards.

When a scholar does vouchsafe to address an area outside his special expertise, he inevitably looks upon it with the warped perspective his specialization enforces. Even inside the various departments, scholars see every topic in the overweening light of their own particular research interests. Professors suffer from what one wit described as the "berserk virtuoso syndrome: the tendency of every violinist to turn a symphony into a violin concerto." No matter what academic question is at hand, the berserk virtuoso sees it as an opportunity to wield his own specialized analytical skills and proffer his own specialized solutions.

Needless to say, this fractionalization of the academic departments destroys any sense of community that might have united the university. And this in turn erodes the sense of discipline that should bind a community of scholars. Beyond keeping the plant clean and the payroll funded, what common institutional objectives do the various departments share? Students, too, have their own individual goals — admission to graduate or professional schools, extracurricular pursuits, employment opportunities, etc. — which they seek in their own particular ways. The campus becomes nothing more than a convenient meeting-ground for a diverse group of self-interested parties.

The United States is a country with a strong Protestant heritage, and our society has always evinced the belief that each man must make judgements for himself. Authority is questioned, even in philosophical disputes. Nor is this a recent development; over 100 years ago Alexis de Tocqueville observed, "I think in no country in the civilized world is less attention paid to philosophy than in the United States."[11] The emphasis on separation and compartmentalization within academe aggravates this tendency, by encouraging each student and scholar to judge for himself which studies are of prime importance, and which truths deserve the most reverence. Whether the undergraduate pursues his studies in order to be a teacher or a revolutionary, a saint or a sinner, the university will accommodate him without question — in fact, the university will never know what it is the student seeks. And the university will neither know nor care whether he declares his allegiance to the Christian religion, or the Gross

National Product, or the Playboy Philosophy. He must judge for himself, the relevant authorities demand.

The advent of specialization brings with it a political threat to both the universities and the societies around them. Christopher Dawson, himself an accomplished generalist, noted that as modern scholarship pursues more and more specificity, it ignores more general questions. Scholars still have opinions on broad topics, of course, but in announcing those opinions the scholars hasten to add that they are not making a scholarly judgement. Even the scholars themselves refuse to consider the possibility that their opinions might be more valuable than the opinion of an ignorant layman. Mired in their research, they become unable to contribute to public debate on problems that should be within their analytical grasp. Instead, they leave these questions to be settled in the political arena, to be decided by majority vote or by bureaucratic fiat.[12] The realm of intellectual privilege thereby shrinks, and the political realm expands, until political judgements begin to impinge on philosophical truths. If the trend continues long enough, Dawson warns, there will be no truths that are not subject to political manipulation; the universities will lose dominance over even their own limited sector of society.

Any enlargement of the political realm is dangerous insofar as it increases the risks of tyranny. Traditionally the universities, like the churches and the industrial corporations, have stood as a countervailing force to limit the government's domain. But the twin forces of specialization and politicization now threaten the universities' standing. If academic experts cannot make pronouncements on the basis of their studies, or if their pronouncements are always limited to tangential details, then the stature of the university is hopelessly compromised, and government takes another step toward total dominance of society.

In traditional Western civilization, the government has respected other institutions within their particular domains. The business community (or the nobility) demanded respect in the economic realm, because its members held so much financial power. The churches had their place in the spiritual realm, because the churches possessed so much moral authority. And the universities enjoyed substantial privileges in the intellectual realm, because they were regarded as the repositories of wisdom. But today, when universities forsake wisdom to concentrate on details, and when the scholarly community has no united purpose beyond its own continued existence, academe is rapidly losing its claim to special status.

Ironically, the decay of academic authority has coincided with a dramatic rise in the role individual professors play in our national government. The country's leading social scientists scurry back and forth between their lectures and their appearances before Congressional committees. Does this indicate that the government respects their wisdom? Not at all; the government respects their *knowledge*. The academic specialist come to Washington to advise the government on how it can approach certain political problems. But Congressional leaders are not particularly interested in hearing the professors' opinions on *which* problems should be solved, or on how to create a good and just society. In other words, these academic experts have become a subsidiary element in the political process, rather than a separate and independent power. The government uses whatever insights and information academe can offer. It does not defer to academicians; it employs them.

Is this, then, the level to which the liberal arts have fallen? Is the liberally educated man nothing but a tool which the government can use or ignore at will?

Academic training can be useful; no one will deny that. The professors' advice is helpful to Congressional committees, in much the same way that a college diploma is useful to a graduate seeking employment. Colleges can provide all sorts of grist for society's mill: trained specialists in every popular field. If American higher education aims to furnish the country with a cadre of expert technicians, then the current system of specialization is a step in the right direction.

But if American higher education hopes to operate on a level above everyday economic concerns — if the liberal arts are to serve a truly liberating function — then education must serve a different purpose. True enough, an education can provide students with saleable skills, and teach them how to earn a living.

But liberal education promises more. A liberal education should teach not merely how to *earn* a living, but how to *live*.

CHAPTER TEN

Facts and Values

> Let parents, then, bequeath to their children not riches, but the spirit of reverence.
>
> *Plato*[1]

Everybody always endorses morality. Nobody always practices it. Therein lies the dilemma that has kept preachers, theologians, counselors, philosophers, educators, and reformers busy for thousands of years. Despite all their best efforts, the gap between theory and practice, between ideals and actualities, never closes.

Sometimes it does widen, however. The Watergate scandal frightened the American public by exposing the corruption of public ethics. A few transgressions, scattered here and there, could have been excused. But the Watergate affair, it seemed, went to the very heart of public life. The corruption was not just incidental; it was systematic. The American public, in the aftermath of that episode, has questioned public morality (and, by extension, private morality) with unaccustomed vigor. The public is concerned. Something must be done.

But what can be done? How is it possible to encourage morality? That question has stumped many religious leaders throughout history. People are human: they have human weaknesses. No one has improved on the classic formula that "the spirit indeed is willing, but the flesh is weak."

Human weakness is everywhere: a constant. Yet the tide of morality does seem to ebb and flow at different times and in different places. Some societies — Athens and Rome are most frequently cited — attain fairly high levels of ethical conduct while other — Sodom and Gommorah, or Carthage — are totally depraved. American society today is far from perfect, but ancient Phoenician society, sacrificing its children to Moloch, was far worse. How can this be, if humans are always equally imperfect? Does public morality have another ingredient?

That greatest of moral theologians, St. Thomas Aquinas, furnishes an answer. "Three things are necessary for the salvation of man: to know what he ought to believe; to know what he ought to desire; to know what he ought to do."[2] To *know*! Before we can begin to act rightly, we must have some moral principles on which to base our actions. So culture does play a role in defining morality. We erring humans are always more or less the same in our inability to act out our best ethical principles, but our society helps to determine what those principles will be.

Here education comes into the proceedings, teaching students how to form their moral principles. Post-Watergate opinion made the connection intuitively, and American colleges quickly began to offer seminars in ethics, hoping to erase the obloquy of public life. Almost immediately, the imperial impulse took hold; the universities evolved new programs to study ethics in the various professions. Harvard's President Derek Bok called for the creation of a "new profession" in government service, with a new code of professional ethics; the (Harvard) Kennedy Institute for public administration responded. At Princeton the Dean of the engineering school advocated programs that paid closer attention to the canons of that profession. If ethics was what the public wanted, ethics is what the universities would teach.

If, that is, the universities could teach ethics. Even as they set up their new programs, the universities warned that they could not indoctrinate the students with moral righteousness. They could analyze the ways in which moral decisions are made; they could provide crucial information that would help make ethical choice easier; but they could not teach students to act morally. Bok himself admitted as much with startling candor:

> For example, few educators would assert that it is possible to devise a college program which is likely to help significantly in fostering such important characteristics as honesty, integrity, generosity, or even creative imagination. Under the present circumstances, therefore, it would be arrogant to claim the development of these qualities among the purposes of undergraduate education.[3]

The juxtaposition of these ideas seems untenable. On the one hand the colleges focus new attention on public and professional ethics. On the other hand they admit that they cannot help nurture ethical conduct. The schools will study morality, but to actually encourage morality is not "among the purposes of undergraduate education." Then what good are all these inquiries into ethics and morality? Are they a palliative to calm the public outcries? A futile gesture? Or is it all merely confusion on the universities part? Could they possibly not realize that they are contradicting themselves? It is at least conceivable. Consistency is not a hobgoblin of today's educational theorists.

The confusion stems from the two different dimensions of moral development. The universities can provide students with moral principles, introduce them to the moral dimensions of life, show them how ethical decisions are made, provide them with plenty of positive examples for emulation. But in the end it is the individual student who must make those decisions, and the university cannot eradicate his human weaknesses. What the university *can* do is suggested by Aquinas' word: the university can teach the studen what he *ought* to belive, and what he *ought* to do. Perhaps the student will not drink, but the university can lead him to the moral water. But modern American colleges will not go even that far.

American society is strongly pluralistic. We respect the right of each individual to form his own moral convictions, and our government carefully maintains the separation of church and state, preventing the development of an enforced national dogma. We resent attempts of legislate morality, and by the same token we avoid enforcing our moral judgements on others. So naturally the universities are leery about any efforts to indoctrinate students. Any such effort would go against the American grain.

But surely there is some basic common ground — some moral common denominator that all Americans could share. That *all* people could share. In his brilliant book *The Abolition of Man,* C.S. Lewis shows that there is a fundamental, unchanging conception of morality that all religions and all societies have always shared. The details differ from creed to creed and from age to age, but the same broad principles keep appearing in every culture and every era: murder is bad; love is better than hatred; dishonesty and hypocrisy are evil. Within our own country the consensus is still broader: there is — or should be — universal support for democracy, limited government, and the Constitution.

Supose some analyst could dissect human cultures, layer by layer, to examine them. He could break cultures down into increasingly specific divisions: by era, by country, by locality, by neighborhood, by family. At each succeeding layer, he would find a greater communality of moral beliefs. The smallest unit would share a wide range of values. Within a nation there are several moral doctrines held in common; within a family there are many.

Every moral principle, no matter how universal, has its dissenters. That old nagging human weakness works its inevitable damage. Every culture disapproves of murder, and yet there are murderers. But that doesn't stop the culture from condemning the murderers, nor should it. The shared values take precedence over the perverse ideas of people who reject them. Similarly, American society should have little patience with people who preach anti-democratic doctrines. Those people might find a hearing in some other country, but the founding values of our own country — the very values that make it a society — must be honored. And so for the universities: some people might argue that books should be burned, but the university cannot countenance that argument.

Universities do represent share values, and they should not blush about conveying those values to their students. As long as they are American schools, they should actively support the democratic ideal. If they are universities in any sense of the term, they should imbue their work with the reverence for truth. If they are Christian schools, they should emphasize the wisdom of the Christian faith. Each school could choose its own particular community, and inculcate the values of that community. This does not mean that the colleges would persecute all contrary beliefs. Just as an American citizen is free to think anti-democratic thoughts, a student is free to hate the library and a Christian student to toy with Islamic ideals. The institution cannot prevent such deviations, and should not try. But neither should it encourage them, or feel abashed about discouraging them.

Most contemporary universities, alas, will not take even this first step on the road to moral education. Instead they cling to the old bedraggled ideals of secular humanism, and profess their absolute neutrality on moral issues. They shun in terror anything that might be taken as a moral stand. The slogans of moral neutrality abound on campus: "If that's what you believe, then I guess that must be right for you."; "That's just a personal opinion."; and, above all, "That's a value judgement."

The idea, you see, is that one can talk about facts — that is the purpose of the university: to assemble and sort out facts — but not about values. According to this theory, the ideal argument is one in which a set of scientific facts is arranged with mathematical precision. Two and two make four. A body in motion tends to stay in motion. Water freezes at 32 degrees. These are good solid statements; one can test them, and they will prove true. But when someone says that abortion is immoral, the educationists flinch. No experiment could prove or disprove that statement; it relies on a subjective judgement. It is unscientific, and therefore (here is the crux of the matter) presumed unfit for scholarly discussion.

Ultimately, this reliance on facts gives birth to the philosophical school of Logical Positivism, which insists that anything not translatable into a quantifiable fact is not logical. The truth, for the Logical Positivist, consists of a set of empirical facts — scientific building-blocks — and the task of philosophy is to arrange these facts into a comprehensive world view. Ludwig Wittgenstein drew the argument to its logical extreme early in this century. In the philosophical world, Wittgenstein argued, anything that cannot be discussed in mathematical terms should not be discussed at all.[4]

Logical Positivism itself is a philosophical school of very recent vintage, yet already it has lost its grip on academic discussion. But the underlying theory — the theory that there are no facts but scientific facts — has roots deep in the Western philosophical tradition. Maybe it began with Descartes, when he decided to doubt everything that he could not logically prove. Certainly it was in full swing with Immanuel Kant and his *Critique of Pure Reason* (which, come to think of it, is a much stronger critique of everything *other* than pure reason). The original idea was to bring new rigor to philosophical discourse. Too often, these thinkers worried, philosophy must contend with emotions, and prejudices, and other inhibitions. If only somehow one could stand detached from his feelings — if only the philosopher could separate his reason from his emotions — then philosophy would become objective.

Now take science. There was an objective approach! Scientific facts could be proven by experimentation, and empirical results were incontrovertible. So philosophers, following Descartes, began to express their ideas in scientific language. Scholars began to concentrate on empirical facts, and set up experiments to test all their theories. Eventually, as the philosophical movement gained momentum, scholars became loath to study anything outside the empirical realm. The ideas trickled down to the other academic realms, and American professors joined the fold, studying facts and avoiding value judgements; concentrating on realities and avoiding ideas.

Ironically, scientific research — pure scientific research — has meanwhile headed off in the opposite direction. The truly profound scientific truths, as it turns out, are not reducible to simple, uncomplicated mathematical truths. Quite the contrary. The greatest scientific discoveries of this century have revolutionized the exploratory process. Einstein has shown that scientific judgements are relative, not absolute; the facts depend upon the viewer's frame of reference. Heisenberg has shown that the smallest subatomic particles — the most basic discernible units of physical reality — do not behave according to any sort of mathematical formulae. At the very frontiers of pure research, scientists realize that the most fundamental truths involve ideas rather than things, and theories rather than empirical facts.

Meanwhile, back in academe, professors stick to the facts in the dogged belief that they are being scientific. And still the irony is not exhausted, because invariably the scholars fail to be scientifically detached and objective. Every scholar is influenced — in selecting the problems he will study, in selecting the hypotheses he will test, and in analyzing his findings — by his personal views and institutions. For any given scholarly problem, there are innumerable possible approaches. Yet perforce the professor must select only one approach. How does he choose? By following his personal inclinations. Especially in the social sciences, there are myriad different explanations for every observable phenomenon; different scholars study the same problem, and notice different aspects of that problem. No matter how hard he tries to eradicate his personal ideas (and many scholars don't even try), his work is based on assumptions and hunches. Value-free scholarship is a fantasy.

But suppose — just for the sake of the argument — that scholars could become objective. Suppose they could subjugate their own opinions and impulses totally, and act with utter detachment. Should they? Would it be desirable to stick to the pure, unblemished, objective facts, if such facts could be found? I think not. The compilation of facts can never furnish a true education, still less a liberal education.

The school of thought that once dominated scientific studies, and now dominates our colleges, is rationalism. It holds that the answer to human problems lies in the right use of reason. If we could only sit down and think our problems through, we could solve them; so say the rationalists. I don't know how to answer them, except in their own language. We have tried the experiment, and it has failed. Mankind has tried to reason its way through problems since the beginning of time, and the problems still exist. Real life — as opposed to academic abstractions — is always too complex for reason to handle.

Reason is never enough. Rationalistic solutions always leave out some crucial human element; they become cold, hard, inhuman. The lines of logic are so clear, but individuals keep getting in the way. Humans cannot be used as cogs in a rationalistic machine: either the machine or the humans will be broken. When rationalism is taken to its extremes, the result is hideous. Orwell's *1984* is a stark warning: Hitler's "Final Solution" is a sickening illustration.

No, rationalism cannot solve all problems. But perhaps the universities are not interested in solutions, after all. Professors earn their living by discussing problems: if the problems were to evaporate, the professors would lose their livelihood. Once the problem is solved, the reason for studying it vanishes also, and the experts become expendable. Maybe professors would rather dither with their sets of facts and theories, free from the fear that a real concrete solution might interfere with their amusement. The Ivory Tower is comfortable — much more comfortable than the hubbub outside — to someone who enjoys the secure life of intellectual banter. By keeping themselves at a safe distance from everyday realities, professors can preserve their comfort.

Rationalism does preserve that safe distance. By amassing facts, and refraining from any judgements about how the facts should be valued, academic experts can remain aloof from the rigors of moral controversy. There will always be more facts to find, more theories to generate. Concrete solutions — answers to tough ethical questions — will not arrive as long as rationalism reigns supreme. Value-free scholarship cannot find solutions — cannot even suggest solutions. To propose a solution is to say that we ought to do something, and value-free scholarship can never make a statement involving the word "ought." "Ought" implies a value judgement, and the true rationalist never speaks about value judgements.

Take a hypothetical example. Suppose I have a surplus of food, while my neighbor is starving. Scholars can tell me about nutrition, about food storage and transportation, about costs and benefits. They can provide all sorts of practical information. Still, they cannot show that I should give food to my hungry neighbor. The facts, taken by themselves, do not indicate what action I should take. Positive statements do not add up to imperative statements: "is" cannot make "ought." If they really want action, the scholars must break down and make a value judgement: I should not allow my neighbor to starve. Then, and only then, the argument is complete. I should help my neighbor not because of any set of objective facts, but because of one moral truth: men should help other men. Rephrase the moral point however you like, but the point must be phrased. The facts do not speak for themselves. They never do.

All this must seem terribly obvious, to anyone outside academe. But in the Ivory Tower one can avoid the obvious facts with great success. Professors can insist that they avoid value judgements, although without value judgements even the most primitive moral decisions are impossible. Some academicians will go even further in their flight from common sense. While their colleagues claim that we cannot know what is right, some champion skeptics proclaim that we cannot even know what *is*. How do we know that everyday facts are not illusory? That sort of systematic skepticism leaves the professor quite fully insulated against the perils of practical life. How can he solve the world's problems, until first he is sure that those problems exist? That the world itself exists? Of course he cannot; he must sit in his study and reconstruct the meaning of everyday reality, starting from scratch. And he will be comfortable, as long as he believes in the reality of his monthly paycheck. Usually he does.

Rationalism and value-free scholarship, working in tandem, lead students to the mistaken conclusion that they can understand a problem simply by compiling facts about it. Or even simply by naming it. A psychologist diagnoses a patient's malady as schizophrenia — perhaps he even alludes to a cause in the patient's childhood — and believes that he has solved the problem. (Who is he to say that schizophrenia is a bad thing? How can he suggest what should be done about the patient's condition?) Botanists confidently explain that plants derive their energy from a process called photosynthesis. They can even name the states of that process, and the parts of the plant involved. But botanists do not understand photosynthesis: if they did, men too could use sunlight and chlorophyl to produce energy. And psychologists do not understand schizophrenia; if they did they could cure it. Engineers know that electricity turns on lights, but they do not know, really, what electricity is.

My point is this: naming a process is not the same as understanding it. Newton codified the laws of physics, but he did not explain them. The laws of science explain how nature works, but not why nature works the way it does, and no other way. Science gives us fascinating insights about the world, but not about the significance of the world. So science provides only a part of the information we need to live a useful, balanced life.

Science, like value-free scholarship, tells us something about the world around us. It tells us very little about how we should respond to that world.

Take the sun, for instance. Science tells us that the sun is a ball of fiery gases undergoing a massive nuclear reaction. So far, so good. But so what? What does that mean to us here below, for our everyday lives? Some primitive people worshipped the sun as their god. Admittedly their view was inaccurate, and ours is accurate. But did their view prevent them from ordering their lives? On the contrary, I suspect it helped them in a way that our scientific, factual knowledge could never help us. I am not suggesting that we should go back to worshipping the sun, or even that the sun-worshippers were on the right track. All I mean to say is that moral values are far more useful than bald scientific data. For the ordinary conduct of life, values are the catalysts that make facts useful.

For consistency's sake, a scholar who refuses to discuss moral values is forced to argue that one man's morality is as good as another's. He must believe that discussion and study do not improve morality. (Otherwise he could be morally obliged to discuss the subject.) To their credit, most scholars are reasonably consistent on these points. They teach their students to respect each and every individual in his moral judgements. The schools are full of students (and society is full of the schools' graduates) who will not and cannot question a man's judgement on moral matters. Schooled in the belief that the subject cannot be discussed, they have no way to combat obvious immorality. So students have a difficult time condemning Soviet communism, despite the evidence of the Gulags. How are they to judge whether the systematic repression is justified by the aims of the state? That would be a value judgement. And Hannah Arendt, questioning American school children closely, found that most students could not flatly condemn Adolph Eichman. If he *really believed* that he should execute hundreds of thousands of Jews, how could they argue with him?

Thus are the most important and necessary moral judgements reduced to a level alongside questions of taste. Do you prefer peace or genocide? chocolate or vanilla? In either case, value-free scholarship will not attempt to sway you. *De gustibus non disputandum*: one cannot argue about tastes.

Needless to say, this attitude represents a complete reversal of the classical attitude toward education. In bygone eras, education consisted of teaching the student the values by which he should conduct his life. Teachers had no scruples about value judgements; they encouraged them. Aristotle made no mistake about it: "Hence we ought to have been brought up in a particular way from our very youth, as Plato says, so as both to delight in and be pained by the things that we ought; for this is right education."[5]

In our society, one group of people (generally called conservatives) believes that education should preserve and defend our cultural institutions. Another opposite group (radicals) believes that the schools should be agents of change. In either case, the group accepts Aristotle's notion that education should foster likes and dislikes — that education should inculcate values. Not surprisingly, then, conservatives and radicals concur in the belief that value-free scholarship is both impossible and undesirable. But a third group (liberals) supports neither preservation nor change. This third group sees no reason either to defend our culture or to attack it. And this third group dominates our colleges.

Each group has its characteristic intellectual weaknesses. Conservatives tend to support institutions even when they should be dismantled; radicals tend to dismantle even the traditions that should be upheld. Sometimes conservatives are too skeptical about change, radicals too impatient with the status quo. But liberals suffer from both weaknesses at once. Too aloof to defend our culture, they are yet too aloof to reform it. They allow traditional institutions to deteriorate, but take no steps to replace them. Since they have no moral postulates from which to work — no values that dictate an approach — they can only work with the situation as it presents itself to them. They cannot call for either revolution or moral rearmament. They can only accept society as is.

Every fact stands in some framework of values, or else it does not stand at all. If a fact is to have any practical implications whatever, it must acquire a moral context in which to operate. The disembodied fact by itself is meaningless, like a skeleton without muscles. Eventually someone must put the fact to work, placing it in a system of moral values and gives it a practical meaning. By refusing to make judgements in that moral realm, liberals (as defined above; not necessarily political liberals) have renounced their power over the facts they produce. The scholars who disdain value judgements tacitly yield control to those practical men who do make such judgements. Practical men make the facts work for them. And indirectly, since scholars produce the facts, practical men make scholars, too, work for them. Students taught by such scholars fare no better; having been taught to avoid judgements, they have no way to dispute those who do. So value-free scholarship has an effect directly opposite the desired effect of liberal education. Instead of liberating the student (and the teacher), value-free education enslaves him. Unable to provide his own system of values, he becomes a tool to be used by more practical men.

"Knowledge is power." That simple discovery, advanced by Francis Bacon, revolutionized attitudes toward education. Previously education had been seen as a process of moral development. Now is viewed as a means toward an entirely different end. The facts could be put to work; knowledge could become power. But power for what? Toward what end?

Such questions posed no problem for Bacon and his contemporaries. To them knowledge was power to make the world a better place, and they had a common understanding of what that meant. Knowledge was power to harness nature for men's purposes: to eliminate hunger and disease. Western culture provided a fine, clear picture of the good life, and the ends toward which that power should be used. The excitement of the discovery, and the cornucopia of possible uses for scientific knowledge, postponed serious considerations of the problem. Scholars were too busy solving problems with their newfound methods to be bothered worrying about the underlying dangers of the power they had uncovered.

But gradually the dangers became apparent. Goethe's Faust craved knowledge and power so ardently that he sold his soul to the devil. Frankenstein longed for power, and created a monster. But those were only fictional treatments. Real-life scientists searching for knowledge and power in this century furnished the final example: the atomic bomb. Here, more clearly than ever, knowledge was power. But power toward what end?

The dangerous potential of knowledge is still more evident today. Soviet psychiatrists have demonstrated their ability – and willingness – to control men's minds (if not their spirits). Meteorologists can tamper with the world's climate. And, most frightening of all, biologists are verging on a breakthrough that might allow them to govern mankind's genetic code. All these forms of knowledge can work unspeakable damage in the wrong hands. And by the way, we should not be surprised to learn that knowledge is a mixed blessing. Remember, the fruit Adam ate came from the Tree of Knowledge of Good and Evil.

Bacon and his fellow scientists worked within a society whose basic values were universally shared. But the consensus was eroding even then, and has continued to erode. Today different groups within Western society have radically different moral norms, while other cultures challenge Western values from abroad. And academe has values very different from those of the society that sustains it. Many books have been written about the use of drugs and sex on campus. I do not here want to recount all the familiar stories – merely to indicate that academe does not share the moral attitudes of the surrounding society. Today the universities cannot fall back on some common understanding of how power should be used.

Yes, knowledge is power. And every year the universities send thousands of powerful young men and women out into society. But the universities have not instructed those students in how to use their powers. Value-free scholarship has demanded that the students choose their own moral values. Will they choose to exercize their power for society's good or for their own? Will they model themselves after Schweitzer or Hitler? The university has very little control over these questions.

Education in itself – the mere processing of knowledge – does nothing to guarantee a student's moral fitness. History is replete with the stories of brilliant but immoral men. In fact, such men are the most dangerous of all people. Even the most erudite scholars, innocent of all lust for power, can commit horrible crimes. Martin Heidegger, one of the great philosophers of our era, cast his lot with the Nazis. American intellectuals are still recovering (some of them none too quickly) from their flirtation with Stalinism. Intellectuals are always ripe targets for a skillful ideologue.

Yes, knowledge is power; and power corrupts. Anyone who possesses power inevitably feels the tug of self-indulgent desires, and students are no different. In fact, their weakness is aggravated by the fact that they eschew value judgements. If one thing cannot be better or worse than another, it can only be more or less desirable. Personal comfort may or may not be better than discomfort in an ethical or moral sense, but it is certainly more desirable for the individuals. So students are naturally drawn toward self-gratification and hedonism. If there are no other values available on the moral horizon, self-interest will present itself without hestitation. And the moral conduct of students on campus today suggests that self-interest has indeed seized that opportunity.

The more sensitive students might avoid the dangers of hedonism, but still the values of self-interest influence their decisions. Some students flock to attend self-improvement courses, which promise to remedy one's physical or emotional problems by using some special core of knowledge. The self-improvement may or may not be real; the appeal to self-interest is undebatable. Other students, caught up even more completely in their own problems and desires, become so absorbed in contemplating their own condition that they lost touch with outer reality. They approach paralysis by self-analysis, as one wag put it. These displays of narcissism and self-indulgence are depressing in themselves; still more depressing is the fact that the universities encourage them. Students are constantly admonished to use their own feelings as measures — to "be in touch with your own emotions." They do, and they are. So much so, that they lose touch with every other means of measuring values.

Knowledge abhors a vacuum. A student cannot understand a fact unless he puts it to work — much as a grammar school student does not really know a new vocabulary word until he puts it into a sentence. Any new bit of knowledge should prompt the student to ask several questions. How will this new learning change his life, or his understanding of life? How does it differ from his old, uninformed ideas? If the fact is important, he asks more probing, sweeping questions. What does the new fact mean, in the great flow of history? What does it mean, as Herman Melville asked, in the light of the New Testament? The liberal arts provide some means of answering those questions. The student knows something about the history of ideas, and he knows where new ideas fit into place. He can hazard some informed judgement about the relative importance of each new idea in the larger scheme of things. Although the student is anchored in one time and place, the liberal arts teach him to look at the world through the eyes of eternity.

Stripped of this context, the facts march before the student's eyes in dizzying profusion, never adding up to any firm conclusions. Tidbits of information lose their meaning. Worse still, the student fails to see the subtle ideas that govern other men's minds; he only sees the facts. So he loses his ability to grasp philosophical concepts and literary masterpieces. He reads Plato's *Republic*, and remembers only a proposed form of government; he misses the discussion of justice and truth, since it is not reducible to facts. He sees a performance of *Oedipus Rex,* and remembers only that an unfortunate fellow killed his father and slept with his mother (if his studies have included Freudian psychology, he might see "facts" in the play that the author never intended); the full force of the tragedy escapes him. The relentless quest for facts — and nothing but facts — crushes the artistic impulse, erasing the differences that separate great art from pornography. As Malcolm Muggeridge has explained, *Romeo and Juliet* is a play about love, but there are very few scientific facts about love, so the levelling force reduces the play to a discussion of sexuality, and nothing else. And the levellers then insist that they understand the drama, since they have boiled it down to distill the facts it contains. Everything else, they imply, is mere window-dressing.

Honest scholarship aims at something more than the compilation of facts: understanding. A wise scholar knows that reality comes to us as a whole, and must be grasped as a whole. But today's scholarship takes the opposite path, breaking down everything into academic specialties, into smaller and narrower details. Professors submerge themselves in details, and ferret out minutiae about their subject. But they have little to contribute to a broad understanding. Today's academic researchers grow increasingly familiar with subjects that grow increasingly abstruse; they know more and more about less and less.

Facts cannot be wrenched free of the values that give them meaning. Judgements of value — moral and ethical judgements — permeate all our thoughts. The values we cherish, and the moral principles we obey, constitute the greatest determining factor in our lives. Values and principles bring facts to life, and give knowledge its power. Without some understanding of how values are formed, education is more than incomplete: it has not begun. Unless he has some fundamental ideals, some governing principles to order his knowledge, the student may know everything, but understand nothing.

Educators insist that the university must abstain from value judgements in order to preserve its neutrality. To sponsor any set of values, they argue, would mean putting all other competing values at a disadvantage. The university must be a greenhouse in which all ideas and all values can grow. But these educators worry more about the climate of the greenhouse than about the health of the plants. If they paused for a moment, and considered the ultimate purpose of the university, they might realize that strict neutrality impedes the growth of ideas. Different ideas require different intellectual frameworks, just as different plants require different climates. And a competent florist always knows how to distinguish plants from weeds, so that he can uproot the latter. College officials, on the contrary, make no effort to distinguish among competing values. As long as the institution is neutral — as long as the windows of the greenhouse are clean and shiny — they have no further concerns.

In an institution that has no common set of values, students and teachers constantly talk past one another. Since they cannot discuss their most fundamental beliefs, the scholars can never set the stage for their facts and theories. They must convey their thoughts without fully explaining their theoretical underpinnings. Before long, scholars find that they do not share common assumptions: they do not speak the same language. Since they cannot discuss values, they cannot discuss goals, so the college cannot coordinate its efforts toward any set of institutional objectives. Each individual professor pursues his own studies independently, and assumes that the result will make educational sense. Each propounds his own ideas, and assumes that others will understand him. Remember the Tower of Babel?

How can a self-respecting scholar content himself with details, and omit the single, central issue of primary values? Take the existence of God, for example. If God does exist, all other facts pale in comparison with that one all-important truth. No other fact can begin to approach the importance of that one belief; all other ideas must be subordinate. Much of Cardinal Newman's *Idea of a University* addresses just that question, and Newman dismembers the argument for neutrality quite completely. Herewith a sample: "How can we investigate any part of any order of knowledge, and stop short of that which enters into every order? All true principles run over with it, all phenomena converge to it; it is truly the first and the last."

The university cannot outlaw value judgements. It can discourage students from making such judgements inside the classroom, but inevitably they will make them on their own. As long as they are individuals, and especially if the university fails to foster communal values, students will disagree with one another on judgements of values. Like it or not, the conflicts will come. The university can only choose whether to encourage or suppress the resulting controversies. To suppress controversy is a grave sin for any academic institution, and yet paradoxically that is exactly what our open-minded universities regularly do.

When they come, conflicts over values quickly degenerate into shouting matches. Students are unprepared to argue calmly and rationally; they have been taught that value judgements cannot be debated, so they do not debate them. Instead students try to win support for their positions by the sheer force of their emotions. Rhetoric becomes strident, and demagogues assume control. Civility disappears, and violence is never impossible. Thus the campus radicals of the late '60s, finding that their values were different from those of the college administration, quickly turned to slogans, protests, and ultimately to violent confrontation. Thanks to their value-free training, they knew no other way to argue their point.

The discussion should not degenerate so quickly. Debate about values is difficult and laborious, but not impossible. Suppose I hold a value which you cannot accept. Granted, you cannot refute me by any scientific experiment, but you need not throw up your hands and walk away from the argument. You can question how I came to hold that value. Perhaps you can convince me that I am basing my belief on an incorrect assumption, or that my value judgement in this case conflicts with another, stronger value which I also hold. Or perhaps you can show me that my judgement carries some undesirable implications — that a world run according to my value would be a less pleasant world. In the process, you would learn a great deal about me, and I about you. Education would occur. This dialectical process is long and painstaking, but it is fully possible. Moreover, this process produces the best works of the human mind. After we finish our argument about values (probably sometime in the wee hours of the morning), we shall both be much wiser, and, by the way, much better friends.

Arguments about values produce man's greatest intellectual achievements. What is Plato's *Republic* but one long discussion of values? What is St. Augustine's *City of God*?

Through the use of the dialectial process, men do change others' opinions. Moral progress does take place, however slowly and however tentatively. Once men worshipped their gods by sacrificing their children; now they do not. Once people in our own country held other people as slaves; now they do not. These are advances. And rest assured that they did not come about because of value-free scholarship. They came about because some poeple took the time and effort to change other people's moral judgements.

If I like chocolate ice cream, and you prefer vanilla, our discussion is probably finished before it starts. We could debate the relative virtues of the two flavors, but why bother? It's only ice cream, and it's only a matter of taste. But moral conduct is not just a matter of taste. Before we discuss any form of morality, we must reach some agreements about fundamental values — about how moral life is led. Unless, of course, we do not plan to take the discussion seriously. Any discussion comparing chocolate and vanilla would be entertaining precisely because every argument would be so totally arbitrary. The debate would be ludicrous because it could not possibly lead anywhere. There would be no ground rules, and no common understanding to guide the course of the arguments. All the participants in such a debate could have fun playing the intellectual game, dreaming up new arguments and new rebuttals. Anyone who tried to take the debate seriously — who cared too deeply about vanilla — would become a nuisance.

Debates on our college campuses are often like that ice cream debate, except that serious topics are discussed. Debate is treated as an intellectual diversion, and anyone taking values too seriously disrupts the general amusement. Richard Weaver spotted this suppressed premise in the argument for value neutrality: "How can we who disagree about what the world is for agree about any of the minutiae of daily conduct? The statement really means that it does not matter what a man believes so long as he does not take his beliefs seriously."[6]

By refusing to encourage controversy on the most serious issues, the university shows that it does not really care about ideas, or about the people who have those ideas. A university based on this sort of routinized disregard for values does not deserve the name. At such a university — and there are many such universities in our country today — intellectual controversy is paralyzed. Students argue in slogans, rather than in complete arguments. The entire process of scholarly debate is a game, like the hypothetical ice cream debate. The university parodies the life of the mind, treating serious issues with frivolous unconcern.

Every sort of education imparts some moral values, whether they are positive or negative. If students are not imbued with some sense of the importance of values, then they recognize another message entirely: they come to assume that values are not important. But even that, in a perverse sort of way, is a value judgement. The universities cannot hope to stay neutral. They must furnish a framework within which the student can place the knowledge he acquires. They must show him to distinguish that which is important and lasting from that which is trivial and evanescent. And the universities will do all this, whether they like it or not.

The choice is clear. Universities can either inspire students to higher moral values, or encourage them to ignore values altogether. Sound education — honest education — encourages students to develop values, and to treat those values with the utmost seriousness. By its teaching and its example, the university prompts students to hold some values with almost reverential care. In this sense, all education is, ultimately, religious. Perhaps not religious in the best sense of the word, but religious in the sense that it helps define the student's ultimate moral values. As Whitehead put it, "A religious education is an education that inculcates duty and reverence."[7]

To put the matter simply, a liberal education can either preserve the values that define Western civilization, or else subvert those values. Students must graduate holding our basic cultural beliefs in either reverence or contempt. There can be no middle ground, no moral neutrality, for the university. All education is moral education. Only one question remains: what will that morality be?

CHAPTER ELEVEN

Academic Freedom

> Even John Stuart Mill did not ask more
> than that a question be not considered closed
> so long as any one man adhered to it; he did
> not require that a man, flourishing a map of
> the flat world, be seated in a chair of science
> at Yale.
>
> *William F. Buckley, Jr.* [1]

Liberation: all of us today are familiar with that term. The political scenario is simple. First there is an oppressive government. Then the liberating forces overthrow that government. Finally, the liberators set up their own regime.

In academe, the oppression comes from unexamined ideas and misplaced values. Liberation comes through careful study, discussion, and debate. And the first rule of the new regime is the law of academic freedom. All other rules flow from that first premise.

With our universities in such a state of intellectual disrepair, it should come as no surprise that their fundamental rule is ill understood. And it is. Politicians, editorialists, and even professors themselves make all sorts of grandiose claims about the virtues of academic freedom. More often than not those claims reveal that the speaker has no understanding whatsoever of the meaning of the term.

The silliest definitions of academic freedom come from professors themselves. (Not all professors; of course the best teachers and scholars are too busy to invent new meanings for old terms.) Like anyone else who works in a large organization, the professor maneuvers constantly to protect his own occupational privileges and to enhance his own position in the institutional hierarchy. The more Machiavellian professors soon notice that whenever they cite the principle of academic freedom, their opposition pales. Laymen are uncomfortable debating scholarly issues, and they bow out quickly; other scholars are only too happy to see the principle expanded to protect them more fully. Soon enough, the principle of academic freedom is cited to enable every professor to do what he wants to do, when he wants to do it. Too often that interpretation goes unchecked.

After a bit more sober reflection, most educators equate academic freedom with freedom of speech. A scholar, they reason, must feel free to advance any argument, and to publish any theory, no matter how controversial. Academic freedom protects that right.

Now wait. Why should academic freedom be necessary to safeguard free speech? The First Amendment already does that. The limits of ordinary free speech do not inhibit scholarship; academics have no reason to shout "Fire" in a crowded theater, or to libel their neighbors. Yes, scholars should be free to preach controversial doctrines. But every American has that right. On a street corner soapbox or a classroom podium, any American can espouse any belief. The legal right is clear. So why should academe need a special, redundant protection? Academic freedom must mean something more than free speech, or at least something different.

The most famous argument for free thought and discussion appears in John Stuart Mill's *On Liberty*. Mill's thesis, roughly summarized, is that unrestricted argument is the best way to determine the truth. When ideas compete with each other, their weaknesses are promptly uncovered. Good ideas therefore supplant bad ideas, and even the good ones are pruned and refined by the competition. Mill argues that no idea should be excluded, no argument rejected, as long as any one man still adheres to it. A truth can only be established when every individual accepts and understands it.

Nowadays most universities espouse Mill's argument in some variation. The school views itself as a free market for ideas, and no theory is excluded from consideration. No one idea or theory can claim special authority. Professors can advance their arguments as true, but they cannot write off other arguments as false. The college as a whole is an impartial umpire: defining and

enforcing the rules of the competition, but never joining with
the one side or another. As far as the university as an institution
is concerned, every idea is a viable competitor. No idea is right.

At least that is the theory. But when the university proclaims
that all ideas are equal — that no argument is objectively, absolutely true — it thereby excludes from consideration a certain
class of arguments. It excludes the arguments that claim to
represent the objective, absolute truth. If one argument is simply
correct, then all other contrary arguments are mere distractions,
keeping scholars from their real business of seeking the truth. If
two and two make four, they do not add up to any other number. Once the truth is established, the marketplace collapses; all
ideas are not equal any longer. But the university has committed
itself to equality of ideas, and to the notion that no idea could
be completely right. So our universities stand in a very curious
posture. They will welcome every sort of idea and argument
except one. They will not accept ideas that claim to be true.

Of course they will accept such ideas up to a point. They will
allow professors to espouse any views, including views that
claim the authority of absolute truth. The universiy will take the
ideas seriously, but not the authority. This position is illogical,
even hypocritical. The university claims to welcome all ideas, but
then shuts out ideas that violate its own preconceptions. It
ignores claims to authority, but then arrogates special authority
to itself. The university steadfastly refuses to contemplate one
central and vital possibility: the possibility that some arguments
are right, and others are wrong.

But still we are in the realm of theory. In practice the universities most assuredly do enthrone some ideas and damn others.
Suppose a mathematician suddenly took leave of his senses, and
began teaching that two and two make seven. Of course he would
be free to advance that argument; the First Amendment protects even stupid ideas. But he would have a great deal of trouble
saving his position in the department of mathematics. Similarly,
a physicist claiming that atoms are indivisible, or a biologist
explaining that the blood does not circulate, or a geographer
arguing that the world is flat — these men could never win tenure
in our universities. And if they could not win tenure, then they

could not teach. And if they could not teach, then free speech of campus would not be absolute. The universities *do* put limits on freedom of thought and expression.

Should we say, then, that the universities accept all arguments except the ones that have been proven plainly false or absurd? That would not help too much: who determines when a proof is complete, and who judges when an idea is absurd? Obviously the university does exercise some sort of authority. Moreover, everyone at the university (the lunatic fringe excepted) supports that authority. No one claims that a flat-earth fanatic should be included in the geography department for philosophical balance; no one contends that the exclusion of that fanatic disturbs the free workings of the marketplace of ideas. (Well, maybe the flat-earther himself objects, but his views are surely biased.) So if academic freedom merely reiterates the First Amendment, then academic freedom is universally ignored on American campuses today.

My point, of course, is that academic freedom does not coincide with freedom of speech. The First Amendment protects all ideas, while academic freedom protects only those ideas that advance the cause of truth. In an academic environment, untruth is the dread enemy. Bad ideas violate the student's right to learn the truth, and interfere with the scholar's right to ponder it. Anyone who truly cares about ideas is nauseated by illogical arguments and disproven theories; he wants to uproot them immediately. So as soon as the university is convinced that an argument has no merit, it effectively stifles that argument. Nor does this violate academic freedom, in the accurate sense of that term.

Academic freedom is a special privilege, granted traditionally to scholars because of their special role in society.[2] Western culture has long placed a high value on wisdom, and conferred special status on those who make wisdom their life's work. Our culture (for reasons I think the next chapter explains) reveres truth. So societies make sure that no obstacles impede scholars in their search for truth. That guarantee from society is academic freedom. Academic freedom is the freedom to seek, to refine, and to convey the truth. Truth — that is the key term delineating the scope of the scholar's privilege. Academic freedom serves the truth, and nothing but the truth.

So far, so good. Now the issue becomes sticky, however, Somehow, someone must determine which arguments qualify for the rights of academic freedom, and which do not. Someone (or some organization) must decide what truth is. How can that be done? Not by majority vote, of course, since the majority can often be wrong. But if the majority opinion is not accepted, will some elite dictate to the masses?

The problem need not be so vexing. Our society has been coached for too long by the reigning academic theorists; when we hear any proposal for authority, especially in academe, we assume that the result would be inmitigated dogmatism. Why must it be so? Every other freedom has its limits, yet those freedoms survive. Why should academic freedom be any different? The university need not, and should not, put forth an exhaustive guide to Right Thinking. All it requires is a statement of ultimate values — an explanation of how fundamental conflicts will be resolved.

Most intellectual controversies do not require quick resolution. In all but the most extreme cases, academic freedom is never in question. Literary critics have spent centuries debating over how Shakespeare achieved his incomparable dramatic power, and with each passing decade the debate yields new illumination. That sort of controversy should continue, and if possible it should expand. The university should not become an intellectual dictator, passing judgements from on high.

But what happens when two basic values conflict, and one cannot survive unless the other is suppressed? What happens at a fundamentalist Christian school, when a professor begins expounding theories that clearly contradict the teachings of the Bible? To give professors the full scope of academic freedom, the university must give them some idea of where the truth ultimately lies. If a final test is necessary, will the school resport to the authority of Scripture? majority vote? government edicts? tradition? Will an idea be judged by what it contributes to the Gross National Product? to the glory of God? to equality? Scholars do not need a complete road map, but they do need some notion of the direction in which (as the institution sees it) the truth lies.

All universities already have some ultimate tests, whether they admit it or not. In the hard sciences, experiments are the ultimate tests. A scholarly scientist must agree to abide by the results of the experiments. If a fair experiment disproves his hypothesis, he must abandon it. Every college makes that demand.

Now suppose a sociologist came to campus preaching Adolph Hitler's views on racial supremacy. No college in the country would hire him or give him tenure. Why not? Because racial hatred is inimical to the truths American colleges espouse. Colleges do adhere to some ultimate values. And so they should.

In the chapter that follows I adumbrate a set of ultimate principles that might support an ideal university. I shall not claim that those principles are the only ones compatible with scholarship. I could easily respect a school conducted in accordance with the beliefs of Protestant Christianity, or of Judaism. No doubt Marxist doctrine could support a university, as could democracy, or monarchy, or any other comprehensive political system. Atheistic belief might be enough for a foundation. I can even imagine a university based forthrightly on secular humanism, much as I should hate to study there. Our society is large and pluralistic enough to support any number of different institutions, based on different sets of ultimate values. The conflicts among these different schools would make scholarly discourse much more lively, and give students (and teachers) a much more extensive choice of schools. Students could choose the school whose ultimate values came closest to their own, and rest assured that they would not feel isolated from that scholarly community. The institutions could assure themselves that their students and teachers would feel united in their values, and positive scholarly discipline would become a reality. In short, the brief statement of fundamental beliefs would restore all the forgotten blessings of academic idealism.

Freedom exacts a toll. To protect the beliefs it holds most dear, the college must forego its right to take a stance on other issues. Any political, religious, or ideological issue outside the

scope of the university's fundamental purposes must be resolved
by the individual scholars themselves, lest the university run
afoul of outside pressures. Any institution that takes a stance on
political issues risks political repercussions. If the universities try
to run the government, the government will try to run the
universities. The government will win that battle, because in the
political sphere the government is the highest power. So prudent
university administrators will hold the university off from participation in politics.

Still, at some point the political authorities might cross the
dividing line and interfere in the university's province. If the
government outlaws research on a certain topic, a topic crucial
to the school's mission, the school must respond. If the government's policies set up artificial obstacles in the path of truth,
the universities are obligated to react. In the most frightening
case, when the government acts in defiance of the truths the
university espouses, then too the university must respond. Still,
in each of these cases, when they resolve to enter the political
arena, the universities must recognize the risks. Any political
venture threatens the continued independence of the institution.
Administrators must ask themselves which is more dangerous to
the ultimate purposes of the university: the threat of political
control, or the threat of complicity with unjust government
policies. Is the political issue clear enough to justify abandoning
the institution's neutrality?

This discussion is all very abstract. Let me offer a concrete
illustration. On American campuses today, students are protesting against university involvements in South Africa. The university must take a stand, they insist, against that country's
apartheid laws. A number of schools have acceded to those
demands, and divested themselves of stock in companies that do
business in South Africa. I can appreciate the students' moral
stance, but still I would recommend against their proposals.

On one point the university should have no trouble articu-
lating its position. The South African race laws are oppressive
and immoral. What is more to the point, as far as the universities
are concerned, those laws enforce the belief that men are unequal.[3] Our society — and by implication our universities — re-

jects that belief. The universal equality of mankind is one of the fundamental truths every American university should endorse. Consequently the universities have every right and duty to oppose *apartheid*. The school might well refuse to recognize the legitimacy of the South African government, or to participate in scholarly exchanges with South African institutions run by that government. First and foremost, the universities should take the lead in condemning this inhuman system.

But once that is done, the question of divestiture remains. And that question is fraught with political and economic judgements — judgements the university should not make lightly. First there is the purely practical matter: would divestiture help or hinder the effort to overthrow *apartheid*? If the university sold all its stocks, would other less scrupulous institutions snap them up, and would the university thereby lose its ability to exert moral suasion? Many observers think that divestiture would constitute a blessing for the oppressed black South Africans; others (myself included) think it would be a curse. This is an economic judgement, and a political judgement — not a judgement of ultimate truths. So as long as the university community is divided on the issue, the institution itself should not take a final stand.

Then, even if that political-economic question is resolved, another political controversy looms. Even if everyone on campus agrees that the South African government is unjust, are there other governments still worse? To me the answer is obvious: yes. But this too is a political judgement, from which the university should usually abstain. If the institution takes political steps to eradicate moral evil in South Africa, why not in Eastern Europe? And why should the effort be limited to foreign governments? Why not refuse to hold stocks in American corporations that earn their money by questionable means? If the university sets itself against evil on any front, how can it refuse to fight the battle on any other front? Who decides which wrongs the institution will battle, and which political causes it will serve first?

The university is simply not set up to consider such questions. Political questions are best resolved in the political forums; schools exist to pursue the truth. If the university has substantial capital to invest, then the investments should be made in accordance with ordinary business principles, subject only to the laws of the country and the fundamental principles of the university. Let the politicians make political decisions; let the business managers make economic decisionions; the university has enough work on its own.

A very utopian institution might find one other solution to this problem. A university could, without contradicting itself, simply make a blanket prohibition against economic involvement with any tainted parties. The prohibition would not be contradictory, I say; but it would certainly be impractical. All right; so the university will not invest its funds in corporations that indulge any moral vices. Will it accept foundation grants from institutions that bear some indirect moral blemish? Will it accept tuition paid by a parent who works for some proscribed company? What if one of the university's pet corporations, a model of sweetness and light in itself, began doing business with other less desirable firms? Will the university trace every dollar of its endowment, determining through some soritical process that the ultimate source is immoral? No school could possibly fulfill all these conditions. Every dollar in circulation carries some moral imperfection somewhere in its history. If the university really finds it necessary to be walled off from all economic misdeeds, it must take a vow of institutional poverty. That, too, would be a logically consistent decision. But it would not be much of a university.

Academic freedom, like every other form of liberty, demands eternal vigilance. The university exists to pursue truth, and academic freedom redounds out of that pursuit. Whenever the university takes its eyes off that goal, and pursues some other secondary benefit, academic freedom is endangered. And to fix its eyes in proper focus, the university must first establish where the truth lies. That, not some hypothetical libertarian theorizing, is the first task of the new regime — the first task of academic freedom.

In my own ideal university, the ultimate set of values would be the dogmas of the Roman Catholic Church. Notice that I should propose to rely on the Church only for ultimate values. I should not look to the Vatican for daily orders, or for a model curriculum. Notice, too, that I am speaking of Church dogma, not of the opinions common among Catholics. On most issues the Church is silent, and on still more issues a wide controversy can take place entirely within the bounds of orthodoxy. Good practicing Catholics can differ vehemently on political issues, even on moral issues, and they do. St. Thomas Aquinas and St. Augustine are both perfectly orthodox teachers, and yet on some questions (free will, for example) their differences are enormous.

Next, my ideal university — it would surely be an American university — would adhere to our deepest national beliefs, as they are set down in the Declaration of Independence and the Constitution. Again, the inconvenience would be slight; America enjoys more political controversy than any other nation could want, and universities very rarely feel any pressure from government censors. (Government social planners, of course, are a different story.)

Admittedly these dogmas would limit my university's range of free discussion. A Catholic school might tolerate someone who did not believe in the authority of Scripture, but it could certainly not tolerate someone who ridiculed Scripture. Nor could a patriotic American school allow a professor to preach fascism or revolutionary communism. But, realistically, would either inhibition be a loss to academic freedom? The level of intellectual controversy would not noticeably deteriorate. For those who agree with me, and abhor such ideas, the benefits would be readily apparent. And those, of course, are the people who would inhabit my ideal university.

What of those who disagree? Our society is large and diverse; I have little doubt that fascists, communists, and their ilk could all find a comfortable home at some other university. There they could develop their own perverse truths exclusively, pursuing their own ideas with the same vigor that my own more orthodox university could muster.

Unity would breed discipline, and discipline would breed strength. Students and scholars alike could focus on one theme of study, and enjoy the many rewards of increased concentration. A university consecrated to certain fundamental values would outstrip its indifferent, neutral rivals by dint of sheer enthusiasm.

One final, related benefit. Even today, when they profess to allow absolute freedom of speech, all universities impose some limitations on scholarly debate. But since they never admit the existence of such boundaries, no one can question them effectively. By openly advancing a set of principles, the schools would bring their prejudices out of the closet. So the debate about ultimate values could begin anew. Protestant schools could debate the founding premises of their Catholic neighbors, and both together could dispute the Marxists. So the time-honored dialectical process would begin. In a society such as our own, no school could set itself off from other competing institutions, cloistering its students and teachers. No, every school would send out new ideas — possibly quite heretical ideas, by the standards of other schools — to cross-pollinate with competing ideas. Scholars would be no more inhibited in presenting their arguments, once they attached themselves to a compatible institution. And since they would understand clearly the purposes of their work, and share that understanding with their institutional overseers, they could pursue the truth with renewed vigor. Academic freedom would reach new heights. Now, instead of being a negative concept — an inhibition on administrative power — it would become a positve force for cooperation and mutual dedication.

Yes, I know. There is a drawback to this conception of academic freedom. Some scholars might find themselves so thoroughly heretical that no school would have them. Some ideas might be universally rejected, just as Galileo's ideas were rejected by the ecclesiastical authorities of his time. I shall not argue that no one could ever suffer Galileo's fate again; it is at least conceivable. (Although the First Amendment, operating in a political forum, makes it highly unlikely.) But I do think it is extraordinarily unlikely to happen again in academe. Our society is not disposed to reject novel ideas. On the contrary, some ideas seem to prosper primarily because they are so bizarre. Under different circumstances one might fear for the Galileos of the future, but in the present state of academic affairs, the main danger comes from the opposite direction. True, academic authorities should realize the limitations of their own power;

they should not be quick to pronounce an idea anathema. But can anyone seriously doubt that today's academic authorities would be prudent? Can anyone fail to distinguish between contemporary academe and the Inquisitions?

And by the way, Galileo's views eventually won the debate. The process was long and painful, but the truth did eventually triumph. In any society, no matter how righteously it advertises its open-mindedness, radical new ideas meet with strong resistance. Societies do not usually shuck off their old notions the way snakes shed their skins. The changes are always hard, no matter what the circumstances. But the truth wins out. A good idea can be suppressed, but not forever.

CHAPTER TWELVE

Truth and Beauty

> In a Christian society education must be religious, not in the sense that it will be administered by ecclesiastics, still less in the sense that it will exercise pressure, or attempt to instruct everyone in theology, but in the sense that its aims will be directed by a Christian philosophy of life.
>
> *T.S. Eliot*[1]

What is truth?

Let us start at the very beginning.

As I write this chapter, I am sitting at a typewriter. The typewriter sets atop a table. I am seated at a chair in front of that table. The typewriter, the table, the chair, myself; we all exist. There is absolutely no doubt in my mind about that statement. It is true.

Now I know, and if you have studied modern philosophy you know, that many brilliant men spend years debating the same sort of questions as the ones I have just solved so peremptorily. How do I know for sure that the typewriter, or the chair, or the table exists? How do I even know that I myself exist? I realize that these brilliant men concoct brilliant arguments about these questions. But I don't care. I exist, my furniture exists, and I consider the matter happily closed. And, by the way, the overwhelming majority of human beings — alive, dead, and yet to be born, agree with me.

Perhaps all those brilliant arguments provide mental stimulation, just as chess provides mental stimulation. And believe me, I love chess. But chess is a game, and makes no pretensions to be anything more than a game. When one begins to argue about whether a thing exists — when the thing is physically present in the same room, in plain sight — one must begin to doubt that *anything* exists. One must begin to doubt one's own existence. And that way lies madness.

Now let me introduce a more complicated case. When I first arrived at Princeton, I sat in on an introductory philosophy course for the first few lectures. In his first presentation to the students, the instructor announced the "fact" that human thought and morality do not progress. To one freshman, that claim seemed somehow wrong. What about slavery, he asked? Once slavery was widespread, now the institution is extinct. Is that not moral progress? The teacher was nonplussed. Finally, after a few abortive efforts, he explained his position: yes, he himself thought that the abolition of slavery was a good thing, but other people might have other opinions. Since he could not make a value judgement about the question, he could not condemn slavery as simply, philosophically evil. As a political matter, yes; he concurred with the student's judgement. But as a philosopher (he called himself a philosopher — not a teacher of philosophy) he could not pronounce that judgement true.

Personally, I have less trouble. Slavery is wrong. Freedom is good. As far as I am concerned, these statements are true. Every bit as true as the statement that I myself exist as I write this chapter. I know these statements can all be debated. But I am not interested in debating them.

Let me explain why.

Throughout this book, I have spoken about the search for truth, the power of truth, and the value of truth. I have argued that a university uncommitted to the truth is not worthy of its name. All the time, I have spoken as if the truth were an actual, palpable reality. I think it is. And I believe still more than that. I belive that I *know* the truth. Not perfectly, by any means; I only know it in a rough, flawed way. Second-hand, in fact. And, knowing that my understanding of truth is terribly limited, I am especially aware of the depth of my ignorance. Nor do I claim to have special mystical insights into the truth. Many other people share my knowledge, and the same knowledge is available to everyone. These reservations stated, let me repeat: I know the truth.

Anti-democratic, you say? Un-American? Not at all. There it

is, in the very first public document of American society: "We
hold these truths to be self-evident." Our founders claimed to
know the truth, too. Even before referring to those self-evident
truths, the Declaration of Independence names the source that
makes truths self-evident. The truth is pronounced in "the Laws
of Nature and of Nature's God." In this chapter I want to explore how the university can aim toward the truth. I want to
discuss the place in academe for Nature and Nature's God.

If God exists, then Nature is His writ, and all knowledge is
knowledge about God. So education is not just another industry;
it is, and it has, a sacred object. Western society has always
drawn a close connection between God and the Truth, and in
the New Testament the linkage is explicit. The Judeo-Christian
God has made promises to His faithful people, and His truth is
everlasting. Notice, if you will, that the idea of the university is
exlusively a Western idea, with its roots in that Judeo-Christian
tradition. Oh, yes; every society has always had students and
teachers. But the idea of an institution that purses knowledge,
an institution that devotes itself to an object greater than the
individuals within it, an institution that (unlike the Greek acad-
amies) endures through the centuries without changing its dedication to truth — this idea only sprung up in the pious atmosphere of medieval Europe. Other societies have since assimilated
the same concept, and founded similar institutions. But it was
the Judeo-Christian notion of God, the God who never changes,
that gave rise to the universities.

If there is no God, or if the gods are malevolent, what reason
do we have for believing that knowledge is so desirable? For all
we know, in an atheistic universe every bit of knowledge might
bring new depths of sorrow. And if the gods are not consistant,
how can any knowledge be certain? Perhaps the law of gravity
obtains today, but tomorrow the gods might amuse themselves
by reversing the physical laws. The Judeo-Christian faith obliter-
ates these doubts. Knowledge is a blessing, truth is constant, and
the world is a good place. More basic still, the world has meaning;
nature is worth exploring. Eastern mysticism, with its belief that
all reality is only *maya,* or illusion, would never prompt society
to build universities. There can be no doubt about it: Western

society has excelled above all other civilizations in amassing knowledge, and our underlying religious traditions have fueled that success.

The original European universities — at Paris and Bologna, Oxford and Cambridge — were explicitly religious institutions. Theology was the primary field of study, and teaching was closely allied with preaching. The universities' mission was to flesh out and pass on the meaning of the Christian tradition.

Nor did that value die out in the Renaissance. In our own country, Harvard was founded as a training place for Puritan ministers, and eventually some pious citizens, unhappy with Harvard's theological deviations, established a rival seminary called Yale. Up until recently, the schools' genealogy was still apparent. Yale's President a mere generation ago, Charles Seymour, could still forthrightly proclaim the institution's devotion to Christianity: "We betray our trust, if we fail to explore the various ways in which our youth who come to us may learn to appreciate spiritual values, whether by the example of our own lives or through the cogency of our philosophical arguments. The simple and direct way is through the maintenance and upholding of the Christian religions as a vital part of university life."[2]

Today things are different. Even in his heyday, Seymour represented a dying breed, a remnant. Now universities are pragmatic, unconcerned with enuciating spiritual — let alone religious — values. Sir Walter Moberly, writing forty years ago, prophesied the complaint in a time when the university's pragmatism was not nearly so marked. The deepest mistrust, Moberly predicted, would be the universities' blithe ignorance about the faith that made their existence possible. As he explains, "Though Lucretius, Voltaire, and Marx agree in rejecting religion . . . they regard it as pernicious but not as insignificant. Nietzsche proclaims that 'God is dead,' but to him this is an assertion having revolutionary consequences for life at a thousand points. But in modern universities, as in modern society, some think God exists, some think not, some think it impossible to tell, and the impression grows that it does not matter."[3]

Our universities boast their willingness to tackle any ideas, and question every belief. But when it comes time to tackle the question of transcendence, and to question the belief in pragmatic agnosticism, suddenly the scholars have cold feet. They edge nervously away from theology, or from any broad consideration of the role religious beliefs have placed in shaping our society. As a result, they cannot possibly understand the society they set out to study. How many great thinkers, artists, and poets have been inspired immeasurably by their faith? The great theologians are obvious examples, but what of Dante, Mozart, Michelangelo, Pascal, or Milton? No scholar can grasp the work of these men without first understanding the Christian beliefs that drove them to greatness. The growth of European society is inextricably enmeshed with the practices of religious devotion. Towns grew up around monasteries; institutions hovered around the Church. For entire centuries, the best minds in Europe were governed by one universal faith. Anyone who does not understand that faith cannot understand European history. And anyone living in our society who has no understanding of European history is cut off from his roots. Such a person cannot claim to be liberally educated.

What one book has had the most influence on Western culture? There is no debate: the Bible. Now how can a university study the Bible without considering the faith it fires? One can study the Bible as an historical document, since it does contain immense historical detail. Or one can study it as a piece of literature, since its style often reaches artistic heights. But neither the history nor the dramatic style gave the Bible its power over Western thought. Thucydides provided history, and Aeschylus provided dramatic style; both predate the New Testament, but neither has had a comparable impact. The Bible's influence stems from the fact that it is — that for centuries the best minds have believed it to be — the inspired Word of God. Any other approach to the Bible cannot touch its wisdom. It is, first and last, a matter of faith.

The same logic applies to the question of Revelation. That, too, is a matter of faith, and cannot be understood by ordinary social science methods. The authenticity of Revelation cannot be gain said by any normal process of logic; it is an article of faith, and faith alone can consider it. By narrow, strict, objective standards, neither the existence nor the nonexistence of God — and thus of Revelation — can ultimately be proven. When a mystic claims that God has spoken to him, no scientific arguments could possibly dissuade him, because obviously God, Who makes the rules of science, can suit them to His purposes. Belief and Revelation subsume logic.

Unfortunately, while most people would agree that God's existence cannot be demonstrated scientifically, many cannot see the other side of the coin. Too many scholars emphatically deny the possibility of arguments *for* Revelation, and yet readily furnish arguments *against* it. The old double standard rears its ugly head. Academicians will consider any claim on its own merits, unless the claim is transcendent. Trancendent claims demand transcendent arguments, and scholars will not oblige.

Some months ago, as I dawdled with my newspaper, a television listing struck my fancy: Paul Weiss would be interviewed on the Dick Cavett show that night. Weiss is a highly respected philosopher and theologian, a longtime fixture on Yale's faculty and then a professor at Catholic University. His work has brought him numerous awards, including a favorable mention (albeit very highly qualified) in William Buckley's *God and Man at Yale.* I had never heard Weiss speak, nor had I read his work, so I decided to tune in and explore. My interest was amply rewarded; Cavett (uncharacteristically) choose a fascinating line of questions. Did he, Weiss, believe in the existence of God, Cavett asked? Wording his answer carefully, Weiss replied that he did not; he could respect faith, but he himself was not convinced. Then what would it take to convince him, Cavett wondered? Suppose God Himself appeared to Weiss. Would he then believe? Well, Weiss replied, the question could not be that simple. How could he be sure that the visitation was real? How could he know that his senses were not deceiving him? Cavett pressed the point, however, and Weiss suggested some tests. If a vision occurred, or if the voice of God could answer, he would ask for solutions to the most difficult philosophical problems. And even then, even if he received perfect answers, he couldn't be sure. How would he know that he had not formulated the answers himself, in his subconscious, and only now brought them to consciousness with the help of a hallucination? In short, even if a voice spoke to him, uttering the most profound of all truths, Weiss could never be sure that God himself had spoken. The argument is quite unassailable; one can never exhaust the logical possibilities. Weiss' doubts are fully appropriate, too.

Unless it really is the voice of God!

Then, suddenly, the philosopher's response becomes pathetic, absurd. There, in the direct presence of his Lord and Creator, the philosopher would be playing silly intellectual games. Why is he asking presumptuous questions? Why isn't he on his knees? If he is truly hearing the word of God, all his questions are futile, blasphemous. The problem, you see, is that Weiss would not *consider* that possibility. He relies on his reason. And when reason oversteps its bounds, it becomes, well, unreasonable.

Consider. Suppose a neighbor, a man living down the street from you, announced that he had seen God. If he had always stuck you as a bit eccentric, you would write him off as insane. Fair enough. But suppose he always seemed a sober and level-headed fellow, and suppose he seemed quite clearheaded even as he made his announcement. You would be left with only two possible alternatives. You must dismiss your neighbor as a lunatic, or else admit at least the possibility that he was telling the truth. You need not believe in the vision yourself; you probably would want to hold that question in abeyance, at least at first. But if you were not prepared to guarantee that the man is insane, you must entertain the possibility that he did, in fact, see God. (And if faith means anything, it means believing that God could appear to anyone, anytime. Even to you; even before you turn this page.) Yes, maybe it is all a hallucination. Then again, maybe not.

Ultimately, faith is a gift, not a logical conclusion. Reason alone can never convince the skeptic, nor should it draw a believer away from his faith. A strict rationalist might view all religious belief as neurotic, and reason could never conclusively prove him wrong. (Although reason could certainly prove him arrogant, to reject so many great minds with one cavalier generalization.) But by the same logic, a religious believer might view rationalism as neurotic. Reason has no competence to judge between the two claims.

Is all this discussion futile, then? Not at all, if reason is chastened by the knowledge of its limitations. Reason must learn to respect claims based on faith. The claims may not be true, the faith might be mistaken, but reason cannot hope to refute them alone. Faith belongs to a different, higher province.

Once reason admits its weaknesses in this realm — the realm of faith — then the floodgates open, and the intellect is awash in humility. And humility can be a very handy virtue for the scholar. As Socrates never tired of saying, an admission of ignorance is the first sign of wisdom.

Yet ignorance can be very hard to admit, especially for a scholar. Reason constantly arrogates new powers to herself. The result, as often as not, is itself unreasonable. Take the case of Charles Darwin. Darwin, years after he introduced the theory of evolution, once told a confidant that he occasionally had doubts about his own theory. But he quickly dismissed those doubts, he said. As he explained it, he could not trust the mind of someone who had descended from an ape. But wait. The theory of evolution was put forth from that same mind, descended from that same ape. Why did Darwin trust himself to construct the theory, but not to doubt it? Evidently he trusted his cerebral powers, but not his deeper intuitions? But why?

What, aside from reason itself, suggests that reason is infallible? The evidence strongly suggests that one's intuitions can sometimes be much more accurate. How often does some persistent nagging doubt, a doubt no logic can explain or dissolve, lead to a fresh new discovery? Something, some faculty, keeps questioning, even when the reasoning powers are satisfied. This special faculty must approve reason's conclusions. This faculty, this deeper reason, if you will, delegates its powers to ordinary everyday reason, but never surrenders those powers too completely — or at least should not. It stands behind reason and validates it.

For want of a better term, let us assume that this faculty is . . . the soul. Only under its tutelage can reason reach its finest heights.

This is not a book about theology, and I am not a theologian. If I were being precise, maybe I should realize that "soul" is not exactly the proper term. Still it is the best term I know. Aristotle spoke of a faculty called *nous*. Today we translate *nous* to mean mind, or reason, but that translation misses much of the Greek word's flavor. Aristotle explains that *nous* is man's most elevated function: it is the part of human nature that touches on divinity. When Christians say that man is made in the image and likeness of God, Aristotleans recognize the reference to *nous*. (Notice, by the way, the striking similarities in the world's great philosophies. Everything that rises must converge.)

Somewhere in human nature, then, there is a faculty for reasoning of the most profound sort — reasoning much more serious than the everyday logical process. Call it the soul, or *nous*, or what you will. The name is not important. The task of liberal education is to develop that faculty and put it to work. Dispelling our prejudices, questioning our beliefs, studying the works of the philosophers and poets: all these practices help us to hone this faculty. We roam through our mental faculties as through a cave, exploring new chambers and following shafts of light, even occasionally striking sparks of our own. But our object is not spelunking; our object is to find the mouth of the cave and the light outside. And only our souls can guide us, because only our souls share the life of the outer light. When we approach the mouth of the cave, our souls will recognize what our reason has never before encountered. "You shall know the truth, and the truth shall set you free."

The universities' flight from faith has been sudden and dramatic. Until 1972 every President of Princeton had been either a Presbyterian minister or the son of a Presbyterian minister. Now the new President, William G. Bowen, professes no Christian beliefs. Just one generation ago, William Buckley was shocked to learn that the incoming President of Yale, Whitney Griswold, would not speak plainly in support of Christianity. Today Buckley would probably be even more shocked (although more happy, too) if the President of Yale *would* preach Christianity.

Today's university presidents often boast of the university as a counterweight against the pressures that govern our society. But would any leading university president dare to repeat the words of Charles Seymour, Griswold's predecessor at Yale? This is strong stuff: "I call upon all members of the faculty, as members of a thinking body, freely to recognize the tremendous validity and power to the teachings of Christ in our life-and-death struggle against the forces of selfish materialism."[4]

No, our universities today are not ready for that sort of advocacy. Religion is all very well in its place, but its place — the universities suggest — is outside the classroom. Each individual in the university community may worship as he chooses, but once he enters the curriculum itself, he cannot fall back on his faith. Belief cannot be certified by reason, and since reason alone rules the university, belief is therefore intellectually suspect. No wonder, then that students so often lose their faith during their undergraduate years. The university promises to fill every vital need in their lives, and then ostentatiously omits any reference to faith. The conclusion seems implicit. As far as the university is concerned, faith is not a vital need.

Every now and then university officials do make some effort to encourage students in their religious beliefs. Religion, they say, is a pillar of society. But in such statements, the ultimate value is not the religion itself, but the institutions it supports. If the student accepts that argument, he sees religion as a means toward an end, with the protection of society — not his soul — as the end. If that attitude is religious, it is clearly not transcendent.

Or sometimes academicians point out that everyone has some ultimate values, and the ultimate values of each individual constitute his own personal religion. In once sense that idea is elevating: it brings all everyday values up to the level of religious experience. But in another sense it is degrading: it brings religious experience down to the level of everyday values. What about the poor soul whose ultimate values are sex, power, and the almighty dollar? Is he religious? A definition that broad denigrates the value of true religious beliefs. Religious beliefs are by definition ultimate values, but ultimate values are not necessarily religious beliefs.

In baseball, a home run is the batter's ultimate feat. But no one has suggested that whenever a batter does his utmost, we should define the result as a home run. (And even the best batters hit home runs fairly infrequently: ultimate values are not frequently encountered.) Likewise with religion and religious values. One cannot define away the distinguishing character of religious thought, and still claim the special status accorded to religions.

In liberal education, teachers should always goad their students on to new levels of moral understanding, urging them to keep setting their sights higher. Defining a student's private values as "religious" defeats that purpose; the student becomes complacent about his system of beliefs, and stops searching for loftier truths. If his private beliefs reflect a shallow approach to life, he never realizes it. Instead, sheltered behind the professors' assurances that his values are religious, he assumes that all "other" religious sentiments are as base and uninspiring as his own.

The late political theorists Leo Strauss made the same point in a different context. One cannot judge great truths on the basis of small notions. Unless one appreciates the fundamental truths, he will be incompetent to make judgements of value. In Strauss' own vivid words,

> By teaching in effect the equality of literally all desires, it teaches in effect that there is nothing that a man ought to be ashamed of; by destroying the possibility of self-contempt, it destroys, with the best of intentions, the possibility of self-respect. By teaching the equality of all values, by denying that there are things which are intrinsically high and others which are intrinsically low as well as by denying that there is an essential difference between men and brutes, it unwittingly contributes to the victory of the gutter.[5]

Strauss was speaking of what he called "the new political science." But he could as well have been speaking of education in general; indeed on other occasions he did address the same criticism to more general academic practices. When the intrinsically higher things are viewed from the perspective of the base values, Strauss pointed out, those high things are debased. But when the baser things are viewed from the higher perspective, they are seen all the more clearly for what they are.

But students know no better, because the universities teach them no better. Undergraduates desert their faith because the college makes faith seem benighted; they never confront the inexhaustible riches of religious thought and worship. Then, troubled by their lack of transcendent purpose, many turn to bizarre cults, or second-rate mystics, for spiritual guidance. Students swear allegiance to the Maharishi because they are unacquainted with Saint Theresa or Saint John of the Cross; they do not realize that mysticism has found a more fruitful ground in the Christian tradition. Others turn to the teachings of social revolutionaries, unaware of the history of social action in Christianity, or the magnificent contemporary witness of Mother Teresa of Calcutta. Still others do turn to Christianity, but in their new zeal insist that they must abandon scholarship; they have not been introduced to the works of the many great saints and scholars who have melded the twin virtues of piety and scholarship. The omission of religion from the university curriculum — or the inclusion of religion as a sociological and historical subject — leaves students stunted in their intellectual growth. Religious knowledge is a type of knowledge, and an important type at that. To lack that knowledge is to see only a part of the truth. If liberal education guards against unexamined ideas and ignorant conclusions, then liberal education must include some attention to the spiritual realm, so that students are protected from folly.

One unavoidable consequence of learning is the realization that the scholar's reach exceeds his grasp. The earnest scholar soon realizes that he can never hope to master the whole of knowledge; he will always remain at least partially ignorant. The more he explores a topic, the more unexplored paths he uncovers. He cannot, in a limited lifetime, hope to accomplish all he would like to accomplish on the intellectual front. He will always be left in the dark. He will never *fully* understand anything.

To this realization, the scholar can respond in one of two

ways. He can respond with the optimism furnished by religious faith, confident that all truths will be revealed to him in eternity. He can approach the world with a happy sense that ultimately there is a purpose in life, although he cannot fully understand all its many moments. Albert Schweitzer spoke of this feeling as "secondary naivete." A child is naive, Schweitzer explained, because he knowns so very little. A wise adult, however, knows a great deal, but his wisdom warns him that he still is ignorant — more ignorant than ever, in a way. Appreciating his new ignorance, and acquiring this secondary naivete, is a first step toward wisdom. It is Socrates' message, again, couched in a new form.

But the frustrated scholar could respond otherwise. He could notice, more and more, that he never reached a full understanding of any topic. He could begin to wonder whether the meaning of life is fully impenetrable — even whether life has no meaning. If the scholar takes that route, he divorces himself from ordinary values, and lives a life of anomic depression. The scholar becomes morbid, plunging ahead with his studies although he feels sure he will find no understanding there.

This pitiable attitude is not a mere theoretical possibility; it is a veritable regime on our campuses today. Scholars deny themselves the solace of faith, and suspect strongly that knowledge interferes with their happiness. Still they plug onward, driven by the belief that they are somehow demonstrating their own moral character by refusing to flinch in the face of meaninglessness. Optimism is unfashionable, pessimism is the rage, and suicide is an occupational hazard. To profess a love for truth would not be chic; scholars compete to demonstrate their intellectual machismo — their ability to withstand the constant disappointment. The heroes of this new stoicism are the intrepid souls who have pushed themselves to the limits of their endurance, and looked into the abyss of despair. Some of these heroes never recover from the depths of their depression; that is the price they pay for their status.

How can this attitude lead toward truth, unless truth is suicidal? And how can suicide solve the problem, since suicide only begs the question? The stoical, pessimistic attitude cannot lead to truth. But then again, possibly the scholars are not terribly interested in truth. Perhaps once again they have taken another goal in view. Leo Strauss thought so. He complained of the prevalent attitude, "Intellectual honesty is not love of truth. Intellectual honesty, a kind of self-denial, has taken the place of love of truth because truth has come to be believed to be repulsive and one cannot love the repulsive."[6]

Still, armed with a supportive faith, one can find the confidence to see beauty, and love the truth.

So far I have argued that ignorance of religion distorts the truth, and corrupts the intellect. But my deeper point is the converse: religious faith informs and supports the intellect. Faith and reason are partners; faith shows reason the paths it should follow, and reason guides faith in explicating the truth. Neither alone will produce enduring statements of the truth.

But what are enduring truths, and how do we find them?

Scientific truths are determined by the scientific method. Observation, hypothesis, experiment, conclusion. Simple and straightforward. Or so it seems, at first glance. But actually the process of scientific discovery is bewilderingly complex. Why do some scientists observe some critical facts, while others are preoccupied with trivia, or following blind leads? And when the facts are observed and collated, how do some scientists have the inordinate elasticity of mind that allows them to frame a radical new hypothesis — one which the experiments confirm? Newton and Einstein had no special access to information; the facts available to them were available to scores of other top scientists of their day. The observation of facts is selective, and the selection of a hypothesis is largely subjective. So the individual's research skills are not enough. At two different stages, serendipity rules the scientific process.

Serendipity. Yes, but we cannot be content with such a superficial explanation, particularly if our ultimate objective is to uncover the truth. Many scientists have pondered at length, trying to understand how they selected their observations and their hypotheses. At first the picture that emerges is even more confused. Time after time, scholars reveal that they solved their problems by what seems to be blind luck. Time after time, they admit that a problem stumped them, and they decided to relax and forget it all for a while. Then, without warning, the answer suddenly struck them like a thunderbolt: in the middle of the night, or while they were riding on a bus, or just as they embarked on another unrelated experiment. Ordinary conscious reason is not at work here. Often it is just when they take their minds *off* the problem that scientists find the answer. A great French mathematician, Henri Poincaré, theorized that the answer comes from unconscious intuition — from some "subliminal self" that mind-straining concentration suppresses. As soon as the scientist lets his mind relax, these intuitions come to the fore, and the problem is solved.[7]

Relaxation, or, if you prefer, a sense of proportion, is the key to another aspect of discovery as well. As he begins to research a question, the scientist has no way to know which facts are most important to his eventual solutions, and which are irrelevant. He cannot afford to select facts in advance; he must wait, and observe, and sift out the facts that seem most pivotal. Quietude is an absolute necessity; his own personality cannot interfere with the process of observation. The researcher must sit passively, not straining to anticipate conclusions. He must soak up all the available knowledge until he understands the parameters of the problem. Then, and only then, can he begin selecting the most important facets of his study.

First the scientist must learn to appreciate his subject. Then he must give free play to his imagination. Only after that, when his observations and hypotheses are aligned, does inductive logic assume a dominant role. "The supreme task is to arrive at those universal elementary laws from which the cosmos can be built up by pure deduction. There is no logical path to these laws; only intuition, resting on sympathetic understanding of experience, can reach them." Those are the words of a man who knows the route to scientific discovery: Albert Einstein.[8]

Now consider another path to enduring truths: artistic creativity. A great artist, unlike a merely popular one, produces works that strike all audiences with equal force. Shakespeare's plays were magnificent when performed for Elizabethan audiences, but they are equally magnificent in our country today. Why? John Keats, a man who surely knew the paths of artistic genius, suggested that Shakespeare's greatest attribute is his "negative capability" — his ability to put his own personality aside, and appreciate characters for their own sake. If Keats is right, much of Shakespeare's dramatic success springs from the same sympathetic observation of which Einstein speaks. Everyone readily acknowledges the importance of intuition in art, so perhaps the two modes of discovery are really quite similar. First the artist (or scientist) empties himself of his own preconceptions, and observes his subject with an open, passive mien, accepting whatever information he finds. Then, armed with that information, he unleashes the creative power of his imagination.

Imagination: another ambiguous word. The artist and the scientist require imagination in the best, broadest sense of that term. They need the ability to take abstract ideas, and form mental images of them — the ability to give abstract thoughts a concrete form. Samuel Taylor Coleridge argues that imagination, taken in this essential sense, is a companion of reason, equal in stature and in function. Reason leads us to the truth by following clues in nature, and advancing logically to conclusions. Imagination takes the opposite tack, starting with intuitive truths and working back to concrete manifestations of that truth. Artistic imagination enables us to convey truths even before we ourselves understand them; the artist expresses his intuitive feelings without analyzing them. And logical reason enables us to analyze truths even before we appreciate their significance. Each provides insights that are incomplete, even if they are accurate. But together they lead to a comprehensive understanding. Eventually the two paths converge, at the pure essential truth.

Some societies place extraordinarily high value on art, and some on reason. In either case, society acknowledges that this special emphasis is leading them toward the truth. In the Western tradition, of course, truth is closely associated with God Himself. Thus the philosopher Jacob Burkhardt: "Yet there remains with us the feeling that all poetry and all intellectual life were once the handmaidens of the holy, and have passed through the temple."[9]

Still one more point remains about the power of artistic imagination. Great art provokes in all of us a sort of longing — a pang of mysterious loneliness. What are we longing for, and why are we lonely? We do not really understand. Still, it does happen. Some artists compare the phenomenon with memory. When we experience a great work of art, a chord of memory is struck. "Yes," we say, "that is how it is." That is how *what* is? We are reminded of something we have never known. Our "memories" recall another, better, life — one we have not lived. Great art lifts our spirits to the recollection of that ideal life, and so the pangs of loneliness begin.

In both art and science, the enduring truths come through creative synthesis. Creativity takes place only when the creative individual abandons his self-regard and immerses himself in his subject, letting his inner beliefs guide him. Through it all, he is guided too by a persistent recognition that he knows something of a better life, where truths are expressed and understood more fully.

Does all this sound familiar?

Allow me to translate the same simple arguments into a different context. The terms are different, but not the ideas.

The enduring truths of this life come through creative synthesis that conjoins faith and reason. Faith teaches the scholar that the universe is basically good, since it is God's work. So he can accept the world lovingly, and step outside the limitations of his own personal perceptions in order to appreciate the aspects of nature which he sees all around him. His confidence in God enables him to love all creation, and thereby to see facts for what they are, rather than trying to alter them to suit his own purposes. When he relies wholly on his own reason, he cannot solve problems. But when he admits his limits, and relies on God's grace to solve the problem, the answer comes to him. The scholar is driven to the truth by the knowledge that truth is a manifestation of God Himself. He knows that his work is especially blessed. And through it all, the scholar never forgets that he belongs, ultimately, in another world. He always keeps in mind the importance of God's eternal life, where the truth is fully revealed. All his work, and all his creative insights, point toward that eternal life.

When I make this interpretation, I do not claim that all creative scholars are religious, although an inordinate number of the most brilliant thinkers seem to be. God does not restrict His blessings to those who believe in Him, and the grace of an unusual insight could easily come to an unbeliever, or to a sinner of the worst sort. My point is this: the path toward truth is the path of faith. A creative scholar or artist might not be spiritually upright, but whatever his failings, his creativity is a positive moral act. Like any other blessing, the grace that informs a creative genius can be ignored, twisted, or used to advance immoral causes. Still the creative act itself is a moral act, because genuine creativity is an approach to truth, and truth is a manifestation of God's presence. In short, creativity is, properly, a form of religious worship.

Werner Heisenberg, the Noble physics laureate and author of the Uncertainty Principle (and a staunch Calvinist), explains that to him all truth is beautiful, and the measure of an idea's truth is the amount of beauty it uncovers. A true theory, he continues, is one that unlocks new vistas of beauty, introducing us to new wonders in God's creation. So the scientist Heisenberg corroborates the poet Keats:

Beauty is truth, truth beauty — that is all
Ye know on earth, and all ye need to know.

God is truth, and truth is beauty. "The heavens declare the glory of God, and the firmament showeth His handiwork."[10] So all knowledge, all wisdom, brings the scholar closer to God. The discipline that constitutes academic freedom, the cooperation that binds a community in a shared quest for truth, the faith and reverence that inspire the academic ideal: all these things make the university an institution of worship.

Christopher Derrick recently wrote *Escape from Skepticism* in praise of a small Catholic liberal arts college in California. But his words apply to more than just the campus of Thomas Aquinas College. His words could apply to any university where scholars dedicate all their actions to the cause of truth.

"On the same principle, in a fully Catholic college of this age, a student should be able to go from morning Mass to the dining hall for a talkative meal with friends, and from there to the library or the physics laboratory, without any feeling that the subject was (so to speak) changed at any point in the progression.

"The subject, throughout, was God."[11]

BIBLIOGRAPHY

Arnold, Matthew. *Culture and Anarchy.* Edited, with an introduction by John Dove Wilson. Cambridge: Cambridge University Press, 1932.

Bird, Caroline. *The Case Against College.* Garden City, N.Y.: Doubleday, 1975.

Buckley, William F., Jr. *God and Man at Yale,* 2d ed., South Bend: Gateway Editions, 1977.

——. *Daedalus: The Journal of the American Academy of Arts and Sciences.* Special issue: "American Higher Education: Toward an Uncertain Future." Vol. 103, #4, and vol. 104, #1; Fall 1974 and Winter 1975.

Dawson, Christopher. *The Crisis of Western Education.* New York: Sheed and Ward, 1951.

——. *Education and the Crisis of Christian Culture.* Chicago: Regnery, 1949.

Derrick, Christopher. *Escape from Scepticism.* LaSalle, Ill.: Sherwood Sugden, 1975.

Eliot, T.S. *Christianity and Culture.* New York: Harcourt, Brace, 1940.

Gross, Theodore. *Academic Turmoil.* Garden City, N.Y.: Doubleday, 1980.

Hofstadter, Richard. *The Development of Academic Freedom in the United States.* New York: Columbia University Press, 1955.

Hook, Sidney. *Academic Freedom and Academic Anarchy.* New York: Cowles Books, 1969.

Hutchins, Robert Maynard. *The Higher Learning in America,* 1st AMS edition, New York: AMS Press, 1978.

Jasper, Karl. *The Idea of the University.* Ed. Karl W. Deutsch. Trans. H.A.T. Reiche and H.F. Vanderschmidt. Boston: Beacon, 1959.

Kelman, Steven. *Push Comes to Shove.* Boston: Houghton Mifflin, 1970.

Kerr, Clark. *The Uses of the University.* Cambridge, Mass.: Harvard University Press, 1963.

Kirk, Russell. *Academic Freedom.* Chicago: Regnery, 1955.

——. *Decadence and Renewal in the Higher Learning.* South Bend: Gateway Editions, 1978.

Lamont, Lansing. *Campus Shock.* New York: E.P. Dutton, 1979.

LeBoutillier, John. *Harvard Hates America.* South Bend: Gateway Editions, 1978.

Lewis, C.S. *The Abolition of Man.* New York: Macmillan, 1947.

Lowry, Howard Foster. *The Mind's Adventure.* Philadelphia: Westminister Press, 1950.

Moberly, Walter. *The Crisis in the University.* London: SCM Press, 1949.

Newman, John Henry (Cardinal). *The Idea of a University.* Introduction and notes by Martin L. Svaglic. San Francisco: Rinehart Press, 1960.

Nisbet, Robert. *The Degradation of the Academic Dogma.* New York: Basic Books, 1971.

Ortega y Gasset, Jose. *The Mission of the University.* Trans. with an introduction by Howard Lee Nostrand. Princeton: Princeton University Press, 1944.

Parker, Gail Thain. *The Writing on the Wall.* New York: Simon and Schuster, 1979.

Pirsig, Robert M. *Zen and the Art of Motorcycle Maintenance.* New York: William Morrow, 1974.

———. *Prospect* magazine. Princeton: Concerned Alumni of Princeton, 1972-1980, vols. 1-8.

———. *The Report of the Commission on the Future of the College.* Princeton: Princeton University Press, 1973.

Roche, George. *The Balancing Act.* LaSalle, Ill.: Open Court, 1974.

Schumpeter, Joseph A. *Capitalism, Socialism, and Democracy,* 3d ed. New York: Harper and Row, 1950.

Snow, C.P. *The Two Cultures and the Scientific Revolution.* New York: Cambridge University Press, 1959.

Trilling, Lionel. *Beyond Culture.* New York: Viking Press, 1965.

Veblen, Thorsten. *The Higher Learning in America,* rev. ed., Stanford: Academic Reprints, 1954.

Wagner, Geoffrey. *The End of Education.* New York: A.S. Barnes, 1976.

Weaver, Richard. *Ideas Have Consequences.* Chicago: University of Chicago Press, 1948.

Whitehead, Alfred North. *The Aims of Education.* New York: Macmillan, 1929.

Williams, Duncan. *Trousered Apes.* New Rochell, N.Y.: Arlington House, 1972.

Witonski, Peter. *What went Wrong with American Education.* New Rochelle, N.Y.: Arlington House, 1973.

Wolfe, Tom. *Mauve Gloves and Madmen, Clutter and Vine.* New York: Farrar, Straus, Giroux, 1976.

Wolff, Robert Paul. *The Ideal of the University.* Boston: Beacon, 1969.

Young, Michael. *The Rise of the Meritocracy.* London: Thomas and Hudson, 1958.

NOTES

CHAPTER ONE: ACADEME IN REVOLT

(1)   Adam Ulam, "Where Do We Go From Here?" *Daedalus*, 103 (Fall 1974): 81.

(2)   *Boston Herald Traveler*, April 9, 1969, p. 1.

(3)   See Steven Kelman, *Push Comes to Shove* (Boston: Houghton Mifflin, 1970), p. 78, for a description of the event and its aftermath.

(4)   Later I learned that the victim was a personal acquaintance. He lost several teeth in the incident.

(5)   Although the suggestion was made to a crowd of over one thousand students — and more than a few members of the press — it has never, to my knowledge, been reported elsewhere.

(6)   Joseph Conrad, *The Secret Agent*.

(7)   A plethora of information about the Harvard "Bust" can be found in various reports. Among the best are Steven Kelman's *Push Comes to Shove*, and: "Academic Calm of Centuries Broken," *Life* magazine, April 25, 1969; "And now, Harvard," *New Republic*, April 21, 1969; "Bust at Harvard," *Newsweek*, April 21, 1969; "Harvard and the Police," William F. Buckley, Jr., *National Review*, May 6, 1969; "President Pusey and the Harvard Radicals Deserve One Another," A.S. Kaufman, *New York Times Magazine*, May 4, 1969.

(8)   See Kelman, *Push Comes to Shove*, and Kaufman, "President Pusey."

(9)   Nick Gagarin, *Harvard Crimson*, April 13, 1969.

(10) See the author's "Recriminations Against Myself," *Hillsdale Review*, Spring 1981.

(11) *The Daily Princetonian*, December 4, 1975, p. 1.

(12) *Ibid.*, May 5, 1976, p. 1.

(13) *Prospect* (Summer 1978): 18.

(14) Any random sampling of editorials in the 1968-1969 volume of the *Harvard Crimson* will yield a dramatic picture of the paper's editorial stance. To be fair to Fallows, one should note that subsequent volumes were far more radical in tone. Nor was Fallows himself notable for radical views.

(15) Gilbert is a faculty member at the University of Denver.

CHAPTER TWO: THE LEISURE CLASS

(1) Irving Kristol, "Toward a Restructuring of the University," *New York Times Magazine*, December 8, 1968; later reprinted in *On the Democratic Idea in America* (New York, Harper and Row, 1972).

(2) Charles Wilson, testimony before the Senate Armed Services Committee, January 23, 1953.

(3) George Gallup, *Attitudes of College Students on Political, Social, and Economic Issues, 1975* (Princeton: American Institute of Public Opinion, 1975).

(4) *The Report of the Commission on the Future of the College* (Princeton: Princeton University Press, 1973), p. 14.

(5) W. Allen Wallis, "Unity in the University," *Daedalus* 104 (Winter 1975): 75.

(6) James Q. Wilson, "Liberalism versus Liberal Education," *Commentary*, June, 1972, p. 51.

(7) "Freedom of Speech at Princeton," *Prospect* 1 (No. 2): 9-11.

(8) *Ibid.*

(9) Russell Kirk, *Decadence and Renewal in the Higher Learning* (South Bend: Gateway Editions, 1978), p. 14.

(10) Robert Pirsig, *Zen and the Art of Motorcycle Maintenance* (New York: William Morrow, 1974), p. 1420.

(11) Clark Kerr, *The Uses of the University* (Cambridge, Mass.: Harvard University Press, 1963), p. 9.

(12) Friedrich Nietzsche, "We Scholars," *Beyond Good and Evil*, #206.

CHAPTER THREE: THE MULTIVERSITY

(1) Clark Kerr, *The Uses of the University* (Cambridge, Mass.: Harvard University Press, 1963), p. 18.

(2) One interesting, but rarely noticed, evidence of the change in attitudes toward higher education is the increasing uniformity of students' stays in college. Unlike their grandfathers, today's undergraduates find it quite extraordinary to think of spending 5 or 6 years studying for an undergraduate degree. A man of leisure could afford the extra years; an apprentice professional cannot.

(3) Kerr, *Uses, passim.*

(4) *Ibid.*, p. 39.

(5) Robert Nisbet, *The Degradation of the Academic Dogma* (New York: Basic Books, 1971), Introduction.

(6) The same drive for growth occurred more or less simultaneously in the American industrial world. Perhaps universities were taking a cue

from their brethren in the profit-making sector. But in industry, growth-at-all-costs is eventually brought to a halt when profits decline; not so in academe.

(7)   Kerr, *Uses,* p. 20.

(8)   John Henry Cardinal Newman, *The Idea of the University* (San Francisco: Rinehart Press, 1960), p. xl.

(9)   Nisbet, *Degradation,* p. 176.

(10)   Quoted in *Prospect* 6 (January 1977): 18.

(11)   Perhaps the best account of the proliferation of allegedly academic concerns is supplied by Russell Kirk in *Decadence and Renewal in the Higher Learning* (South Bend: Gateway Editions, 1978).

CHAPTER FOUR: WHO RULES THE ROOST?

(1)   Quoted by William F. Buckley, Jr., in his new introduction to the second edition of *God and Man at Yale* (South Bend: Gateway Editions, 1977), p. xxviii.

(2)   See *Prospect* 5 (September 1976): p. 14.

(3)   This student-faculty committee, set up at the suggestion of Dean of the College Ernest May, discussed curriculum reforms for over a year. Then, like so many other such committees, it vanished without a trace. To the best of my knowledge, it left behind no written record of its discussions or recommendations.

(4)   Philip F. Lawler, "Harvard Embraces Curriculum Reform," *Prospect* 7 (Summer 1978): pp. 23-25.

(5)   In addition to the Report of the "Rosovsky Committee" itself, see: James Q. Wilson, "Harvard's Core Curriculum," *Change,* November 1978; and B.J. O'Connell, "Where Does Harvard Lead Us?" *Change,* September 1978.

(6)   Buckley, *God and Man at Yale,* p. xlvii.

CHAPTER FIVE: PAYING THE PIPER

(1)   Thomas Sowell, "A Black Conservative Dissents," *New York Times Magazine,* August 8, 1975, p. 156.

(2)   *A.P. Smith Manufacturing Company vs. Barlow,* New Jersey, 1953.

(3)   William F. Buckley, Jr., *God and Man at Yale* (2d ed., South Bend: Gateway Editions, 1977), pp. xl-xliii.

(4)   *A.P. Smith vs. Barlow.*

(5)   See *Prospect* 6 (January 1977).

(6)   Dwight David Eisenhower, "Farewell Radio and Television Address to the American People," January 17, 1961. Published by the National Archives in *Public Papers of the Presidents of the United States.*

(7)   William G. Bowen and W.J. Baumol, *Performing Arts: The Economic Dilemma* (Cambridge: MIT Press, 1966).

(8)   *Prospect* 6 (January 1977).

(9)   Kingman Brewster, speech before the Fellows of the American Bar Foundation, Chicago, March 27, 1975. Quoted in the *Wall Street Journal,* March 28, 1975, p. 4.

(10) George Gallup, *Attitudes of College Students on Political, Social, and Economic Issues, 1975* (Princeton, American Institute of Public Opinion, 1975). See also *Prospect,* Volume Four, Number 5, and Volume Four, Number 6 (September-October 1976).

(11) See *Prospect* 6 (Janaury 1977): p. 21.

(12) Irving Kristol, *Wall Street Journal,* March 24, 1977, p. 33.

(13) Gallup, *Attitudes of College Students on Political, Social, and Economic Issues, 1975* (Princeton, American Institute of Public Opinion, 1975).

(14) Daniel Patrick Moynihan, "The Politics of Higher Education," *Daedalus* 104 (Winter 1975): 141.

(15) See John Howard, "The Responsibility of College Trustees," *Policy Review* #1 (Summer 1977): pp. 71-81.

CHAPTER SIX: THE ADMISSIONS LOTTERY

(1)   American Academy of Arts and Sciences, Assembly on University Goals and Governance, "Recommendations," *Daedalus* 104 (Winter 1975): 329, #8.

(2)   As this book goes to press, the young athlete in question, Ralph Sampson, is — to the surprise of all who speculated on the matter a few years ago — entering his final year at the University of Virginia. The point remains, however, that the coaches competing for his talents did not anticipate that he would graduate with his entering freshman class. And his decision to remain in school for the full four years is an exceptional one; he had received several lucrative offers from professional teams, and a dozen of his college contemporaries left school early to accept lesser offers.

(3)   *Report of the Commission on the Future of the College,* (Princeton: Princeton University Press, 1973), pp. 84-90.

(4)   See Geoffrey Wagner, *The End of Education* (New York: A.S. Barnes, 1976).

CHAPTER SEVEN: GRADING AND DISCIPLINE

(1)   Alfred North Whitehead, *The Aims of Education* (New York: Macmillan, 1929), p. 41.

(2)   *Ibid.*, p. 25.

CHAPTER EIGHT: THE CULT OF DISSENT

(1)   *Newsweek*, May 8, 1970.

(2)   C.S. Lewis, *The Abolition of Man* (New York: Macmillan, 1947), p. 16. Here Lewis was speaking of an English primer.

(3)   *Prospect* 1, No. 4 (December 1972): p. 11-13, explains both the poll in question and the controversy that it provoked.

(4)   Everett Carll Ladd and Seymour Martin Lipsett, *Academics, Politics, and the 1972 Election* (Washington: American Enterprise Institute, 1973). Reports based on the authors' continuing research appeared serially in the *Chronicles of Higher Education* during the academic year 1975-1976. See also *Prospect* 5 (May 1976): *passim,* for analysis of their findings.

(5)   William G. Bowen, *Annual Report of the President* (Princeton: Princeton University, 1975).

(6)   Joseph A. Schumpeter, *Capitalism, Socialism, and Democracy,* (3d ed., New York: Harper and Row, 1950).

CHAPTER NINE: ON GIANTS' SHOULDERS

(1)   Woodrow Wilson, "Princeton in the Nation's Service," October 21, 1896, *The Papers of Woodrow Wilson,* edited by Arthur S. Link and others (Princeton: Princeton University Press, 1971), 10: 11-31.

(2)   Matthew Arnold, *Culture and Anarchy* (Cambridge: Cambridge University Press, 1932), p. 6.

(3)   C.S. Lewis, *Miracles* (New York: Macmillan, 1947), pp. 15-16. The same point is made, on another level of seriousness, by Plato's famous metaphor of the Cave.

(4)   G.K. Chesterton, *Orthodoxy* (New York: Image Books, 1959), p. 48.

(5)   Werner Dannhauser and L. Pearce Williams, quoted by Alan Bloom, "The Failure of the University," *Daedalus* 103 (Fall 1974): 59.

(6)   See the *Report of the Commission on the Future of the College* (Princeton: Princeton University Press, 1973), p. 168.

(7) Lionel Trilling, *Beyond Culture* (New York: Viking Press, 1961), pp. 4-5.

(8) *Report of the Commission on the Future of the College* (Princeton: Princeton University Press, 1973), pp. 166-169.

(9) Robert Weaver, *Ideas Have Consequences* (Chicago: University of Chicago Press, 1948), pp. 52-69.

(10) Robert Maynard Hutchins, *The Higher Learning in America* (First AMS Edition, New York: AMS Press, 1978), p. 59.

(11) Alexis de Tocquerville, *Democracy in America*, Book One of Volume II.

(12) Christopher Dawson, *The Crisis of Western Education* (New York: Sheed and Ward, 1951), Introduction.

CHAPTER TEN: FACTS AND VALUES

(1) Plato, *Laws*, #739. See also #653.

(2) Saint Thomas Aquinas, *Two Precepts of Charity*.

(3) Derek Bok, "On the Purposes of Undergraduate Education," *Daedalus* 103 (Fall 1974): 162.

(4) Ludwig Wittgenstein, *Tractatus Logico-Philosophicus* (London: Routledge and Kegan Paul, 1922), #7.

(5) Aristotle, *Nichomachean Ethics*, #1104.

(6) Richard Weaver, *Ideas Have Consequences* (Chicago: University of Chicago Press, 1948), p. 130.

(7) Alfred North Whitehead, *The Aims of Education* (New York: Macmillan, 1929), p. 26.

CHAPTER ELEVEN: ACADEMIC FREEDOM

(1) William F. Buckley, Jr., *God and Man at Yale*, (2d ed., South Bend: Gateway Editions, 1978), p. xxxvi.

(2) In making this argument, I am endebted to Russel Kirk's compelling case for traditional notions of academic freedom. See his underappreciated, invaluable book, *Academic Freedom* (Chicago: Regnery, 1955).

(3) There are arguments in favor of *apartheid* that do not assume fundamental inequalities among men — arguments claiming that *apartheid* laws are conducive to eventual true equality. These arguments are outside the scope of my point here. In fact, my point becomes more straightforward if one assumes simply, for the sake of the argument, that *apartheid* is inherently unjust.

There are other governments which, in my view, provide even clearer cases of institutionalized evil — notably the governments of the Soviet bloc. But unfortunately the evils of those governments are less universally recognized for what they are than the comparatively minor peccadilloes of South Africa. Thus my choice of this example.

CHAPTER TWELVE: TRUTH AND BEAUTY

(1)   T.S. Eliot, "The Idea of a Christian Society," in *Christianity and Culture* (New York: Harcourt, Brace, 1940), p. 30.

(2)   Quoted by William F. Buckley, Jr., in *God and Man at Yale* (2d ed. South Bend: Gateway Editions, 1978), p. xxiv.

(3)   Walter Moberly, *The Crisis in the University* (London: SCM Press, 1949), p. 55.

(4)   Buckley, *God and Man at Yale*, p. 3. The quotation is taken from Seymour's inaugural address as President of Yale.

(5)   Leo Strauss, "The New Political Science," from *Essays on the Scientific Study of Politics*, edited by Herbert J. Storing (New York: Holt, Rinehart and Winston, 1962), p. 327.

(6)   *Ibid.*, p. 322.

(7)   Henri Poincaré, *Science and Hypothesis* (New York: Dover, 1952).

(8)   Albert Einstein, as quoted by Robert Pirsig, *Zen and the Art of Motorcycle Maintenace* (New York: William Morrow, 1974), pp. 106-7.

(9)   Quoted by Richard Weaver, *Ideas Have Consequences* (Chicago: University of Chicago Press, 1948), p. 22.

(10) Psalm 19, verse 1.

(11) Christopher Derrick, *Escape from Scepticism* (LaSalle, Ill.: Sherwood Sugden, 1975), p. 84.

ABOUT THE AUTHOR

Philip F. Lawler was born and raised in Boston and received his primary education at local parochial schools. As an undergraduate at Harvard, he majored in Government, and graduated with honors in 1972.

After doing graduate work in Political Science at the University of Chicago, Mr. Lawler moved to Princeton, New Jersey, to become the editor of *Prospect,* a magazine published by the Concerned Alumni of Princeton. He also served as the education editor of the *New American Review.*

In 1979, Mr. Lawler moved to Washington, D.C., to become the Managing Editor of *Policy Review,* a quarterly journal published by The Heritage Foundation. In 1981, he became the Director of Studies for the Foundation — a position he still holds. He is also the founder and President of the Catholic Center for Renewal, a Washington-based think-tank.

Mr. Lawler is married to the former Leila Elmaghraby, and lives in Washington with their two children.

His written work has appeared in dozens of newspapers around the United States, and in Journals such as *Policy Review,* the *American Spectator, National Review, Modern Age, Chronicles of Culture,* the *New Oxford Review, Hillsdale Review,* and others. He is the editor of *Papal Economics.* This is his first book.